'Side-Show' Theatres
of the Great War

'Side-Show' Theatres of the Great War

British Campaigns in Africa & the Far East
During the First World War

British Campaigns in Africa and the Pacific:
1914—1918
Edmund Dane

The Fall of Tsingtau (extract)
Jefferson Jones

LEONAUR

'Side-Show' Theatres of the Great War
British Campaigns in Africa & the Far East During the First World War.
British Campaigns in Africa and the Pacific: 1914—1918
by Edmund Dane
and
The Fall of Tsingtau (extract)
by Jefferson Jones

First published under the titles
British Campaigns in Africa and the Pacific: 1914—1918
and
The Fall of Tsingtau

FIRST EDITION

Leonaur is an imprint
of Oakpast Ltd

ISBN: 978-1-78282-146-5 (hardcover)
ISBN: 978-1-78282-147-2 (softcover)

http://www.leonaur.com

Contents

British Campaigns in Africa and the Pacific: 1914—1918   7

The Fall of Tsingtau (extract)   181

British Campaigns in Africa and the
Pacific: 1914—1918

Contents

Preface   11

The Germans in South-West Africa   13

General Botha's Campaign: First Phase   32

General Botha's Campaign: Second Phase   50

The Story of East Africa   71

East African Campaign 1914-1916   81

The Campaign of General Smuts: First Phase   96

East African Campaign: The Closing Phases   114

The Campaign in Togoland   139

The Campaign in the Cameroons   145

The War in the Pacific and the Siege of Kiao-Chau   165

Preface

The Campaigns in Africa have an interest of their own. They present aspects of the Great War associated with varied, and often strange, adventure. And as illustrations of military resource and skill they well repay study.

In order that they may be the better understood, a succinct account has been given of German colonial policy and dealings. Some of the facts may appear incredible. There is, however, not one that is not based upon well-tested proof. German rule in Africa portended a revival of chattel slavery upon a great scale, and had the contemplated German Empire in Africa been established, the desolating social phenomenon of chattel slavery could not have been confined to the so-called "Dark Continent." Happily, in the campaigns in Africa the evil was rooted up. The effect of these campaigns on the world's future will be deep.

Both the causes of military operations and the character of the terrain over which they take place have to be presented clearly to the reader's mind before they can be followed with ease. Often military events have been dealt with as a kind of poetic history, or in the dry technical manner which, save to those with expert knowledge, is repellent. There is no reason why they should not be narrated at once truthfully and lucidly. That attempt, at any rate, has here been made. Finally, the relations of these campaigns to each other and to the Great War as a whole have been touched upon as far as necessary.

London, May, 1919.   E. D.

CHAPTER 1

The Germans in South-West Africa

Immersed up to that time in schemes of aggrandisement on the continent of Europe, or in Turkey in Asia, the rulers of the German Empire did not openly enter the field of colonial undertakings until the year 1885. Their departure was marked by the Berlin Congo Conference. In November, 1884, on the invitation of Prince Bismarck, representatives of the European Powers met at Berlin to consider more especially the future of Africa and the welfare of its native races. The diplomatists were in session until February, 1885. Besides dealing with certain boundaries, such as those of the French possessions on the Lower Congo, until then not definitely delimited, and the claims of Belgium over the Congo hinterland, they solemnly resolved that it was the "sacred duty "of the represented Powers to preserve the native races of Africa; watch over their interests; and cultivate their material and moral advancement. To that resolution, of course, the Government of the German Empire was a subscribing party.

Five years later—in July, 1890—there took place at Brussels a European Anti-Slavery Conference, and at that conference, in which German diplomacy had an active part, the "emphatic desire of the conferring powers to protect the native races of Africa from slavery and oppression," was registered with like solemnity. Because these were the declared lines of German colonial policy, and the declarations were presumably accepted by the British Government on their face value, the agreement was arrived at which in 1890 enabled the Government at Berlin, without further overt protest or opposition, to annex the territories afterwards known as German South-West Africa and German East Africa.

Then opened, notwithstanding the German Government's solemn professions, probably the blackest in all the black pages of human cruelty.

As deemed by the Anglo-German Agreement, German South-West Africa comprised that part of the South African plateau lying to the west and north-west of the Kalahari desert. Including 322,450 square miles of territory; extending from the Orange River in the south to the Kunene River in the north, 900 miles, and at its broadest part 500 miles from the coast inland,[1] this vast region, more than two and a half times as large as the United Kingdom, is marked out by its geographical features into three areas. The southern tract, Great Namaqualand, is a highland country, crossed by parallel ranges of mountains in height from 4,000 to 8,000 feet, the culminating summit, Mount Omatako, 8,800 feet above sea-level. Between the ranges lie fertile valleys.

The central area, Damaraland, is, save on the west, a great rolling plain, affording excellent pasture. To the north, and divided from Damaraland by a dry belt, is Ovamboland, a sub-tropical country of rounded hills and wide productive hollows. Not the least notable feature, however, of South-west Africa is the zone lying between the coast and the interior plateaux, and marked off from the latter alike by their boundary mountains and by its own lower level. On an average some seventy miles in breadth, this coastal zone is a waterless and forbidding desolation of stone, sand, and scrub. And the peculiarity of the coast, as a whole, is the lack of natural harbours. In all the 900 miles there are but two breaks in its dangerous inhospitality—Walfish Bay, where a sheltered anchorage is afforded by a sandbar; and the indent named by the Portuguese Angra Pequena.

With the Kalahari desert on one side of them, and the arid coastal tract on the other, the inhabitants of South-west Africa were among the last to come into contact with Europeans. Apart from the tribelets of Bushmen thinly dispersed over the coastal desert, and gaining a scanty living by the chase, the natives were divided into three national groups. Great Namaqualand was the home of the Hottentots. Considered by ethnologists one of the most peculiar of African peoples, for their traits are more Mongolian than Negro, these mountaineers— warriors, hunters, and herdsmen—were separated into some twelve independent tribes, or cantons. Their natural bravery was extreme. Though small of stature, they were active and very hardy, not wanting in intelligence, and endowed with acute sight and hearing. Probably at one time they inhabited the whole of the south-west African plateau

---

1. This was exclusive of the Caprivi enclave added later, and carrying German South-west Africa inland to the Zambesi.

south of Ovamboland.

Since, however, they only numbered about 20,000 all told, this occupation of a country larger than the Spanish peninsula must have been very scattered. Hence when, about two centuries ago, the Hereros, a people of the Bantu race, migrating with their flocks and herds across the continent in search of fresh pasturage, came upon Damaraland, the feeble numbers of the Hottentots enabled the immigrants to settle in that country. From the plain the Hottentots were driven into the mountains, south and north-west. This movement made the two peoples hostile, and the hostility became traditional. The lifting of Herero cattle was one of the most esteemed of Hottentot activities.

Of a people in the pastoral stage of civilisation the Hereros offered an unusually interesting example. They were a group of clans under a paramount chief, each clan holding its allotted pasturage as the common property. Their herds and their flocks of sheep and goats, providing them with milk, meat, and clothing, were alike the basis of wealth, and of their customs regarding tribal rights, marriage, and inheritance, for as in all societies the customs were designed to safeguard the standard of life. Skill as a herdsman, or shepherd, was held the most valuable accomplishment. Bound up with all their experiences of well-being, their cattle were the objects of their veneration, and the increase of their herds their utmost care. The heaven of the Herero was a heaven of shepherds.

As the country into which they had immigrated was among the most favoured spots in the whole continent of Africa for a pastoral life, its climate temperate and healthy, they had thrived, and it is estimated that at the date of the German annexation the Hereros possessed 150,000 head of horned stock besides their flocks. Like other peoples of the Bantu race, they were tall and of fine physique, but they had two traits which marked them off. Unattacked they were peaceable, though naturally by no means unwarlike, and their usages disclosed a high respect for their womenkind. The Herero wife was not treated as a chattel. The Herero, too, had a very defined notion of honour, distinguishing in war between combatants and non-combatants, and one of the tribal sayings was that he was not a barbarian. Reliable computations put their number at 80,000.

The most powerful, however, of the three native groups were the Ovambos. In point of civilisation they had reached the stage of agriculture, and had evolved a feudal system. With the natives to the south their relations seem only to have been slight and casual, a fact

15

sufficiently accounted for by the intervening belt of arid territory. Whatever the cause, the Ovambos remained the most isolated of African nations, and this apparently on their part was a settled policy. They were not negroes. The characteristics of the Ovambos were their powerful physique; their almost Gallic gaiety shown in a love of music and dancing; their suspicion of strangers, and not least of Europeans; and their disinclination to adopt European usages, except as regards arms and ammunition, of which, whenever the chance offered, they were steady purchasers. They were presumed, though the figure is no more than a guess, to number 150,000 and were able therefore to muster some 30,000 fighting men, and it was always uncertain to what extent they might prove to be armed with weapons of precision, the value of which they keenly appreciated.

The association of Germans with South-west Africa began through the Rhenish Missions Society of Berlin, and the work of its agents among the Hottentots. Of that work the pioneer was a German missionary named von Schemelen. Sent into Great Namaqualand from Capetown in 1814 by a British society, he opened up a correspondence with compatriots in Berlin. The result was that about the year 1840 the Rhenish Missions Society formally took Great Namaqualand within its field of activity. Conversion of the natives, however, made slow progress. For its outcome in converts the mission was expensive. This lack of satisfactory consequences was put down to the Colonial cattle traders from across the Orange River, and their importations of arms and liquors. To counteract the influence and at the same time to lessen expenses, it was decided to turn every German mission station into a trading post, and the scheme from the financial point of view answered so well that trading activity soon became the more important. The next step was, in 1870, the flotation at Berlin of a limited liability company to develop German trade in Great Namaqualand and Damaraland. Each missionary was to receive one-half the trading profits of his post.

From 1864 to 1870 there was a Hottentot-Herero war. Headed by the most powerful of them, the Whitboois, the Hottentot tribes had joined together and subjected the Hereros to tribute, but the latter, advised by two English traders named Green and Haybittel, had signally defeated the Hottentot confederation and thrown off the yoke. Seemingly in this struggle German sympathy was with the Hottentots. The Hereros looked to British protection.

Trade jealousies now began to enter into the matter, and the effect of representations from the Cape Government was that in 1876 a British Commissioner, Mr. W. C. Palgrave, was sent out to inquire and report. In an interview with the paramount chief and sub-chiefs of the Hereros, Mr. Palgrave was handed a petition signed by fifty-eight chiefs and headmen asking that Damaraland might be placed under British authority. The immediate motive was, no doubt, desire for tranquillity, for the war with the Hottentots had then just ended. Palgrave's recommendation, endorsed by the High Commissioner at Capetown, was that the whole coast line of South-west Africa should be annexed. The British Government at home, however, declined to take that course, and the reason was beyond question the German footing already established in the country. After a delay of two years the British Government compromised by the annexation, in 1878, of Walfish Bay, considering, it would seem, that by taking possession of the best harbour on the coast the *hinterland* would be rendered value-less to any other European Power.

But German projects were not thus to be thwarted. A scheme was set on foot for enlarging the original limited liability company into a much more ambitious affair, and in 1882 the promoters sent out Adolphe Luderitz, a Bremen merchant, who landed at Angra Pequena, and began to look into commercial possibilities. That the German Government was behind this scheme was evidenced in 1884 by the arrival at Angra Pequena of a body of German scientific and commercial prospectors, charged to inquire into mineral and agricultural resources. The result was the annexation forthwith of the port of Angra Pequena, renamed Luderitzbucht, and some 4,000,000 and more acres of territory said to have been bought from the Hottentots. A kind of Chartered Company was now set up under the administration of a Dr. Goering as Government-controller. It is worth noting that on hearing of these events the Hereros once more, and in that same year 1884, petitioned to have their country taken under British protection. For a second time, however, the petition was refused by the British Colonial Office.

From the neighbourhood of Angra Pequena Goering lost no time in pushing the limits of the Protectorate northwards. Guided and introduced to the native chiefs by a missionary, Carl Buttner, he promised them, in return for trading facilities, the protection of the German Government. Where an agreement of that kind was entered into the country was presumed to have become German.

And now occurred an episode which threatened to prove awkward.

William Jordaan, a Boer, had with a company of associates trekked to Grootfontein in the belt of country between Damaraland and Ovamboland, and in that until then unclaimed district had set up what he called the Republic of Upingtonia. From neighbouring chiefs Jordaan had obtained a concession of the territory and of its mineral rights. One of his concerns was to keep on good terms with the Ovambos. In 1886 he was on a visit to Ovamboland. He was there assassinated. The allegation, a German story, is that he was murdered at the instigation of a Herero chief, but it is, if a coincidence, peculiar that after his "removal" his followers were forthwith informed by Goering that their Republic could not be tolerated on German territory. Their settlement was broken up.

As understood by the native chiefs the palavers with Goering were of a purely friendly character, but as interpreted by Goering and his underlings they gave an implied authority to exclude from Southwest Africa every white not of German nationality. Since the trade between the natives and Cape Colony was much larger than that carried on with the Germans through their missions, the attempts at exclusion led to friction. At the instance of the Colonial traders the Government of Cape Colony forwarded protests to the British Government at home. The government at home, however, was swayed much more by the European situation than by affairs at the Cape, and there then prevailed in high quarters a belief that an understanding with Germany was both feasible and desirable. This belief the government at Berlin did its utmost by smooth professions to foster. It was, on the other hand, plain that were German policy in South-west Africa to go unchecked and a German trading monopoly to be established, the interests of the native population commercially would be gravely compromised. No surprise therefore can be felt that the native chiefs leaned to the side of the Colonial traders, and became alarmed by their warnings.

The most popular and influential of the Cape traders among the natives, and the man in consequence most obnoxious to the German administration, was a Robert Lewis, who now took a leading part in the opposition. Goering demanded his expulsion from Damaraland. On the refusal of that demand, the German Government-controller with his chief officials came to see the chief Kamaherero at Okahandja, and claimed enforcement of the order on the ground that the country now belonged to the German Crown. Astonished by the pretension, Kamaherero ordered *them* out of his territory within twelve hours. Their lives, he told them, would be forfeit if they declined to go. And having no force at the back of them and "bluff" having failed, the "administration" had no choice save to comply. They sought refuge at Walfish Bay, and from there sailed to Europe with an appeal for armed intervention.

To begin with, the German Government vetoed, or appeared to veto, the proposal. A Press outcry was then raised. Needless to observe, both the seeming veto and the newspaper agitation were calculated moves. Not less calculated was the next step—the ostensible climb down of the German Government in deference to "public opinion;" and yet the next—the sending out to Luderitzbucht of twenty-one men, which trivial force was intended to indicate Germany's docile and for- bearing policy. By means such as these, joined to the professions put forward at the Brussels Anti-Slavery Conference, and, it may be added, a certain element of backstairs diplomacy, the British Government was, despite opinion in Cape Colony, induced to hand over the native peoples of South-west Africa to the fate that might await them at the hands of German colonial enterprise.

We have now to see what that fate proved to be.

In 1890, when South-west Africa was formally annexed, the situation with regard to the natives broadly was that the Hottentots, as without doubt the Germans had already found out, were a people who could not be reduced to serfdom; that the Hereros, considered pro-British, were looked upon as hostile; and that the Ovambos were too strong to be disturbed without war on an expensive scale. In the circumstances, what was the principle which guided German policy? On the one hand there was the declared "sacred duty" of furthering the natives' moral and material advancement, and the alleged "emphatic desire" to protect them against slavery and oppression. But, on the other, there was the opinion reflected in the book, entitled *German Colonial Policy*, written by Dr. Paul Rohrbach, at this date a high official in the German Colonial Office. And the opinion of Dr. Rohrbach was that German colonisation could, after all, mean nothing else than that the natives must give up their grazing lands in order that the white man might have them for grazing his stock. That, of course, was, without just compensation, robbery. Some, Dr. Rohrbach anticipated, might question the dictum from a moral law point of view. He wrote:

"The answer is that for nations of the *kultur*-position of the South African natives, the loss of their free national barbarism, and their development into a class of labourers in the service of and dependent upon white people is primarily a law of existence in the highest degree."[2]

Reduced to plain terms, this jargon meant that the lot of the natives was to be bondage. Presumably because the "*kultur*-position" of the German riff-raff who were sent out to South-west Africa was higher than that of the Herero, who was as much above the average German colonist as any natural nobleman is above any natural cad, every rule of honest dealing was to be set aside.

Whether in South-west Africa German colonial enterprise was conducted on the lines of the German Government's declarations or on those laid down by Rohrbach, will appear in the sequel.

In 1892 the German garrison was increased from the stage army of twenty-one to two hundred men, and from that date the administration, set up at Windhuk in the south-west of Damaraland, entered towards the Hereros upon a policy of provocation. At the same time, attacks by the Hottentots upon the Hereros were encouraged, and were then made the pretext of complaints against the Hottentots. The incursions of the chief Hendrik Whitbooi, head of the Whitbooi tribe, into Damaraland gave rise to protests from Windhuk, and so long as a force of twenty-one men alone was at hand, the matter was limited to protests. On the arrival, however, of the draft which brought the German armed strength up to two hundred men, it speedily became another story. The landing of this contingent happened to coincide with the conclusion of a peace between Hendrik and the Hereros. The latter fact made no difference. Hendrik then had his chief location at the native town of Hornkrantz, lying at the foot of the western mountains.

Now at peace, he apprehended no danger. But he had addressed to the British resident at Walfish Bay a letter detailing the cruelties practised by the Germans at Windhuk upon natives, and in particular the inhuman floggings there inflicted. The details cited are unprintable, for the punishments, or rather tortures, were carried out without regard to sex, and five of the victims had failed to survive. It is clear that, informed as to this correspondence, and suspecting its import, Captain von Francois, the German governor at Windhuk, having received his reinforcement, was resolved upon revenge. He allowed time enough to go by to throw Hendrik off his guard. Then, in April, 1893, with, to quote his own statement, "the greatest secrecy," his force stole at

2. P. Rohrbach: *Deutsche Kolonial Wirtschaft.*

night across the hills into the valley, stealthily formed a cordon round Hornkrantz, and just as day was breaking closed in.

They fired into the huts of the sleeping inhabitants, killing men, women, and children alike and slaughtering without distinction of sex or age all who sought to escape. But though taken by surprise Hendrik, with some sixty of his warriors, cut their way through the cordon and retreated to the mountains, from which they looked back on their homes, now given up to the flames. They became outlaws. Hornkrantz was wiped out. The natives of South-west Africa had felt the first contact of the "mailed fist," or ought it to be said of the "emphatic desire "to shield them from oppression?

Von Francois was recalled after this affair, but was so far not recalled in disgrace that he received promotion to the rank of major.

He was succeeded by von Leutwein whose arrival had been preceded by the formation in Germany of a South-west Africa Land Settlement Syndicate, which disposed of cattle ranches as yet in *nubibus*. To give effect to this speculation the German governor, in virtue of his supreme authority, set up as paramount chief of the Hereros a native named Samuel Maherero. Samuel was not in the direct line of succession, and both on that account and because the sub-chiefs had had no voice in his election as demanded by tribal custom, he was never recognised by them or by the Herero people. In the eyes of the Germans, however, Samuel Maherero had an important qualification for his "office." He was a drunkard, and so long as he was supplied with rum could be relied upon to sign any document put before him. And the administration at Windhuk lost no time in requiring his signature to an "agreement" which assigned to the Land Settlement Syndicate 4½ millions of acres in Damaraland extending from Windhuk eastwards.

It was further alleged, though no proof of the statement has ever been found, that Samuel also signed a concession which enabled the Germans to seize for trespass any Herero cattle found straying to the south of a boundary line drawn across the map of Damaraland west to east for a distance of four hundred miles. Thus by one compact, on the face of it a swindle, the Hereros were deprived of part of their best pasturage, and by another, which if ever entered into was yet more flagitious, were open to have their most cherished property stolen from them. Worst perhaps of all, they were left to find out the existence of the latter "treaty" by the impounding of several thousands of their horned stock. This, of course, reduced many families among

21

Kunene R.

OVAMBOLAND

Tsumeb
Grootfontein
Otjiwarongo
WATERBERG MTS
Omaruru
DAMARA
Okahandya
LAND
Otundya

Swakopmund
WALFISH BAY
Swakop
WINDHUK

Kalahari

Desert

Hornkrantz
Naawkloof
GREAT
Gibeon
NAMAQUALAND
Tses
KARAS MTS

Luderitzbucht

Keetmanshoop

Molope R.
Kuruman

Kalkfontein
Warmbad
Nababis
Upington
Orange R.
Port Nolloth
Steinkopf
Ookiep
Orange R.
Prieska

Swamps

Coastal

Desert

Approximate Contours
at intervals of 1,000 Feet
Railways
Boundaries
SCALE
0   50   100   150 MILES

them to penury, and naturally it caused excitement, described by Governor von Leutwein as "war fever." In some districts the seizures led to violence. The Herero people as a whole, however, had decided to exercise forbearance, and the main result was that, warned by experience, they gave the alleged boundary line a wide berth.

Such passive resistance was not to the German taste. Needy adventurers, they wanted not only land and cattle but labour, and all three, if possible, for nothing, and it was evidently hoped that studied provocation of the natives would supply the pretext for continued and continuous confiscations. In face of the attitude of the Hereros these measures threatened to become abortive, or, in any event, too slow. Other measures, judged to be more speedy, were therefore adopted. One of them was the facility afforded to every newly-arrived and would-be German *ranchero* to open a trading account with the natives on the basis of bartering goods for cattle.

Cut off from trade with the Cape Colony, the natives had now no means of obtaining articles they needed save from these German traders, and on the traders' own terms. On the one hand, the traders did not hesitate to demand £20 for a coat, and £10 for a pair of trousers, [3] ten times over the price at which such articles had been supplied by way of the Cape; on the other, the traders fixed the price of a cow at £1, half the amount given by Cape Colony dealers. On these terms a German trader reckoned to get a herd of thirty cattle for two pieces of shoddy clothing. Coffee and tobacco were sold at corresponding rates. To give these impositions a business face, the natives were allowed credit, but that device meant that the debtor might be seized and condemned to labour in consideration of the debt, in a word, be made a slave.

Here a reference is apposite to the German "Courts of Justice." Their character is disclosed by the regulation which enacted that the evidence of a white witness could only be rebutted by the testimony of seven natives, and by another laying down that natives must regard every white man as a "superior being." In these tribunals "justice" became worse than a farce; it was a tragedy. The tribunals were part of the machinery of despoilment. It is hardly necessary to add that no native ever appealed to them. The truth, as disgraceful as incontrovertible, is that for the natives, after the German incoming, law and justice in South-west Africa ceased utterly to exist.

---

3. Report of the Union Administrator on the Natives of South-west Africa and their Treatment by Germany, p. 47.

In the liquidation of their credits, besides the seizure of "debtors," the Germans picked the best cattle out of the Herero herds. Considering the pastoral usages and traditions of the now unhappy Hereros, this was a bitter injury. But the last word on a superior "*kultur*-position" displaying its superiority has yet to be spoken. About the burial places of their dead the Hereros planted groves, which they held as sacred, and of these the most venerated was that in which were interred their supreme chiefs. The German administration cut it down, broke up the land and turned the place into a vegetable garden. In short, no measure likely to drive the Hereros to desperation was overlooked.

Meanwhile the relations of the administration at Windhuk with the Hottentots were by no means easy. After the affair at Hornkrantz the Hottentot attitude was, as might be expected, one of distrust. But the mountain tribes were comparatively poor, as the Hereros were, taking the native standard, rich. And besides being relatively poor, the Hottentots were manifestly a tough proposition. As for the Ovambos, the Germans left them for the time alone, not even taking the trouble to let them know that the *Kaiser und König* had been pleased to extend his All-highest protection to that part of Africa. So far as can be gathered, indeed, the Ovambos do not appear to have been aware that the white man advanced any claims to their country. The sleeping dogs were suffered to lie.

Fear at Windhuk was occupied with the likelihood of a confederation between the Hereros and the Hottentots, and the chance of their common hatred of the white oppressor becoming deeper than their old hostility. In 1896 there was a disquieting symptom. Arising out of the credit system disturbances occurred in the eastern districts of Damaraland bordering on the desert, and in these the Kausa Hottentots made common cause with the Hereros, of the Ovambandjera sub-clan. A battle with the German troops took place at Otyunda. Thanks to their superior armament, the Germans prevailed. Then, in pursuit of the policy of forbearance, Nikodemus, the Herero supreme chief by tribal right, and Kahimema, chief of the Ovambandjera clan, went to Okahandja to protest against German dealings and arrange terms for their people. They were seized, tried by court-martial, and shot as rebels, being taken to the place of execution in an ox-cart which, as it paraded through the town surrounded by an armed escort, called forth native wailings from every house.

As time went on the lot of the natives sank from bad to worse, and feeling between them and the Germans grew more bitter. Any spark would now start a flare. The spark fell in October, 1903, at Warmbad in the Bondelswartz area. The German official in charge there was a Lieut. Jobst, who cited the aged chief of the Bondelswartz Hottentots, Willem Christian, to appear before him on a trivial charge. The chief declined to comply. Thereupon Jobst with an escort went to the native location. Christian resisted arrest, well knowing the kind of treatment meted out to native prisoners. Seeing him roughly handled, his men turned upon Jobst and his party and slew the whole of them. When this news reached Windhuk the administration there, though Jobst had been the aggressor, prepared to exact a signal revenge, and on their side the Southern Hottentots made ready to defend themselves. Thus broke out the Hottentot War. It dragged on for the next four years, and cost the Germans thousands of casualties and many millions sterling in outlay.

The administration at Windhuk relied not so much on its numerically feeble garrison as on native auxiliaries, chiefly the Whitboois, and the Bastards, a community of half-breeds settled at Rehoboth. Hendrik Whitbooi was known to be a leader of no mean military skill. After the massacre at Hornkrantz, he had betaken himself to his location at Naauwkloof, a mountain stronghold difficult of access, and there for more than a year he had set the Germans at defiance. Finally they moved out in force to attack him, and after bombarding the place tried to take it by storm. The assault failed with heavy losses. A regular siege was then entered upon, and for three weeks the Germans sat before the defences.

At the end of that time Hendrik and his garrison, starved out, were compelled to surrender, though on terms. The terms of the capitulation were that the chief should accept a Protection Agreement. Having hastened to offer the troublesome Hottentot an accommodation, von Leutwein strove to use him as far as possible as a tool. Towards the Bastards likewise Leutwein had deemed it prudent to be conciliatory. He needed the support of both to keep the Hereros in subjection. The Hereros had possessions worth plundering, which was the main point. But on their part the now revolted Hottentots of the south threw up a leader in every respect the equal of Hendrik, and in guerilla tactics much more than equal to the German officers pitted against him. This was Jacob Marengo, a man of mixed Herero and Hottentot parentage. He was as distinguished for chivalry as for personal daring.

Accordingly, in the opening engagements of the Hottentot War von Leutwein found his Punitive Expedition by no means the walkover he had thought it would be. He and his auxiliaries got as good as they gave, if not more. While engaged in this fatiguing campaign among trackless mountains hunting an always elusive foe, the German governor received news that the Hereros had risen in arms.

Knowing that with regard to them it was a fight to the death, von Leutwein had no choice save to patch up a hasty peace with the Bondelswartz "rebels," and hurry northwards. The Hereros, mustering some 8,000 fighting men, of whom about 2,500 were armed with rifles, more or less antiquated, had swept over the German settlements, but while destroying buildings and driving off cattle—more than half their herds had passed into German hands through the operation of the credit system—had, according to their custom, spared German women and children, and, though they had but little reason to love them, German missionaries. From Windhuk, meanwhile, frantic cables had been sent to Germany calling for military aid. In answer to these the division of troops which had been engaged in putting down a similar native rising in German East Africa, under the command of Lieut.-General von Trotha, were ordered forthwith to South-west Africa.

The days of modest contingents of twenty-one men were long past. The world in general, and Africa in particular, was now to know German might, and the thoroughness of German protection. And on that point it is, to say the least, remarkable that two native risings in far distant parts of Africa should have so coincided in time as, with notable advantage to the German Imperial Exchequer, to allow of one overseas expedition dealing with both. The coincidence can hardly have been accidental, and as a fact the same policy of studied provocation was followed in each instance. In each instance, too, the campaign was carried on as a campaign of extermination.

Until these forces under von Trotha landed, von Leutwein could do little. No sooner, however, had von Trotha and his troops begun to arrive than characteristically the Germans in the colony openly boasted that without distinction between friendly and hostile the natives were to be disarmed, their chiefs deposed, and their customs abolished. The effect of these boastings was to cause Hendrik Whitbooi to withdraw his allegiance, throw in his lot with Marengo, and renew the Hottentot War.

Concentrated at Windhuk, the forces of von Trotha were, in June, 1904, launched against the Hereros. In the face of modern rifles, machine-guns and artillery, the natives were helpless. They had entered upon the war with not more than twenty cartridges for each rifle, and that ammunition spent, though from sheer desperation they opposed the Germans in one pitched battle, were, of course, heavily defeated. After this engagement in which, besides killed, some two thousand and more were taken prisoners, mostly left wounded on the battlefield, they had no choice save to retreat east and north. They separated into two bodies. The smaller with their herds and flocks made an attempt to cross the Kalahari Desert, notwithstanding that that desolation takes on foot six weeks to traverse.

The horrors of this journey, however, were less than those of German rule. The larger body, always driving their cattle and small stock before them, sought refuge in the Waterberg mountains, and in the wild bush country forming the inland and desert confines of Southwest Africa. They sued for peace, but the request was peremptorily refused. In place of peace, von Trotha issued to his troops the order that the Hereros were to be wiped out wherever found, old and young, male and female. This was in August 1904. Pursuant to the order, the German troops proceeded to hunt the fugitives out.

Then began a succession of atrocities which has rarely had a parallel. Droves of little children clinging in terror to their mothers were day after day driven from place to place. The feeble, the old, and the exhausted, fallen out and left helpless by the side of the track, indicated by the prints of many feet, were by the Germans as they followed up butchered in cold blood. Women unable to rise were disembowelled where they lay. Often their infants, torn from their arms, were tossed upon the bayonets of the brutal soldiery before their eyes. In one instance at least, and the fact has been attested on oath, this was done in the presence of von Trotha and his staff. [4]

The aged had their brains dashed out with the butt ends of rifles. Young girls were openly outraged, and then thrust through. As for the cattle, they perished by thousands from lack of fodder and water. What enraged the Germans was to see lines of carcases lying along the route of flight. They had hoped to despoil the Hereros of the remainder of their stock at one stroke. But so long as a beast could stand upon its hoofs the fugitives drove it before them, and at the end of this appalling man hunt, and women and children hunt, which went on, not for weeks only, but for months, out of all the mighty herds of Damaraland there were left and fell into the hands of the "conquerors" a miserable

---

4. See evidence of natives taken on oath at Windhuk by Union of South Africa Administrator, *Report on Natives of S.-W. Africa, p. 63 et seq.*

remnant of some three thousand head.

Regarding the valour of the Hereros, let it be added that of the 80,000, or thereabouts, who formed at the outbreak of the war their united community, all save some 15,000 perished. Rather than accept slavery they waged from first to last during nearly two whole years a totally hopeless fight against impossible odds. No civilised nation has ever been known to pay such a price for freedom.

It might have been supposed that this signal bravery would have extorted respect even from Germans. But by far the deepest and most indelible stain upon the German name is the treatment meted out, to begin with, to the prisoners of war, and next to the wretched remnant, who after weeks of starvation dribbled back from the wastes of the Kalahari. They were partly sent to Luderitzbucht and to Shark Island, and partly distributed among the German ranchers. Of those sent to Shark Island all save a few, underfed and worked beyond their strength, or beyond any strength, died of hunger and the lash. The young girls and female children were prostituted by the German guards, who regularly broke into the women's compounds at night; the women, yoked together in teams, were used to draw carts loaded with sand or stone.

But, if anything, the fate of the remainder, assigned to German ranchers, was yet worse. It was, it seems, settlers themselves who, in the hope of loot, had fanned the Herero rising by spreading the false report that Leutwein had been defeated in the south and killed. Their disappointment regarding the loot had enraged them. The fault was not theirs; it was that of the Hereros. Every Herero as a pig-headed savage became an object of revenge. During the war any adult male Herero taken exhausted yet alive was hanged, and for that purpose when rope ran short the Germans used fencing wire. After the war every German rancher used the *sjambok* to all intents as he pleased.

The *sjambok* is a whip cut from hippopotamus hide, square at the handle, which is from a half to three-quarters of an inch across each face. From about six inches above the handle end the lash is twisted like a screw. Dried, this throng is as hard and nearly as heavy as iron, but elastic and tough. A blow from it tears into the flesh, leaving with every stroke a long, jagged wound. Twenty or more strokes applied to any human back leaves it a mass of wounds, and the wounds even when healed cause scars which are horrible. Not only was every German rancher free to inflict this inhuman punishment at his caprice, but every German sergeant in charge of a police post, whether formally authorised or not, in practice, and on complaint from a rancher, inflicted the like punishment without trial or inquiry.

Often the lashing, as much as any human being could endure without perishing under the shock, was renewed after a fortnight's interval. That is to say, while the old scars were still tender they were by the same process of torture ripped open afresh. And lest it be inferred that this brutality was casual only, let the fact be added that on the German police records themselves "convictions"—followed by such floggings and with few exceptions for utterly trivial offences, or alleged offences—numbered between 4,000 and 5,000 a year with a total of nearly 47,000 lashes imposed. [5] This was among a miserable native remnant of less than 15,000 of all ages and both sexes. With regard to the women, their honour was considered by the Germans as of no account, and the children of both sexes were bound to an employer from the age of seven years for life, at wages not only nominal, but as a rule never paid.

Such proved to be the translation into acts of the German professions. German rule had made South-west Africa a hell. Where there had once been prosperity there was now a desolation amid which filthy vultures from the mountains gorged unmolested upon the carrion. Swept bare of its herds and flocks, and emptied of its people, the land relapsed into a rank and weedy waste.

Part of the nemesis, however, was even more speedy. The renewal of the Hottentot War was to all intents coincident with the issue of von Trotha's extermination fiat. The Whitboois and the Bastards alike refused to take part in the massacres, and the former joining up with the other Hottentot tribes, harassed the Germans in the Herero campaign by hanging in turn upon their rear, and raiding their supplies. As soon as he was able, von Trotha turned the main body of his forces upon these new antagonists, but, like Leutwein, he soon found guerilla warfare in a wild and difficult country no game of skittles. The Hottentots knew all the ins and outs of this tangled region. The Germans did not. The Hottentots, skilfully led, and with few exceptions excellent riflemen, appeared when and where they were least looked for.

Over and over again they ambushed contingents of Germans in the hills. There were fatiguing and fruitless pursuits, and expensive retreats. The parallel ranges of mountains made attempts to surround the native bands futile. The bands could always double back across paths known only to themselves. Where encounters took place they were to

---

5. Official German Police Record from January 1, 1913, to March 31, 1914. *Report on Natives of S.-W. Africa*, p. 119.

the last degree desperate. For a year this went on, and seemingly the Germans were no nearer to any result. Their losses too were decidedly the heavier. The natives never fought save at an advantage. The German procedure was to destroy food supplies, and to hunt women and children out of caves. Here again they sought to strike terror by extermination.

The only effect was that the war became one without quarter given or asked on both sides. With every German contingent wiped out the guerillas obtained more arms and ammunition, and they were ceaselessly on the watch for such chances. The original division of German troops, reduced by casualties and fatigue to a skeleton, had to be heavily reinforced, and again reinforced. For Hendrik, dead or alive, von Trotha offered £1,000, to a native a fortune beyond estimate. Not a soul was tempted by it.

Hendrik headed the revolt, Marengo acting as his lieutenant, until October, 1906. Then, in the battle at Ases, Hendrik fell. He was eighty years of age. Seeing him fall the Germans charged in, every man eager to obtain the coveted money. The Hottentots beat them back. The attack was more than once repeated, but every time was similarly repulsed. And this went on for so long as it was necessary to the Hottentots to dig a grave on the field and lay in it the remains of their great leader—for great he was. Nor did they retreat until darkness made it impossible for their mortal foes to discover the spot.

The mantle of Hendrik fell upon Marengo, and he kept up the fight to the bitter end. Von Trotha was recalled, for this campaign had been costly in men and money beyond the German Government's widest estimate. It was only by slow degrees that the Hottentots' resistance weakened. They had lost their cattle; their homes had been swept away; they were reduced to eating the flesh of dead and abandoned horses and mules. A new German governor, von Lindquist had meanwhile superseded Leutwein, and the policy of extermination was dropped; it had turned out to be a game not worth the candle. Offers of accommodation were addressed first to one tribe then to another, and one by one their remnants accepted the terms. Marengo alone declined to trust to German pledges. He would most probably have been sorry for it if he had. Wisely he preferred exile in Cape Colony.

In summary, that is the story of German rule. It is often assumed that while the struggle of European peoples for freedom is, even in misfortune, noble, there is in the fate and sufferings of African peoples no interest. But this fight of small and primitive nations clinging

30

against hope to an inborn love of liberty, and declining to purchase peace at the price of degradation, is an epic of bravery, and colour of skin can make no difference to any generous human heart.

CHAPTER 2

General Botha's Campaign: First Phase

On the outbreak of war between Great Britain and Germany in 1914 an attack upon German South-west Africa by the forces of the South African Union does not at Berlin appear to have been looked for, though incidentally for such an attack preparations had been made. It was evidently German official belief that prevalent opinion in the Union would prove to be against an active part in the conflict, or that that opinion would be so sharply and so evenly divided as to put prompt and vigorous action beyond the probabilities.

There were several grounds for this view. In the first place, the issue of the war at that date seemed for the Allies to be at best uncertain, while by way of contrast with allied doubt, German supporters and sympathisers in South Africa made it known that the German Government looked in Europe for a swift and decisive success. In the event of success, the German Government were ready not only to recognise the Union as politically independent, but were also to enter into relations with it on friendly and favourable terms, or terms which would forthwith and finally ensure the supremacy in its affairs of the settlers of Dutch descent.

In the second place, the military forces of the Union were organised purely on a defensive footing. There was a standing or permanent force on the distinctively South African model; that is to say, a force in the main of mounted infantry with the usual equipment of light artillery and field apparatus. The features of this force were its mobility, and the skill of its riflemen. And in a country of enormous spaces where, besides, the coloured population outnumbered the white in the proportion of eight to one, if not more, the maintenance of this armed police was a necessity. But that it was a police and not an army in the European sense of the word was clear from the limitation of its numbers. They were not more than were demanded by the strict duty of ensuring order and public security.

Under the Defence of the Union Act, white citizens might enrol for annual training, those of the rural areas in the mounted commandos, those of the urban areas in the infantry and reserve artillery. The enrolment, however, was voluntary, and the statutory service undertaken did not extend beyond the Union territories. The Reserve, in short, was a measure against possible invasion. Service was on a voluntary footing, because, in fact, compulsion was not called for. In the rural areas and towns alike the common desire was to serve, and the force was always up to establishment strength. While the Defence Act gave the government the power, in case of shortage, to make it up by means of the ballot, the authority was precautionary and formal, and in view of the active and adventurous spirit of the white population was not likely to be anything more.

But though in case of invasion the Union could put into the field a powerful force of excellent and hardy soldiers—for their numbers as fine a territorial army as could be found in the world—to employ that army, or any part of it, in offensive operations outside the Union was a departure upon which the South African Government could not embark without formal permission of the Federal Parliament, and it was evident that to secure the permission they must have an overwhelming weight of opinion behind them.

To the Germans that did not seem probable. And it appeared to them, coming to the third point, the less probable because the strategical difficulties of an attack upon German South-west Africa were not slight. It was not a question of distances alone, but of the character of the country to be crossed—a wide belt singularly unfavourable for military transport. Taking, then, to begin with, the assumed neutrality of Cape-Dutch feeling as between themselves and Great Britain, next the political obstacles to be overcome, and finally the manifest expense of such a campaign, the chances, in German estimation, were that the Government of South Africa would keep out of the struggle.

This formed, as it were, the Germans' jumping off position, and they had made ready in a manner peculiarly Prussian to exploit it. For the working of the German possessions in Africa, as well as those in the Pacific to the best profit, there was floated in 1890 the German Colonial Company, a kind of South Sea undertaking with a very large capital, and, on paper, very wide rights. Collectively, these colonies were about twelve times the area of the German Empire in Europe, and as they had been very rapidly acquired and owed their existence in effect to Germany's military prestige, large ambitions had been based upon them. They were no more than a beginning. One of the ambitions was the eventual predominance of German influence in South Africa. In 1891 the Colonial company had emphasised the importance of the South-west African acquisition on that ground.

Afterwards the aim was less openly advertised. Indeed, it may be said to have been withdrawn from public view. Nevertheless, as a goal it was always there. One of the proofs is the administration set up in South-west Africa. The organisation was military. The other proof is found in the covert intrigue steadily carried on throughout South Africa with the object of fostering hostility to the British connection, and ostensibly of keeping alive Cape-Dutch sentiment in favour of independence. The more German organisation in South-west Africa is studied the more saliently does the use of that territory as a means to a larger end stand out.

Even in 1914 the white population, and all save a small percentage were Germans, numbered less than 15,000 all told. But of that total one-third were garrison and another third reservists. Administratively, the colony involved a heavy annual loss. To say nothing of the cost of the native campaigns, the current expenses exceeded the receipts by nearly a million sterling a year. Seemingly, however, this deficit was willingly incurred. An expensive system of railways had been laid down. From Tsumeb in the north on the frontier of Ovamboland a main line ran south until, after various sinuosities, it terminated at Nababis in the extreme south-east corner of the Colony on the frontier of the Union, and a few miles from the Orange River. Branches from this trunk had been constructed in the north from Karibab to Swakopmund, the small and artificial port which the Germans had by means of a jetty laid out just beyond the Walfish Bay lagoon, and in the south from Seeheim in Great Namaqualand across the coastal desert to Luderitzbucht.

In all there were close upon 1,500 miles of track. Business to justify this outlay there was not, nor near prospect of it. The railways were military and strategical, designed at once for getting up troops and supplies from the coast to the interior, and for a massing of forces either against the Ovambos on the north, or against Cape Colony on the south-east. In addition, the accumulation of military equipment and stores of all kinds went far beyond the needs of such a white force as the German administration could put into the field. Tsumeb in the north, and Kalkfontein in the south were arsenals on a scale larger than the largest demand of mere defence. As in the instance of the railways a good many millions sterling must have been spent in providing reserves of arms and ammunition at those depots. It is a fair estimate to say that the total reserves would have equipped an army of 50,000 men for a campaign of many months.

The inference is, too, that the policy of terrorism and thinning out pursued towards the natives was a studied policy—an insurance against any rising in the event of the German forces being drawn off for operations beyond the borders. No German administrator would have dared systematically to have carried out such a policy from personal views and on his own initiative. Every principle and practice of German officialdom negatives the conclusion. In a word, German South-west Africa, as a so-called colony, was armed to the teeth for an ulterior purpose. And the heavy, and for the time, wholly unprofitable, outlay in money clinches the demonstration. Either the frugal and close-fisted German Imperial Government was making ducks and drakes of its resources, or it was engaged in what it was believed would in the long run prove a handsomely paying speculation. No sane man can doubt on which foot the boot really was.

In all these calculations there was cunning. Yet there was no depth of sagacity, and, as it proved, little prevision. When war broke out opinion in the Union soon revealed itself as of three shades. The settlers of British descent were without disguise eager for hostilities, and their feeling was shared by those of Dutch descent who relished the prospect of active service. The great majority, however, of the National Party, loyal to the British imperial connection on a footing of self-government, and content with it, were prepared to follow the lead of General Botha. If he decided for war they would accept war; if against war they would equally support him.

A minority, not very considerable, thought the opportunity favourable for severing the tie with Great Britain. Swayed by that feeling, they were disposed to take a favourable view of German chances. The number who were actively pro-German, favourable, that is, to German predominance within and over the Union, were, however, a mere fraction even of this minority.

It will be seen therefore that General Botha held the decision in his own hands, and unfortunately for their projects the Germans had reckoned without him. The oversight was fatal. Not only were General Botha and General J. C. Smuts[1] men of military experience who could not fail to see the meaning and intention of German measures in South-west Africa; they were statesmen capable of taking and of acting upon long views. To them, as to every reflecting man, it was clear that German policy towards the natives involved a grave danger. If among the coloured population it became a settled conviction that from the white man there was to be expected neither justice nor mercy, then, even though it might be slow, there would gather, as the natives learned more of European ideas and resources, a terrible rebound. The natural disgust of the Union statesmen at German cruelties was sharpened by the consciousness of the short-sightedness of the policy. German cruelties tended to bring the white population into disesteem.

On those lines the development of South Africa was impossible. But the Cape statesmen also knew that German professions regarding the independence of the Union were hollow. The nominally independent Union was meant to be a German dependency, and between a German dependency and a British dependency the choice was between military and commercial constraint and freedom. Hesitation there could not be. Looking towards South-west Africa and the cloud there gathered; knowing that it was at once a menace to freedom and the common welfare; and having now the control of their own affairs and the power to undo past mistakes of British imperial policy, the Union Government speedily made up their minds that it was alike their duty and their interest to rid the sub-continent of this threatening portent.

Having so decided they lost no time in passing to acts. The formal requisition to move came from the British Government at home. At Windhuk the Germans had set up a wireless installation powerful enough to receive messages directly from and transmit them to Berlin, and it was one of a chain of similar installations, which, as a series, put the German Government into immediate communication with its remotest possessions. Designed as the chain was to facilitate the raids of German commerce destroyers, and to harass Allied overseas communications, it was important that it should be broken, and the capture of the Windhuk installation would go a long way to break it. The reply of the South African Government to the requisition from London was prompt and affirmative.

1. *With Botha and Smuts in Africa* by W. Whittall also published by Leonaur.

There was some difference of view in the Federal Parliament, but the overwhelming weight of opinion both in the House and outside proved to be with General Botha, and when the necessary proportion of the Reservists were called up they responded unhesitatingly. Put to the test, German propaganda was found to have had little effect. The Germans had earned for themselves too bad a name.

The South African Government, however, did more than decide promptly. General Botha had thought out a sound plan of campaign. According to all the available indications the Germans, in the event of hostilities, expected the main attack from across the Orange River. On the face of things, indeed, it did not seem probable that an inroad would be attempted with large forces from the coast across the desert belt. Such operations were not, it was apparently thought, likely to be more than a diversion. The water and transport problems were deterrent. Besides, even assuming that the coast desert could be crossed in force, there were the boundary mountains to penetrate. On their slopes facing towards the coast these are totally bare of vegetation, masses of rock worn and broken by time into the wildest and most fantastic outlines.

To destroy or poison the water-holes; tear up the railway tracks section by section, and finally, when pushed back, to fortify the passes, and put down land mines seemed to afford easy means of checking any such movements. And those means, on learning that war was the order, the Germans in the Colony laid themselves out to utilise. On their side, too, plans had been elaborated, and it is clear long elaborated. Part of their equipment consisted of large consignments of land mines. They were of two kinds. One variety was the contact mine, a great iron case filled with dynamite exploded by a rod, the end of which was left just sticking out above the ground surface, and hidden by stones or sand. A pressure of the foot upon the end of the rod, or a stroke of the foot against it instantly fired the mass of explosive below. The second variety was electrical, fired by a concealed watcher from an observation post. Both were employed on a lavish scale.

Such were the preparations along the approaches from the coast, and to round them off a German force, when hostilities were declared, took possession of the port and buildings at Walfish Bay. During June and July, 1914, some thousands of men who had served with the German forces in the colony and passed into the reserve had been sent out again to bring up the garrison to war strength. The main body of the troops were now concentrated to the south, less, however, with the intention of standing upon the defensive than of launching, when the moment came, a counter-offensive in association with disaffected elements in the Union, whose numbers and influence the German Government had been led greatly to exaggerate. This proposed counter movement was the substance of the German plan. Safe on the side of the coast, they had apparently little doubt in any event of being able to obstruct an advance from south to north across Great Namaqualand.

Whether or not he surmised the nature of the German plan, and the probability is that he did, General Botha's scheme was calculated most effectively to circumvent it. His main operations were to be conducted from the sea. The difficulties were not light, but they could be overcome. General Botha justly relied upon the hardihood and endurance of his troops. The mounted men, the *burghers*, were accustomed to ride long distances on frugal fare and a minimum of water. The marching powers of the infantry were phenomenal. Most, *burghers* and infantrymen alike, were veterans.

The combined toughness and mobility of the Union forces were plainly points of the first importance, and they were points which a skilful general like Botha would assuredly turn to the fullest advantage. If, in face of an attack of that character from the coast, the Germans changed front, a formidable flanking movement could be thrown against them from the landward side; if they did not change front, they would be taken from seaward in flank and rear, and rounded up as they fell back. Either way their discomfiture was only a matter of time. The campaign was meant to be a campaign of manoeuvre, and, when once fully in train, swift and decisive.

Just because this was General Botha's plan the opening moves on his side gave no evidence of it. Like a skilful player he began with what appeared to be a gambit, and seemingly fell in with the German scheme. The first of the Union forces, five regiments of the South African Mounted Rifles, the Witwatersrand Rifles, and three batteries of the Transvaal Horse Artillery, under the command of Brigadier-General Lukin, sailed from Capetown on September 2. They landed at Port Nolloth in Little Namaqualand. From Port Nolloth through the hills, which here south of the Orange River come close to the coast, there is a light railway. It runs inland some fifty miles or so to Steinkopf, and then turns south to O'okiep, a copper mining centre.

At Steinkopf Lukin was to establish his base, since he was then within striking distance, a matter of forty-five miles, from Raman's Drift, one of the main crossings of the Orange River. The country

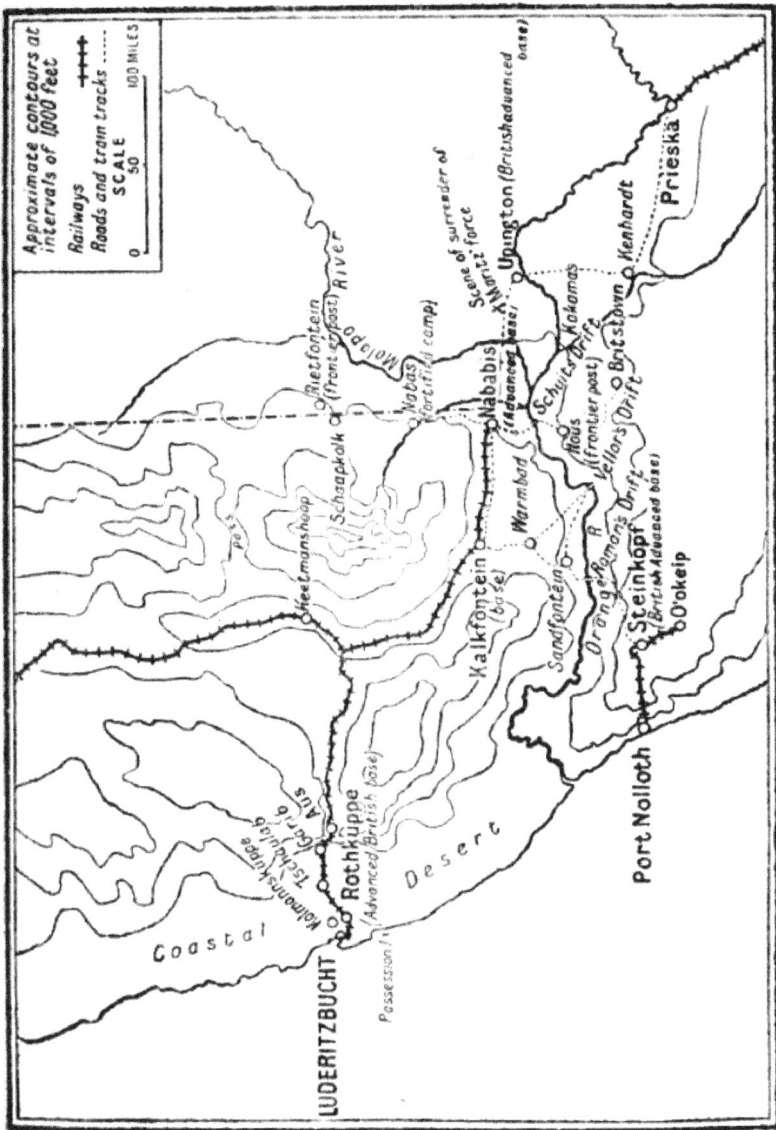

Approximate contours at
intervals of 1,000 feet
Railways +++++
Roads and tram tracks -------
SCALE
0   50   100 MILES

LUDERITZBUCHT

Coastal

Desert

Possession N

Keimanskuppe
Tschaukaib
Garub
Aus
Rothkuppe
(Advanced British base)

Port Nolloth

Pot 3

Heetmansheop

Schaaphoek

Kalkfontein
(base)

Sandfontein

Riet River

Rietfontein
or (Front outpost)

Nabas
(Fortified camp)

Nababis
Warmbad
Orange R.

Steinkopf
(British Advanced base)
O'okeip

Scene of surrender of
X Maritz force

Ukamas
(advanced base)
Rous
(frontier post)
Schuyts Drift
Kakamas
Vellors Drift
Britstown
Ramans Drift
Kenhardt
Upington (British advanced base)
Prieska

between is difficult, very hilly and rough, and almost wholly devoid of water. On its face this move was intended to check any German incursion into Union territory from Nababis. But it served incidentally to divert attention from the next step—the seizure of Luderitzbucht, and the more so because at Upington, 100 miles east of Nababis, preparations were afoot for an advance by a column of Union Mounted Infantry to co-operate with Lukin.

A fortnight after Lukin's force had embarked there sailed from Capetown in four transports an Expedition of Union regulars, two regiments of infantry, a section of the Cape Garrison Artillery, a battery of the Citizen Artillery, and a squadron of the Imperial Light Horse. The destination of these troops, who were commanded by Colonel Beves, was Luderitzbucht, and the flotilla, escorted by H.M.S. *Astræa*, arrived off that place on September 18. Some opposition was looked for, or at all events an unopposed landing could not be assumed, and the intention was to throw part of the troops ashore from the open sea so that they might, while an attack from the bay was going on, advance sufficiently inland across the sand dunes to cut the railway and isolate the German garrison. This intended procedure, however, was frustrated by a gale which made the landing of troops and stores outside the bay impossible. The only men who got ashore, though at great risk owing to the heavy swell, were several boatloads of scouts.

In view of the weather, and the danger of standing close in to such a shore, *Astræa* headed the transports into the bay. The anticipated resistance was not met with. Instead the scouts were found already to be in possession of the town. On the news that an attempt was being made to land troops outside of and to the south of the bay, assuming that the attempt might succeed, and knowing that retention of the town, even were it possible, was less important than control of the railway, with the power to destroy it, the German commandant had ordered an immediate evacuation, and had retired along the railway to Kolmanskuppe, some ten miles inland. The desolate little port of Luderitzbucht was formally surrendered by its *burgomaster* without a shot being fired. At first the civilian inhabitants were left at liberty within the boundaries. Some of them, however, took advantage of this freedom to convey information to the Germans at Kolmanskuppe of the strength and composition of Colonel Beves' force. When that was found out they were all rounded up and deported to Capetown.

In the meanwhile, having established his base at Steinkopf, Lukin had thrown forward his advance guard, two regiments of the Mounted

Rifles, to Raman's Drift, and the force had, after a sharp combat, captured that crossing. In this lower reach the Orange River is broad,
and in the flood season swift. The *drifts* are ferries, worked by boats
for passengers, and by pontoons for goods and cattle. Raman's Drift,
and Shuit's Drift, a hundred miles or thereabouts farther upstream
and close to Nababis formed the chief crossings between Great and
Little Namaqualand, and the scheme of operations at this stage of
the campaign was that while Lukin's men moved against the one, the
Mounted Column from Upington, under the command of Lieut.-
Colonel Maritz, was to seize, or at all events to blockade, the other.
Maritz was an officer of the Union Regulars, and there had been no
reason to suspect his fidelity.

No sooner, however, had he established contact with the enemy
than he transferred his *commando* to the German service. In this district
of Cape Colony men who held extremist views formed a local majority. They were a majority among Maritz's force. Whether he initiated
the sedition, or was influenced by the malcontents under his command, is somewhat uncertain, and his later conduct would suggest that
he was half-hearted.

Be that as it may, the immediate effect was totally to upset Lukin's
enterprise. From Raman's Drift the two advance regiments of Mounted Rifles pressed upon the retreating Germans as far as Sandfontein,
where the enemy had established a camp, which with its equipment
was taken. Sandfontein is distant from Raman's Drift twenty-five
miles, and it is so named because of the well or water-hole at that spot.
It was found, however, that the Germans, besides wrecking the pumps,
had poisoned the water. This was the first instance in the campaign of
what proved to be their settled practice. To hold Sandfontein in any
strength was in the circumstances out of the question. The country
round about was scoured by patrols, and no signs of the enemy met
with anywhere. Concluding, perhaps somewhat too hastily, but not
unnaturally, that the hostile evacuation was deliberate, and ascribing it
to pressure of the converging force from Upington, the commandant
of the advance guard, leaving only a patrol at Sandfontein, fell back
to the *drift*.

The *drift* was regained on September 24. On the following day
the squadron holding Sandfontein was attacked by a German force of
some 1,500 men, headed by Colonel von Heydebreck. That officer,
commanding-in-chief the German troops in South-west Africa, and
handling in person the present main concentration, had, on finding

himself reassured from the side of Upington, decided to sweep the other Union troops from the north of the Orange River, and in doing so to defeat them if possible in detail. When news of the attack upon Sandfontein reached the Union camp at the *drift* a relief—another squadron of Mounted Rifles, and a half-battery of Transvaal Horse Artillery—was at once sent out under the command of Lieut.-Colonel Grant. This was what Heydebreck had expected.

On the approach of the relief his troops, under orders, dispersed. Grant advanced to Sandfontein without encountering any resistance, or indeed without meeting with the enemy anywhere. The ruse seems to have convinced him that the attack had been merely an attempted surprise. But just as his men had dismounted after their long and thirsty ride, the Germans, hidden in the hills, swarmed down upon the post. This time they did not come to close quarters. In view of the marksmanship of the Union riflemen it did not pay. They opened upon the camp with shell fire. Very soon Grant realised that he had been surrounded. His two guns gallantly entered upon the unequal duel. They kept up the fight for several hours, and though in that time they put various enemy pieces out of action, were themselves at the finish knocked out.

The only hope now lay in getting up a second relief from the *drift* to break through the beleaguerment. But after the movements which had already taken place—first the advance to Raman's Drift from Steinkopf, then the ride to Sandfontein and back—the only part of the force still fit to face another ride of twenty-five miles with a stiff battle at the end of it were two squadrons of the 4th South Africans. Even they and their mounts were fagged. Fagged as they were, however, they set out, and though outnumbered by five to one, essayed to break through. The feat, it is hardly necessary to say, proved impossible. From within the cordon Grant, notwithstanding that he had been wounded by a shell, led the co-operation.

Fearing that he might escape, the Germans now closed in. He beat them off. Since the sound of battle with the relief force had died away, it was clear that the relief effort had failed. Repulsed in his assault, the enemy renewed his bombardment, and the fight dragged on. Of the total force holding the post when the combat began, less than 400 men, more than half, were by this time casualties. Further effort at relief could not be looked for. Finally, late in the day, Grant sent out a flag of truce and surrendered.

This was to all intents the first brush in the campaign, and the

Germans had scored the honours. But far too much was made of the episode at the time. Nothing more than one of the ups and downs which have to be expected in any armed struggle, it was magnified into a grave disaster. In a country lending itself to surprise and ruse, it would be astonishing if every ruse proved abortive. The real importance of the check, almost negligible from a military standpoint, lay in its political consequences.

Combined with the defection of Maritz, a much more serious matter, it stirred into activity the extremist elements whose ordinary antagonism to Botha and the Nationalist majority had been further embittered by the Union Government's policy. Their armed rising in the Transvaal and the Orange River State was headed by Beyers and De Wet. Neither desired to see the South African Union under German rule. What they opposed was the war. Most of all, however, they were swayed by party feeling. Very wisely, in the Union Government's dealing with the rising, that fact was recognised. Severity would have poisoned political difference. The forbearance of General Botha and his colleagues under provocation went far to heal it.

But besides detaining General Botha at Capetown during the next four months these events had the effect of prolonging the campaign in South-west Africa by at least that length of time. The intended descent upon Walfish Bay while the Germans were busy upon the Orange River was judged now to be premature, and the force of two brigades of infantry with artillery support placed under the command of the veteran General Sir Duncan M'Kenzie for that purpose, and embarked at Capetown immediately after the departure of Beves's column, were diverted to Luderitz Bay, where therefore there was a very strong concentration of Union troops. And the concentration served a useful purpose.

It was evident that, in association with Maritz, the Germans meant to launch a counter-offensive into Little Namaqualand, and had they acted promptly, and while the political trouble within the Union was as its height, it is not unlikely that a good deal of mischief might have resulted. The powerful force at Luderitz Bay acted as a deterrent. The Germans hesitated to commit themselves finally to an expedition into Cape Colony while their own bases and line of communications lay open to be attacked and cut. After the affair at Sandfontein they had retaken Raman's Drift, but they were not yet certain that the Union effort to move a large body of men across the coastal desert would end in failure. On his side Botha played up to this hesitancy. He now wanted time, well aware that if the German counter-move did not synchronise with the Beyers-De Wet rising, it could do little harm.

Hence it was that M'Kenzie at Luderitz Bay soon began to show signs of activity. He thrust the German garrison in the first place out of Kolmanskuppe, and pushed on to Rothkuppe, more than twenty miles inland. And there for the time he sat down. But the leisure was eyewash. Behind him a body of labour, skilfully controlled by that able engineer, Sir George Farrar, was hard at it relaying the ripped up railway track. This done, and it took little more than a fortnight, M'Kenzie made another bound forward. The second move was to Tschaukab, forty miles inland. There again there was a halt. But also once more the reconstruction of the track, and the protection of it against sand drifts, was taken in hand. The feat of moving in force across a region where there is neither food nor water looked the more impracticable because it was now the height of the southern summer, and the season of sandstorms.

One of the natural curses of this coastal tract are the hot winds laden with fine dust blown off the dunes. The air becomes like a fog, and the particles penetrate into everything, food and drink alike, and insinuate themselves into clothing, until life seems a cross between a perpetual itch and a perpetual choke. Nothing but the irrepressible cheerfulness of men of British race under adversity enabled the troops to put up with the conditions. Of course conditions were not like that always, though the sandblasts were frequent enough.

There was the expectation also that sooner or later a real brush would occur with the enemy. Hitherto he had proved distinctly illusive. Skirmishes up the line towards Garub, another twenty miles' trek, were always going on for the purpose of spoiling his wrecking tactics. Once when the Union force pushed right on to Garub the foe put up a genuine fight. After that, about mid-December, he moved his advanced base from Garub, no longer safe enough, to Aus. Garub lies at the foot of the outer or seaward slope of the mountains amid a landscape almost Dantesque in its wild singularity. Aus is on the other side of the heights, and in habitable country. Between the two points runs a pass, and the railway is carried through it. The Germans had elected to fight at Garub because they wanted time to fortify the pass and sow it with land mines.

But M'Kenzie, as soon as the track to Garub was in working order, moved his advanced base there, and resumed his prevention-is-better-than-cure procedure, giving enemy mine-buriers a nimble life. The

Germans thought much of the difficulties of this pass, and they spared no pains to obstruct it. It was here where their treatment of the natives began to tell against them. At the foot of the hills the British force came into contact with the Hottentots, and as the Hottentots were sworn foes of everything German they soon let it be known that there were ways round.

Thus when the time came the Germans at Aus could be dropped upon, as it were, out of the clouds, and all their labour rendered futile. M'Kenzie at any rate had now manoeuvred his forces across the whole breadth of the desert, and he had the railway behind him both secure and operating well. And it was clear that the Germans did not like the development one bit. At the beginning of December, reinforced by Maritz, they had indulged in an incursion over the Cape border and had taken the village and police post of Nous. But they had in that quarter shown caution. The thrust from the coast disconcerted them.

Unfortunately, at this juncture M'Kenzie's column sustained an irreparable loss. Sir George Farrar, whose energy was indomitable, and who was up and down the line in all weathers and always on the spot where reparation was in progress, travelling, as was his wont in a motor trolley, came into collision during a sandstorm with a light engine. It was one of the risks he had habitually run, and as habitually escaped by a hairsbreadth. This time it cost him his life. Happily for the welfare of the force whose very existence depended upon his resolution and skill, for he almost more than any man had made this seemingly impossible advance possible, the work he had undertaken to do was then nearly complete.

To the men of M'Kenzie's force the war appeared slow. It was not quite the kind of campaigning they had anticipated, and not knowing the real meaning of their movement, their patience was tried. Nevertheless, things *were* moving. The time had now, at the end of December, arrived when the main movement of the campaign on the side of the Union was to be set on foot. On December 21, under the command of Colonel Skinner, there were embarked at Capetown the 3rd and 4th Brigades of Union Infantry, the 1st Imperial Light Horse, Grobelaar's (mounted) Scouts, a brigade of Heavy Artillery, and machine-gun details. The force steamed to Walfish Bay. Seeing the flotilla of transports enter the lagoon, the small German contingent holding the town retired. Opposition would have been futile. Beyond the exchange of a few shots with the last of the retreating enemy, the landing, which took place on Christmas Day, was uneventful.

The next fortnight was taken up with the unloading of ammunition and transport, the landing and housing of stores, the construction of water condensing plant—before retiring the Germans had destroyed the town supply apparatus—and the other work of laying out a base camp. On January 13, however, Skinner threw out a reconnaissance in force towards Swakopmund. Since that place was the terminus of the railway line to Karibib, the chances seemed to be that the enemy would try for a time to hold it, and the Union commander desired to measure the exact strength of the opposition. The road to Swakopmund, about twenty miles, skirted the bay. The mounted men had to ride across the dunes, the sand in many places so loose that the horses sank up to their knees.

But no evidence of opposition was forthcoming. Not until the troopers were close upon Swakopmund, and negotiating the last ridge of dunes overlooking the place, did anything exciting occur. Then, at the seaward and lower end of the ridge, four land mines went off in quick succession. The explosions threw up vast clouds of dust, and for the moment nobody could tell exactly what had happened, or how many men had been lost. But when the dust cloud cleared the loss was found to be two troopers and their horses. The mines, it was afterwards ascertained, were electrical, and had been fired from an observation post. The loose sand had, however, rendered them to a great extent harmless, and it must vastly have astonished those of the enemy still in Swakopmund to see this body of horsemen, who *should* have been annihilated, dashing towards the town at a gallop.

The German detachment deemed it prudent to dash out at the other end, and hustle at their best speed inland. They had relied for defence, not only on the land mines, but on the poisoning of the water supply. Discovery of this latter fact caused General Botha, when he learned of it, to send to Colonel Franke, who had succeeded von Heydebreck in the command of the German forces in the colony, a warning that if such a violation of the usages of civilised warfare continued Franke would be held personally answerable. Franke's reply was that water-holes were never poisoned without a notice being left to that effect. If left, the notices had somehow got lost, or been stolen. None were ever found. Heydebreck had lost his life by the explosion of a new type of bomb while witnessing experiments with it.

It may have been to allay alarm at Windhuk of this threatening approach that the local newspapers came out with startling accounts of how whole troops of the Union attackers had been blown to pieces.

Bloodcurdling details of the havoc supported by circumstantial personal narratives adorned their columns, and possibly enough, since there was not a word about the poisoning of the wells, Germans, both in the capital and in scattered ranch houses about the country, read these accounts with satisfaction. Before long they were to find out that, like so many other German stories of the war, the "battle" was only a masterpiece of lurid fiction.

In calculating upon their various devices the Germans had left out of account the native population. Following upon the outbreak of war the natives had deserted from farms and ranches almost *en masse*. They betook themselves to the hills, or wandered in bands about the country. Wherever the Germans poisoned a well or laid a mine or contrived a trap, hostile eyes were upon them, and if their contrivances were not secretly made harmless, and their wires cut, the Union troops, as soon as they appeared, never failed to receive warning. As scouts and guides with their unrivalled knowledge of the country, the natives were invaluable. And they were heart and soul with the invasion, for to them it meant deliverance. The whereabouts and movements of German forces, the camp conversations on German plans and orders, the safe though little-known ways over heights and through the wide and almost roadless wilderness, were all reported.

Thanks to German inhumanity, the Union forces had at their disposal, without the trouble of organising it and without cost, an Intelligence Service at once first class and absolutely sure. It enabled the Union forces to undertake with boldness and confidence movements which otherwise could only have been essayed with caution, and time and again to bring off surprises. Nearly every native had at least a smattering of the *lingua franca* of South Africa, the Dutch Taal. There is no doubt this state of things acted upon the Germans as a discouragement, but confident in the successful issue of the war as a whole, though they might be beaten in South-west Africa, they promised themselves an ample revenge.

As already pointed out, it was an essential feature of General Botha's plan that the attack from the coast should be supported by an attack from overland. The overland attack, consequent upon the defection of Maritz, and the repercussion of his desertion on the fortunes of Lukin's Column, had been reshaped, and amplified. The Union forces operating from overland were entrusted until General Smuts was free for active service to the command of General van Deventer, and the strategy designed was, while holding the enemy in the centre, to en-

velop him on both wings. This was the traditional South African manoeuvre, and, being suited to the country, and to the mobility of the
Union columns, it could not in skilful hands miss success. So little,
however, did the Germans and their auxiliaries under Maritz suspect
what was impending, that from Nous, which they had held from the
beginning of December, they advanced to attack Britstown. At Nous
the Union commando, though five hundred strong, had declined action, and abandoned the position. Most were politically opposed to
the war, and serving without zeal.

The Germans and Maritz expected the same thing to occur at
Britstown. In part it did. Some of the Britstown commando dispersed
as soon as the enemy opened fire. But the remainder stood firm to
the orders of their commandant, Major Breedt, and with him fell back
upon Kakamas. It was not until January 23 that the Germans and
Maritz moved to attack Upington. The delay of more than a month,
however, had made all the difference. In the meantime General van
Deventer had taken charge, and already Colonel Bouwer, who had
been put in command of the column at Steinkopf, had recaptured
Raman's Drift. Deventer was now at Upington. That place, which is a
hundred miles within the Union boundary, on the Orange River, and
an important jumping-off position, was one of the four prospective
starting points of the overland converging movement.

On the right wing, Colonel Berrangé was, with a flying column of
two thousand men, to set out from Kuruman in Southern Bechuanaland; cross the Kalahari Desert, and strike the boundary of South-west
Africa near Rietfontein. On the left wing, Bouwer was to strike up
from Raman's Drift. In the centre, from Upington and Kenhardt, the
main forces were to move upon Schuit's Drift and Vellor's Drift. In
the meantime, the terminus of the Cape Railway at Prieska was being
pushed rapidly forward so that it might in due course be linked up
with the German system at Kalkfontein.

Undoubtedly it would very seriously disconcert these arrangements if the enemy could seize Upington. In that case, the intended
movements of the Union troops on the wings would have been left
in the air. General van Deventer, however, was not the man to allow
arrangements thus to be thrown out of gear. It does not appear to
have been known either to the Germans or to Maritz that Deventer
had at Upington a strong backing of artillery. They attacked up the
Orange River in force, but with at most only two batteries of guns;
these, however, were considered ample to overawe the looked-for re-

sistance.

On approaching the town, a German *parlementaire* was sent forward with a demand for surrender. Of course, the demand was refused. Then the German guns unlimbered, and opened fire. To their surprise, they found themselves in the gun duel outweighted. It was decided, therefore, forthwith to rush the town by assault and to capture the Union guns, a valuable spoil. But the Union gunners shot the attack to pieces, and when the on-rush had been thrown into confusion, Deventer, who had his mounted force on the leash, launched a counterattack. The enemy's repulse speedily became a rout, and the battle a mad, galloping flight and pursuit, kept up for a distance of fifteen miles until those of the enemy who had not been cut down had been raced to a standstill. Having completed a long ride just before the battle, they and their mounts were done.

Now surrounded, there was nothing for them except surrender. Kemp, the associate of Maritz, with forty-four other ex-Union officers, and 563 men laid down their arms. Maritz himself, fearing to face the consequences of his treachery, desperately cut his way out, and with the wreck of the rout, scattered into small parties, dribbled back into German territory, or, following the western confines of the Kalahari to the north, sought refuge in Portuguese Angola. There, later, Maritz was discovered and arrested.

Since this severe reverse had disclosed what was impending, the Germans, in another attempt to queer Deventer's plans, delivered an attack on February 3 upon Kakamas. They were repulsed again. The failure marked the end of their offensive.

CHAPTER 3.

General Botha's Campaign: Second Phase

M'Kenzie's dash from Aus to Gibeon—The action at that place—
M'Kenzie's tactics—Botha At the beginning of February General
Botha assumed the active command, and the circumstance may be
regarded as opening the second phase of the campaign. Up to this
time, though—in the seizure of Swakopmund and in M'Kenzie's advance to Garub—the foundations for swift developments had been
laid, and securely laid, the struggle had proved indecisive. It had now
been protracted for five months; that period should have sufficed, had
no complications arisen, to bring the operations to an end. There had
been complications, and they had incidentally helped the enemy to
maintain an active defence.

The German counter-attack, however, as already seen, had failed,
and the rising of the extremists within the Union had been a fiasco.
If, so far, little headway had been made by the Union forces operating
against South-west Africa from overland, from the coast the gains had
been important. M'Kenzie's enterprise, to begin with and on appearances the least promising of any, had been steadily successful. No unto-
ward incident had interrupted it. Skinner also was firmly in possession
of Swakopmund, and his arrangements both there and at Walfish Bay
had been rapidly advanced. Everything was ready for pushing these
undertakings home.

Coincidently with General Botha's departure from Capetown
there were embarked there strong commandos of mounted men
under the command of Brigadier-Generals Myburgh and Brits and
Manie Botha, all experienced and skilful leaders; a brigade of infantry entrusted to the command of Brigadier-General Beves; a force of

field artillery, and a complement of heavy guns. All these troops with their equipment were destined for and in due course landed at Walfish Bay.

On his way to that base General Botha went ashore at Luderitz Bay, and journeying inland, inspecting the work done on the railway line, visited the camp at Tschaukab. For nearly two months, the hottest and in this region the dustiest time of the year, the troops there had waited for the word to advance. In honour of the general's visit they were drawn up in parade order. Despite all they had gone through their health had continued good, and their fine discipline was now reflected in their bearing. It extorted from the commander-in-chief a tribute of admiration. Warmly in sympathy with his men, and knowing, as all able generals do, the value of the moral factor, he expressed his keen appreciation of the work they had done.

The British Empire, he told them, was grateful for it. They had waited and with patience for the day of advance. They would not have to wait much longer. Their loyalty and their steadiness had gone far already, and he knew would go farther, towards carrying through the task to which the Union of South Africa had set its hand, and with the determination that the task would be achieved. One purpose of his visit was to discuss the situation with General M'Kenzie. "I hope," he concluded, "you will soon have the order to go forward. I wish you all possible success. God bless you."

Three days later (February 11) Botha reached Swakopmund. The place had been transformed into a centre of activity. For months existence at this remote little port had been utterly dull and uneventful. The German contingent holding it had watched day by day and week by week, and until the arrival of the first flotilla of transports nothing had happened. Now encampments and horse-lines covered the surrounding sand dunes, and artillery rumbled through the mean streets. There was an incessant coming and going. Everybody was busy, for it was not intended that time should be lost.

As its German name indicated. Swakopmund is at the mouth of the Swakop River, which comes down from the interior through a break in the mountains. Some twenty miles up country from the town the Swakop is joined by a tributary, the Kham, and it was along the valley of the Kham that the railway had been laid to Karibib, a hundred miles inland. Both streams flowed across the desert coastal tract. Ordinarily, and always in the dry season, their beds were mere tracks of stones and scrub. Indeed, like all the streams flowing from the mountains into this arid zone, their waters disappeared into the thirsty soil many miles from the coast. Only now and then at irregular intervals of years were the streams sufficiently in flood to traverse the whole expanse, and that phenomenon always indicated exceptionally heavy rains on the plateaux. It was now the southern autumn and the beginning of the wet season.

The more immediate geographical objective of Botha's intended advance was the railway junction at Karibib, since the capture of that point would sever the main German communications with the important northern districts of the colony. But the problem of reaching Karibib was, like the problem of reaching Garub, one chiefly of water supply. Thousands of men and thousands of horses need in the aggregate and from day to day a respectable total of gallons—the contents, in fact, of a fair-sized reservoir, and to move the contents of such a reservoir daily over miles of rough country, much more to keep up with a movement which would be of no effect if not rapid, was no trifling enigma.

This was the proposition which had first of all to be solved, and upon a workable basis, for hitches in such a matter could not be risked. To have a strong force on the spot was all very well. But it was only the A B C of the situation. How to lift the force across the desert was the rest of the alphabet. And of course, knowing this, the Germans had neglected nothing to obstruct the lifting. They had sown the valley of the Kham with mines and barred it with entanglements. Every day's delay, they were well aware, would add to the embarrassments of the invasion. If the advance could be prolonged for weeks, and it very well might be, the water trouble would become more than acute; it might wreck the enterprise.

But within a week of Botha's arrival the Swakop River came down from the mountains in flood, and it was one of the rare and phenomenal floods which carried the waters on and into the sea. Now when that takes place, even though the flood speedily runs off and the stream sinks on the surface to a trickle, or becomes apparently dry, there is always for a long time afterwards water to be found by boring in the river bed. General Botha seized upon this phenomenon at once. It simplified the problem enormously. Giving the Kham valley and its mines and entanglements a miss, he could, without undue anxiety as to water, throw his main force inland along the bed of the Swakop. And the advance, in part relieved of the necessity of transporting water daily from the coast, could be swift, with all the chance, while the enemy was occupied in watching the valley of the Kham, of seizing the pass opening up the road to Windhuk.

Meanwhile, all the appearances had to be kept up of an intention to advance along the Kham valley, assisted by threats from other quarters. M'Kenzie received orders to move his main camp to Garub, and by February 19 had completed the move. Botha thereupon pushed out from Swakopmund and occupied Goanekontes, at the confluence of the Swakop and Kham Rivers, and away to the south-east Deventer also suddenly became active. Following a rapid march from Upington, he attacked and drove the Germans out of Nakob (February 26), and crossed the frontier to the north of the Orange River. While a flying column on his left, detached for the purpose, was sent along the Orange River to seize Schuit's Drift and Vellor's Drift, he himself struck straight for Nabas.

Nabas was a fortified post on the main road, or track, from Upington to Kalkfontein, and the Germans had here laid out an entrenched camp, the advanced base of their counter-offensive. They now defended the position obstinately. At all costs the dash of the Union forces upon Kalkfontein had to be delayed. For a good half-day the enemy held out. Deventer, however, steadily closed in, and at the opportune moment, for which he had proved himself to possess a sure eye, rushed the entrenchments by storm. This had been, so far, one of the stiffest fights of the campaign. The severity of the German reverse was disclosed by their disinclination from that time to come to close quarters. Deventer now had them on the move, and meant to keep them moving.

On March 6 Berrangé set out from Kuruman with his desert column. His force was made up of the 5th South African Mounted Rifles, the Kalahari Horse, Cullman's Horse, and the Bechuanaland Rifles. This advance was one of the most romantic and adventurous movements in the war. Berrangé had for hundreds of miles to cross an utterly lonely wilderness, lifeless, and save for the few and extremely dispersed wells, or water-holes, totally arid. Disappearing into its solitudes, he and his men were for a fortnight lost to sight. He was to follow westward the bed of the Kuruman River, the depression which meanders through the waste, and, except at the rare intervals of unusual rainfall in Bechuanaland, dry. They had therefore to carry their water supply with them, and use it with severe economy. But by the end of the fortnight the column had struck the Molopo river, which flows north to south along the western confines of the desert, and close to the foot of the Great Namaqualand hills.

Just at the other side of the Molopo was the frontier of South-west Africa—the 20th degree of east longitude. Among the foothills, and upon the boundary line is Rietfontein, a Union police post, in pre-war days reckoned the loneliest and most isolated in the service, and close to it, on the western side of the boundary, a German post, Schaapkolk. The Germans had taken Rietfontein, but on the appearance of Berrangé's formidable force, the garrison, evacuating the position, joined up with the Schaapkolk contingent. Together the two attempted a resistance. Berrangé, however, made very short work of this opposition; knocked the German blockhouse and other defences to pieces, and captured the surviving defenders.

From Schaapkolk he struck north-west to Hasuur, another German fortified post, and took it. His column was intended to cross the mountains to Keetmanshoop, and by that manoeuvre to turn the anticipated hostile resistance in the formidable natural position between the Great and Little Karas ranges. There is between Hasuur and Keetmanshoop, which lies in the central valley of Great Namaqualand, and on the line of railway, a "*nek*" or pass, the highest summits of the Great Karas to the south of the track, and other mountains of less though still of considerable elevation to the north. In the pass, at, the Germans had built a blockhouse, originally to check native movements during the Hottentot war, but the post was now useful as barring the way into the central valley.

It is hardly probable that the Germans had looked for this daring threat to their main communications from so remote a quarter as Kuruman, but whether they did or no, their troubles now began to follow in quick succession. In view of the circumstances already related regarding the flood water along the Swakop, Botha might, had his transport been complete enough, have entered upon his advance in February. But, of course, the natural phenomenon had not been taken into account, and he had to wait until the equipment machinery duly revolved. In more senses than one the delay, nearly one month, was unfortunate. It gave the enemy time to move up reinforcements, and to set about obstructing the Swakop valley. As soon, therefore, as transport could be relied upon, the commander-in-chief attacked. Obstructing entrance to the Swakop valley, the enemy had fortified positions at Pforte, Jackalswater, and Riet. These posts were distant from each other rather less than ten miles, and as points of support formed in effect one line of defence. Delivered on March 20, the at-

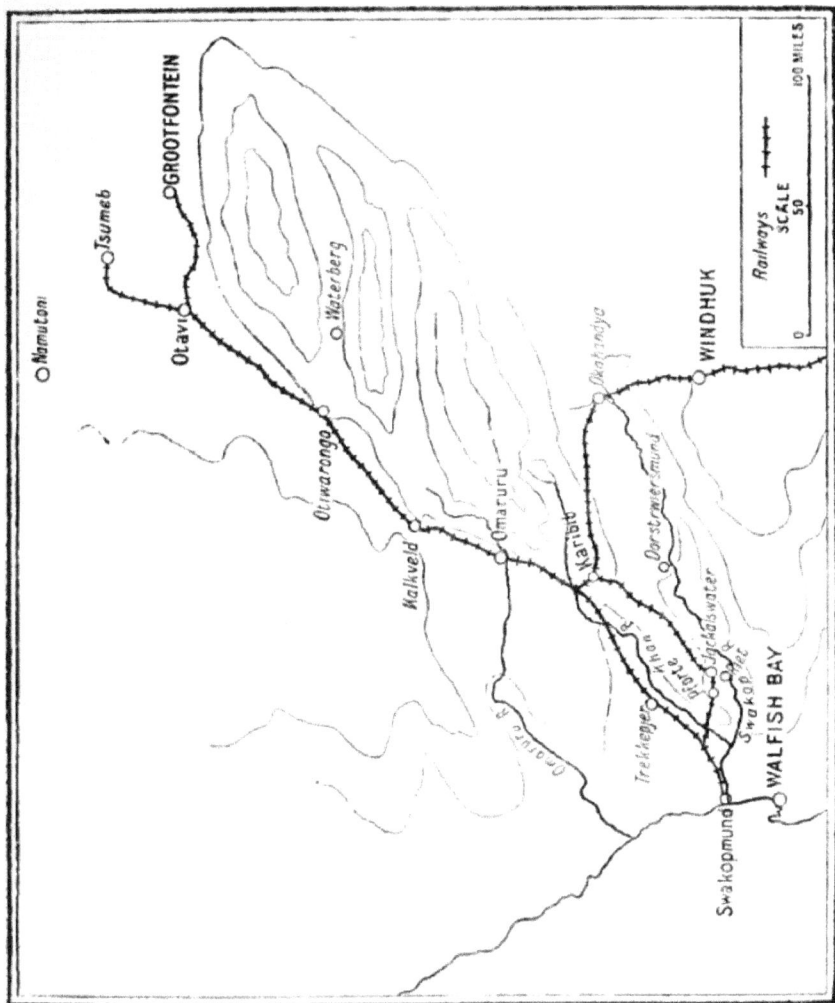

GROOTFONTEIN

Tsumeb

Namutoni

Otavi

Waterberg

Otiwarongo

Walkveld

Omaruru

Karibib

Okahandya

WINDHUK

Dorstrivermund

Salt-water

Trekkoppe
Khan
Arais
Nonidas
Swakopriez

Swakopmund

WALFISH BAY

Groot River

Railways

SCALE

0   50   100 MILES

tack was in three columns, the infantry in the centre, mounted men on either wing.

On the left the *commando* of Colonel Alberts, intended to turn the position at Pforte, scored a swift success. The attention of the enemy was concentrated chiefly upon the attack in the centre, evidently convinced that it was the real thing. Alberts' men, covering their movement by the hollows between the ridges, got well in before their approach was detected, and the Germans here, finding themselves outflanked, no longer stood their ground. The *burghers* forthwith charged home, rode them down as they fled, and rounded up more than two hundred prisoners. What seems especially to have demoralised the resistance was the South African practice of firing from the saddle at a gallop. To the Germans, dexterity of that kind was a novelty, and its deadly effect at short range took them by surprise.

In the centre, where their strength was massed, they had held firm, but at Riet the turning movement proved as successful as at Pforte, though from the longer detour it was not so prompt. The same tactics of unobserved approach were followed. Instead of attempting to assault the position at Riet directly, the mounted column rode round towards the rear. The Germans evacuated their defences. The retreat on both wings leading immediately to a retirement in the centre, from now on the battle became a pursuit. The enemy were shepherded back along the loop railway in the direction of Karibib. This was really the first pitched action in the campaign. All the advantage of position lay with the Germans. They had selected it, and the choice showed skill. In tactics, however, they had been entirely out-matched. At one blow Botha had cleared them out of the Swakop valley, and in that direction he afterwards met with no serious opposition.

While he was making ready for the next bound, the overland operations entered upon another stage—the linking up of Deventer's and Berrangé's forces. On the eastern spurs of the Great Karas mountains the Germans still held several fortified positions, notably at Plattbeen, where they had also an entrenched camp, and at Geitsaub, both places on and commanding the track from Upington to Keetmanshoop. It was the probability, if not something more, that with these posts yet in the enemy's hands, he might thrust a strong force between Berrangé and Deventer, isolating the former, and by a threat in flank holding up the further advance of the latter, General Deventer therefore decided to clear this interlying tract of country. With that object he detached his brother, Colonel Dirk van Deventer, at the head of the

4th Mounted Brigade, to open up the Upington-Keetmanshoop road which joins close under the pass with the road from Rietfontein, the route Berrangé was understood to be following. In this movement Colonel Dirk van Deventer met with considerable opposition, a proof of its timeliness and sagacity.

The Germans resisted in the first instance at Davignab. Worsting them in this combat, he moved on to Plattbeen, covering the forty-miles of mountain country between the two points in two days. He came in sight of the Plattbeen camp on March 24. Despite this sudden appearance, the Germans had prepared to hold out. But time was important, and Colonel D. van Deventer, not disposed to waste it, assaulted and carried the camp by storm. Geitsaub, another forty miles farther up in the hills, and a stiff climb, was an even tougher and riskier job. Here, on April 2, the enemy sought finally to bar the passage, and had they been successful Colonel Dirk van Deventer would have been stranded with his men in the mountains, with 160 miles of wild upland track between them and Nabas. He was, however, a skilful hand at enveloping and invisible approach tactics, and he compelled the Germans to evacuate their defences without on his own side suffering a casualty. He joined Berrangé at Kiriis West on April 14.

The movement from east to west was coincident with another on the part of M'Kenzie's Column from west to east. Receiving the order definitely to begin his advance, M'Kenzie struck his camp at Garub on March 28. By a detour across the mountains his advance guard had reached and turned the surprised Germans out of Aus on March 30. This dash, a notable feat of endurance, cleared the way to Aus for the main force. The effect of the two movements from east and west respectively was now speedily disclosed by the German abandonment of Kalkfontein. Undoubtedly had their line of retreat to the north not been menaced from both sides, all the likelihood was that at Kalkfontein, their military centre in the south of the colony, they would have put up a determined defence, and the more so because of the natural difficulties of the country.

The position of Kalkfontein had been chosen on account of its strength. It commanded a pass narrow and rugged enough to enable a very small force to defy many times their own number. If, however, the way to the north was not open and secure, such a defence would be worse than ill-advised. And this was the reason for the preparations begun so long before both at Luderitz Bay and at Kuruman. For had the enemy been able with a small force to hold up a direct advance from the south, then he could have massed his main strength against the movement from Swakopmund, and with every chance in his favour of rendering it abortive. As matters now were, however, his force was divided, and neither part strong enough for its purpose. The southern troops besides were in jeopardy, and before they could effect a junction with the northern Botha from Swakopmund would have driven his thrust home.

Even at this time, therefore, it was plain that the Germans had been outmanoeuvred. Their southern forces were in full movement towards the north, saving what equipment they could, destroying or leaving behind them the remainder. General van Deventer, moving up from Nabas on April 5, entered Kalkfontein without opposition, and his advance guard penetrated to Kanus, fifteen miles farther up the pass, without finding any signs of the enemy. On his part, Bouwer, coming from Raman's Drift through Warmbad with the 17th Mounted Rifles and Hartigan's Horse, also closed to the front at Kalkfontein, and on April 11 General Smuts arrived to take over the command of the united Columns.

Without further delay Smuts pushed on to Keetmanshoop, the administrative capital of Great Namaqualand. This southern sector of the campaign had become in fact a contest in pace. On the one hand, with Smuts in pursuit the Germans were hustling towards Gibeon; on the other, M'Kenzie was hurrying across country from Aus towards the same point. If the enemy reached and passed Gibeon first, then he would have made good his escape; if not, he would have to fight his way out. M'Kenzie had the greater distance to cover, and also, it may be added, by far the more difficult road. But here the marching powers and endurance of his troops told. In two days he had (April 17) reached Bethany, sixty miles; in another two days he was at Beersheba, another sixty miles.

The last stage, to Gibeon, was seventy miles. Unfortunately, M'Kenzie could not at once set out upon it, for he had far outstripped his transport. The roads in South-west Africa are for wheeled transport not ideal, to put it mildly, and he had to wait four days until the supply columns closed up. All the same, he was at Gibeon by the evening of the 25th. The Germans retiring from the south had not yet passed. They had, in fact, reached Gibeon almost at the same time. During the night after his arrival M'Kenzie sent out a strong detachment with orders to cut the railway line. But the German commander had plainly looked for some such attempt, and he had a much stronger force under arms. And his men, brought to bay, fought desperately. This struggle in the darkness, fitfully lit at intervals by star shells, was bitter. On the Union side, the losses were considerable, and seeing that the South African detachment were outnumbered, and were in action at the end of a week of forced marches, the circumstance is not surprising. What is surprising is, not that their attempt did not come off, but that they, as a body, came out of this combat able to make good their retirement. There could be no more striking testimony to their valour.

Nor can the attempt to cut the railway forthwith be adjudged a mistake. It was a measure which no active general would in the circumstances neglect. The effort was sound campaigning. Besides, as a result of this night fighting, in which a good proportion of his force had been involved, the enemy was next day in no condition to continue his flight. He had to entrench. At dawn M'Kenzie attacked. His tactics, backed by a brisk and effective bombardment, were an envelopment, and his men, who after so many months of waiting had at last got to grips and were not to be denied, worked round the hostile defences on both flanks.

When the South Africans were seen to be closing in the Germans made for the loophole still open. They left behind some of their artillery, and much more of their ammunition and material, and they retired in very broken order. In short, they were nothing like so effective a force as before. Nevertheless, in the mass they got away. As to that, it should be said that these German troops, the largest body of those in South-west Africa, out-numbered M'Kenzie's Column considerably. It was the business of that commander to hold them, if possible, until General Smuts came up; it was not his business—unaided it was impracticable—to round them up. Failing that, he did what was decidedly the next best thing; he seriously damaged them.

At Gibeon the retreating enemy troops were 200 miles from Windhuk, and nearly 350 miles from Karibib, and it was plainly important that General Botha should move his forces across the coastal belt before the Germans could effect a concentration. Accordingly, on the same day that the action at Gibeon was fought (April 26), the commander-in-chief entered upon his advance up the Swakop valley. Suspecting by this time probably that a move of that kind might take place, the German commander in the north thought to check it by a counter-thrust down the Kham valley which would cut Botha's communications. Botha, however, had foreseen the likelihood of just that counter-move.

While, therefore, he set out himself with his mounted *commandos* along the Swakop valley, he sent Skinner with the infantry along the valley of the Kham. A few miles beyond Trekkopjes Skinner fell in with the German column marching in the opposite direction. There was an obstinate battle. The enemy did his utmost to break through. Could he have inflicted a reverse on Skinner's brigade the movement of Botha would have been brought to a halt. Prudently falling back upon Trekkopjes, a position of some strength, Skinner refused to be dislodged from it, and the Germans finally realised that they were only wasting time and losing men. Their retreat was hastened by an attack on the part of a detachment of Naval armoured cars.

To state the position briefly, the Germans had staked their chance upon this move and had lost. While they were engaged in it, Botha was going rapidly forward, his four brigades of burghers disposed in widely-spreading parallel columns; himself and his staff, with a small bodyguard, in the centre. It was a formation suited to swift manoeuvre. The drive was pushed on to Dorstriviermund, nearly 100 miles inland, and at the western foot of the "*nek*" through which the Swakop finds its way seaward. From Dorstriviermund, Myburgh and Manie Botha were dispatched across the pass north-east to cut the railway between Karibib and Windhuk. Their enterprise succeeded. In two days they were back again.

Botha then (May 5) moved upon Karibib. It was a drive of forty miles over very difficult country, and country too without a water supply of any kind. No certainty existed besides that Karibib might not be held in force. The best assurance against such a contingency was speed. Botha set out before daybreak. By noon his advance guard were within sight of the junction. In the early afternoon he had himself arrived. The garrison laid down their arms.

The German force in the Kham valley, with Skinner in front of them and Botha in the rear, had now no alternative save to retreat by a wide detour to the north upon Omaruru. Skinner with the infantry marched up unopposed along the railway line, following the bed of the Kham, and Karibib became the jumping off place for a movement upon Windhuk.

From Karibib to Windhuk, the distance, following the railway track, is 150 miles. The *burgher commandos*, a battery of artillery, and a machine-gun section were sent on in advance. Having ascertained in a conversation over the telephone with the *burgomaster* that Windhuk would be surrendered on demand—Dr. Seitz, the German governor of the Colony had removed himself and his administration to Groot-fontein, and was housed in a railway train—General Botha and his staff set out for the capital in motor cars. Notwithstanding the primitive track—road it could scarcely be called—the journey, despite stoppages in the bush, was completed in three days, the general and his assistants sleeping in the cars at night. On May 11, the date of their arrival, the surrender formally took place. The British ensign replaced the German flag over the *Rathaus*, and the town was placed under the control of Colonel Mentz, a Union Staff officer. Botha, addressing his *burghers* from the steps of the *Rathaus*, thanked them for their zeal.

The German Government of the Colony, which but a few months before had still ruled this great territory with an iron hand, was now fugitive, and its forces, broken and scattered, were partly in the north, partly in retreat somewhere across country to the east. If there was no violent effort just at this juncture to intercept them, the explanation is that the effort would have been wasted. To Botha, at all events, it was perfectly well known that to pin them against the frontier of Ovam-boland meant the end of the campaign. That frontier was a barrier they dared not cross. In the circumstances, he anticipated propositions for surrender, and his expectation was fulfilled. A *parlementaire* from the German commander-in-chief came in next day. General Botha, in reply, agreed to discuss terms at Karibib, and returning to that place concluded a forty-eight hours' armistice as from midday on May 20.

Coming down from Grootfontein to Giftkop, between Omaruru and Karibib, by rail, Dr. Seitz and Colonel Franke there presented their proposals, already formulated. They suggested, first, that hostilities in South-west Africa should be suspended until the close of the war as a whole; secondly, that the forces on each side, remaining under arms, should until the close of the war occupy respectively the territories each held at the proclamation of the armistice; thirdly, that the question of the future of South-west Africa should be left open without prejudice to any settlement arrived at in the general peace.

There was a certain cunning in these propositions, but to a states-man like Botha their ineptitude must have appeared gross. To begin with the suggested suspension of hostilities on such conditions meant keeping in South-west Africa and totally inactive a large force of Union troops. The procedure involved, not only a very heavy public out-lay, but could not fail to cause grave dissatisfaction in the Union Army. Further, it would assuredly give rise, on the grounds alike of expense and inconclusiveness, to serious discontent and criticism within the

Union. Nothing could be more exactly calculated to stir up again the feeling which had found expression in the Beyers and de Wet rising.

Once more to have a large Union force locked up and idle in South-west Africa, and for an indefinite period, would most materially assist the German defence in East Africa. Lastly, there were very good grounds for suspecting—and the suspicion was soon afterwards confirmed—that the Germans had in the colony a large accumulation of arms, ammunition, and other warlike stores, which Seitz and Franke were naturally anxious to save from seizure. Those resources were the mainspring of German policy. With that inflammable material lying about a suspension of hostilities could never be a sure thing. It was not possible to say what use might not covertly be made of these materials in association with further Union disturbances. To imagine that a man of Botha's ability and experience could not see through the move and grasp its implications was presumption pushed to the limit of absurdity. Botha handed back the document to the disgruntled German negotiators with the laconic intimation that at the end of the forty-eight hours' suspension the war would go on.

It seems to have been imagined by Seitz and Franke that Botha would be the more inclined to give ear to their proposals because the last stage of the campaign in the northern area of the colony would, for him, be difficult, and might prove prolonged. He was faced with the prospect of operations hundreds of miles away from his base at Walfish Bay, and still more remote from his bases in the south. And those hundreds of miles were hundreds of miles of wilderness. On the other hand, the Germans had held in reserve at Tsumeb a well-equipped base for this very contingency. Their troops were making for it, and they could confront a renewal of the struggle with a concentration of their remaining strength.

All this, no doubt, inspired the confidence disclosed in their suggested terms. But Botha had formed a much truer estimate of the position. The railway from Kalkfontein to Aus and from Aus to Luderitz Bay was in working order, and the line from Swakopmund to Karibib was rapidly being restored. In short, the difficulties incidental to the coastal zone, difficulties the Germans had all along counted upon as their best ally, had been mastered, and since the difficulties had been mastered it had become perfectly feasible to transfer troops from the south to the north of the colony by sea. With an adequate fleet of transports at hand, it could, in fact, be done more easily than the Germans could struggle across country on foot.

The Union base for this last stage of the operations could be moved up from Swakopmund to Karibib, and if these movements and transfers would take some little time, it would at least take the enemy as long to pull himself together. The risk was that, if enterprising, he might, hurrying his preparations, rebound first. As it happened, however, all the enterprise was on the side of the Union commander. In that matter he had weighed up the men he was dealing with. Since the death of von Haydebreck they had displayed no trace of military genius. Their present intentions were transparent. Botha, and his judgment turned out to be exact, was reasonably sure that he could get in first.

He shaped his measures accordingly. The movement of troops by sea and the transfer of his base were at once taken in hand. Up to the middle of June he was occupied with these rearrangements, and though on the alert, went about the business with an easy mind. As he had foreseen, the enemy during that interval gave him no trouble. The preparations for it completed, he launched on June 18 upon his final drive.

The plan of it was an advance by the infantry, and two mounted brigades, supported by the field guns along the railway towards Grootfontein, by way of Kalkveld and Omaruru, combined with an enclosing sweep by the remaining *burgher* brigades, the brigade of Brits on the left, the brigade of Myburgh on the right. The *burghers* had to cover long distances on light fare and little water, but to such hardships they were inured, and their zest was unfailing. After the South African fashion, they moved at night, well covered by bands of scouts, and chose the hot hours of the day to off-saddle and rest themselves and their horses. By this means they reduced water consumption. It was well known that so far as the natives were concerned they were traversing a friendly country, and their own instinct for discovering water-holes was aided by these volunteer intelligence men. Movement in the circumstances was rapid.

The Germans meanwhile had concentrated at Kalkveld, but on learning of the outflanking movement by Myburgh's brigade—they do not appear to have been aware of that of Brits—fell back upon Otjiwarongo. To cover the 200 miles between Kalkveld and Grootfontein in the confusion following upon a defeat, and with the practical certainty of the railway being cut somewhere in the rear, was not to be adventured. Catching up with them thus became once more a test of the marching powers of the Union infantry. In this race the

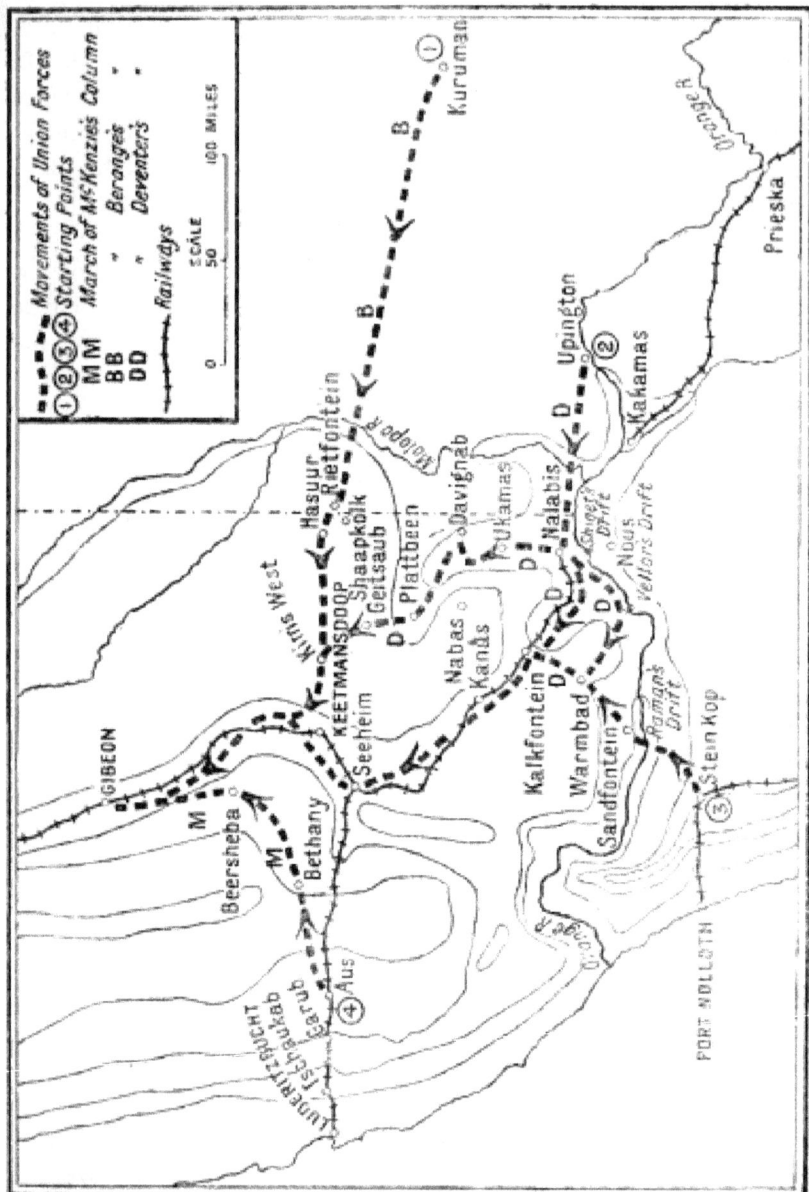

enemy had a long start, fifty miles at a moderate estimate. But the march of Botha's main body stands out as a record, paralleled only by M'Kenzie's dash from Aus. In two days his force had covered the fifty miles to Omaruru. The place was undefended, and without delay the march was resumed to Kalkveld. Here opposition had been expected, and the position which the Germans had occupied, but on the approach of the Union columns had abandoned, was capable of a strong defence.

The next, and third, stage to Otjiwarongo was sixty miles, and that place is 150 miles from Karibib, the starting point. Leaving Kalkveld, General Botha and his force entered upon the dry tract, the Waterberg mountains on their right hand. The general was incurring a risk, but he knew his men, he had weighed the probabilities well, and he pushed boldly on. Including a halt at the former place, he covered the 100 miles between Omaruru and Otjiwarongo in six days. As he advanced the Germans retired. This determination destroyed their *morale*. Abandoned equipment marked their flight. At Otjiwarongo Botha made a brief halt, and then, on June 27, set out for Otavi, another eighty miles. The enemy had fallen back there, and to all appearances meant to accept battle. The march therefore was slowed somewhat, but the pace still averaged twenty miles a day.

Hereabouts the country is rough, ridged by spurs from the mountains, and for the most part bare of vegetation. The advance had to be covered by careful scouting. Otavi is a copper-mining centre, the Germans having reopened and developed the ancient native mines. Amid the stony ridges and workings it was not unreasonable to expect something like a respectable, if not a stiff, defence. The approaches to Otavi, when on June 30 the Union advance guard arrived within sight of the place, were found indeed to have been elaborately mined, and there was a certain amount of open order and desultory fighting at long range. But it did not prove to be the preliminary of a battle. It was nothing more than a cover for a further enemy retirement. Instead of deploying for action the German troops, massed at Otavi, were hastily withdrawn along the branch railway line to Tsumeb. On their arrival Botha's main body marched into Otavi unopposed. As for the land mines, the engineers, sent on ahead, had made short work of them.

Beyond Tsumeb Botha knew the Germans could not retreat. They had there reached the end of their tether, and must either fight or surrender. Accordingly, assuming, as he was in the meantime bound to do, that they meant to fight, he drew out his dispositions for action. But he sent forward a demand for capitulation, giving Seitz and Franke twenty-four hours in which to make up their minds. Just as the allotted interval had expired a German despatch bearer, hurried and breathless, came in under the white flag. The capitulation, this time on Botha's own terms, was agreed to. Pending a final and formal signature of the conditions, a local armistice was declared, for the Union commander-in-chief had no idea of interfering with the enveloping movements of his lieutenants.

It was a wise precaution, and as it turned out a very necessary one. But for such a limitation the Germans would have been free to scatter, dispersing themselves over the country with their arms, and leaving themselves free to give indefinite future trouble. General Botha, however, had no intention of letting himself be put off with an illusory surrender. He had made up his mind to clear the German forces out of the colony, and not only the German forces, but the German equipment. This military menace had to be dug up by the roots.

And the precaution was necessary, because the enemy, given the opportunity, had resolved to destroy the stores at Tsumeb. The opportunity was not given. Myburgh, moving through Waterberg and then striking north across the railway between Otavi and Grootfontein, dashed over the open country straight for Tsumeb. At Gaub, a German flank guard tried to arrest him. He brushed aside the opposition. The defeated enemy galloped for Tsumeb, Myburgh's *burghers* hot on their heels. Just outside the town the leaders of the pursuit were met by a flag of truce. The war, they were told, was over, and Tsumeb was to remain for the present in German hands. Myburgh's men were inclined to doubt the story, and asked for some proof. While they were debating a German battery opened upon them without warning. That was proof certainly, but proof to the contrary, and very unmistakable. Taking the whole proceeding to be a ruse, as in fact it was, and enraged by such an abuse of the white flag, they leapt to their saddles, and charged into the town at full speed. The fight in the streets was short and sharp. The defence was overpowered, and those of the Germans who had not escaped surrendered.

When General Myburgh arrived he was assured that the firing by the artillery had been a complete mistake, arising from the misinterpretation of an order to the contrary. Profuse apologies were forthcoming. The episode was regrettable, but the armistice had really been entered into, and hostilities were in fact over. Myburgh was requested in accordance with the terms of the armistice to withdraw himself and his men from the town. But naturally he wondered why, if this tale was true, he had received no intimation of any kind from his own headquarters. The omission, and the kind of omission General Botha was not likely to commit, raised doubts.

As a test of good faith he asked if the Germans could put him through on the telephone to General Botha, and if so, were they willing to do so? They were now cornered, and without giving themselves away could not refuse. In conversation with his chief, the Brigadier soon learned the truth, and the meaning of it. He announced to the German local authorities, who were, of course, in his power, that he remained in Tsumeb, and in charge of everybody and everything in it.

Investigation speedily disclosed the reason for all this shuffling. On visiting the arsenal Myburgh was astonished alike at its extent and at its contents. There was in it complete equipment for more than twenty thousand men; a great stock of modern rifles, millions of rounds of small arms ammunition, and material and stores of every kind; an enormous haul.

The occupation of Tsumeb by Myburgh closed one back door; the occupation of Namutoni by Brits on July 6 closed the other. Namutoni is a remote place on the Ovamboland boundary. When surrender became imminent much of the German transport and a large stock of munitions had been removed there in order, as it was supposed, to be out of harm's way. Brits, of whom little had been heard, appeared before the position, completely to the surprise of the German garrison. In face of the strength of the Union brigade resistance was out of the question. The German commandant and his contingent, some 200 strong, capitulated.

Considering the German record in South-west Africa, though the full villainy of it had not then come to light, the terms accorded to the defeated enemy by General Botha have been pronounced magnanimous. The officers of the surrendered force were permitted to keep their arms, were released on parole, and were allowed to select their places of abode, subject to the condition that those places were duly notified; the non-commissioned officers and men retained their rifles, but without ammunition, and were to be interned within South-west Africa, the place or places of internment to be named by the Union Government; the reservist German settlers were given leave to return to their farms, and kept their rifles and an allowed quantity of ammunition for self-defence. All the guns, stores and transport of the enemy force were surrendered.

With reference to these terms it has to be remembered that in South Africa to deprive a white man of his rifle is reckoned the last depth of degradation. The concession as to arms did not arise from any sentimental regard for these men as combatants. As combatants they had shown that they merited none. Respect for the usages of civilised warfare they had never displayed; they had resorted to any device, however discreditable. In the conduct of the campaign one of their least forgivable traits had been their treatment of prisoners. The Union soldiers who had surrendered—they had been few—were in every instance brave men, and it might have been supposed that their valour would have extorted respect. It had merely inspired vindictiveness, and barbarous usage.

As combatants, therefore, the Germans had no claims to consideration. But contemptible as they had shown themselves, they were still men of the white race, and to have imposed upon them the degradation of complete individual as opposed to collective disarmament would have lowered the prestige of the white race. The natives would have been offered the spectacle of white men treating white men as other than white. True, the Germans had not allowed such a scruple to influence *them*. But it was not for General Botha to follow an example of that kind, even had he been so disposed. More than anything else this meanness on the part of the Germans regarding prisoners had fired resentment against them and against everything German all through South Africa. For on this matter the feeling among the white minority in South Africa is very strong. To the native, naturally military, a white man disarmed is an object to be despised.

It is indeed a very open question whether the terms of the capitulation, coldly judicious, did not express a deeper disesteem than the extreme of apparent severity. The latter would have indicated some element of vindictiveness. There was none. The Germans were not worth it. Vindictiveness springs partly from fear, partly from a sense of inferiority. Fear, present or prospective, this surrendered crowd did not inspire, and whatever sense of inferiority there was had shown itself on their side. General Botha dealt with them simply for what they were—negligible. They had owed such temporary importance as they had had to the system of their government. That system had been abolished, root and branch.

And so far as the German settlers were concerned, to have sent them back to their farms and ranches without rifles would, in view of the native resentment against them, have been to incur a grave risk, and have made the problem of policing the country trebly onerous. But self-defence in this case *meant* self-defence. It was precisely on that point where the change brought about was so radical. Before the war the native complaint, and it was a well-founded complaint, was that every individual German was himself the government, for in fact, in regard to the natives, every individual German did exactly as he liked. Appeal to courts, or to officials, by coloured people, was not merely useless; it was worse than useless. The native lived under daily exposure to violence and robbery, and the official machinery, so far from restraining, abetted those practices.

In short, the German administration was in practice an anarchy. It was hardly to be expected that the German settlers should adapt themselves to the change forthwith, looking at their character. They did not. Consistently with their character, they repaid the concession made to them as white men—misunderstanding it, and taking it as made to them as Germans—by going along in most instances in the old ways of bullying and brutality; treating the natives persuaded to reaccept their service as legitimate objects of revenge. And threats were added of worse to follow, for it was asserted that in the long run Germany was certain to win the war.

Here, however, the change in authority made itself felt. The worst curse of South-west Africa, a despotic, irresponsible, and cruel police, had been replaced by a police humane and even-handed, and was speedily supplemented by fair tribunals. When assaulted or cheated, the native could without fear appeal for justice, and get it. The prosecutions and convictions of German settlers on these complaints were numerous, and the German element came to consider when fines had to be paid, or in flagitious cases, sentences of imprisonment to be served, or native labour withdrawn, that they were now the oppressed. But on the new administration at Windhuk these murmurs made no impression.

The days of every German a law to himself were over. The able administrator appointed by the Union Government, Mr. E. M. Gorges, was determined to settle the country, and put down anarchy, and he did. German and native alike learned the meaning of the Pax Britannica. It puzzled the native mind to find that the Germans were not cleared out, and were allowed to retain their private possessions. The civilised code which respects the private property of public enemies was to the native a refinement too subtle to be grasped, as indeed it seemingly was to the common German mind. The native knew that the German settlers were a nuisance, and his detestation of the nuisance was not the lightest problem of the new government. It was a problem only to be solved by time and patience. Ovamboland, which the Germans had not dared to enter, was with the full concurrence of the native chiefs entrusted to a British resident, on the same footing as Basutoland.

CHAPTER 4

The Story of East Africa

Natural features and climate of East Africa—Its native communities and kingdoms—Trade From the story of South-west Africa that of German East Africa is different in all respects save one—the effect of German administration. Unlike the native peoples in the isolated south-west of the Continent, those of East Africa had been in contact with Europeans almost continuously since the seventeenth century. Certainly that was the case with the Swahilis of the coastal area. They had had relationships with the Arabs, however, from a much earlier date, and along the coast as well as in districts inland bordering on the Great Lakes, then unknown to geographers in Europe, the Mohammedan faith had won a firm footing. These were the more civilised areas; their civilisation of a distinctively oriental type.

The reason why there had been a greater advance in the arts of life at once along the coast and in the extreme interior is found in the natural features of this wide region. From a coastal belt comparatively low in elevation, hot, and, owing to its humidity, enervating, so far as the heat is not tempered by the sea wind, the land rises in the interior into a succession of plateaux divided from each other by the depressions along which flow eastward the main rivers. The surfaces of the uplands, however, are not flat. They present the prospect of ranges or rugged knots of hills and broad valleys clothed, where the ground has not been cleared by native cultivation, with a dense vegetation, or with tropical woods. In the uncultivated expanses bare of trees the covering is a tropical grass growing to a height of six feet. Still farther inland the plateaux give place to the mighty mountain chain, which, extending in an irregular arc for more than a thousand miles from north to south, forms the barrier imprisoning the waters of the inland seas.

Had the rivers flowing eastward been navigable for any distance from the Indian Ocean, it is more than probable that East Africa would long ago have become the seat of a populous native Power, but the greater rivers, the Congo and the Nile, flow north and west, and those to the east, falling from the highlands, are mostly obstructed by shallows, and rapids, as well as by marked changes of depth according to the seasons. The mountains, forming the backbone of the country, or rather dividing it into two distinct areas, include, as is well known, the loftiest peaks in Africa, the crowning summit, Kilimanjaro, 19,321 feet high.

Even in the highlands east of the mountains the climate is comparatively healthy, and the nights generally cool. But west of the mountains it is yet more so, for the level is there still higher, vegetation more like that of the temperate zone, and the open country park-like. And, the chain of great lakes aiding inter-communication, the remoteness of this part of Africa had led to the formation of a group of native kingdoms. Beginning with Darfur in the north, they included Uganda, Bukoba, Ruanda, and Urundi, most under Mohammedan rulers. These States corresponded with the Sultanates along the seaboard, the more important of the latter that of Zanzibar—which embraced the adjacent coastal zone on the mainland—and that of Witu.

The interlying inland country east of the mountains and marked off from the coastal zone by a secondary chain of heights was occupied by numerous native communities. All broadly were in that tribal stage of development in which custom is strong. Primitive life had passed into a simple agriculture. Every family tilled its own small farm or *shamba*, and, assisted by the produce of its cattle in a climate where the natural wants of man are few and the soil bountiful, enjoyed a rude but sufficient independence. Though some of these tribal confederations, notably the Mazai in the north and the Yaos in the south, were warlike, most, where undisturbed, were peaceable. The chief cause of unrest was the movement of tribes of the Bantu race, pushed towards the equator by the white immigration into South Africa.

Between the native kingdoms on the coast and those bordering upon the Great Lakes trade had long been carried on by way of several established routes. There was the route from Mombasa through Nairobi to Kisumu on the Victoria Nyanza; the route from Tanga through Moshi to Mwanza at the southern end of the same sea; the route from Dar-es-Salem to Ujiji on Lake Tanganyika, and that from Lindi to Lake Nyassa. The most frequented of these was the road inland from Mombasa. When Europeans began to be interested in this region of

Africa they naturally penetrated from the coast along the trade routes, and one of the earliest and most considerable settlements was that of some 300 farmers of British and Dutch descent, who, moving from South Africa, took up land around Kilimanjaro, where the soil, of volcanic origin, is of exceptional fertility. But, as this was long antecedent to the rubber boom, European settlers were few, and for the most part traders or prospectors. The native population of the region between the Lakes and the coast was estimated at some eight millions.

Such in outline was the state of things when, about 1880, the first German prospectors entered the country. They came, however, not as individuals, but as the pioneers of a Society for the Promotion of German Colonisation, then recently set on foot. The moving spirits in this enterprise were Dr. Karl Peters, Count Pfeil, Count Behr-Bandelin, Ernst von Weber, and Dr. Fredrich Lange. They formed the nucleus of an association which sprang from meetings and discussions in a *brasserie* at Berlin, where geography and German expansion were discussed in an atmosphere heavily laden with tobacco smoke. Recognition and support of their views was given by the *Taglische Rundschau*. Having with that backing launched their society, they invited membership and subscriptions. The latter totalled 250,000 *marks*, and the society resolved forthwith to found a German colony. Most of the subscribers looked for a high return. Openings were being sought for German trade, and East Africa, it was thought, offered a field.

There was a commerce between Great Britain and Mombasa and Zanzibar, and between those places and India, as well as the ancient trade with Arabia. German enterprise sought to share it. Realising, however, that on the footing of the "open door" development of that kind would be slow, German prospectors proceeded on a quasi-monopolistic basis to enter into agreements with inland chiefs. Embarking at Trieste in the autumn of 1884, Peters, Count Pfeil, Dr. Juhlke, and a trader named Otto, who knew the ground, arrived in November at Zanzibar. To all appearances they were merely globe-trotters without importance. They passed over to the mainland, and during the next three months were lost to view.

But in February, 1885, Dr. Fredrich Lange received a telegram written in a private code telling him that the adventurers had under a treaty with the local chief acquired the Usambara plateau. It was a success beyond expectation. But in quick succession came the news that Peters and his associates had by like means secured the districts of Nguru, Ukami and Usequha, and in the summer of 1885 Peters returned to Berlin carrying in his pocket "rights" to more than 80,000 square miles of territory—an area larger than Great Britain. On their part the German Government lost no time in recognising so meritorious an enterprise. In the course of a few weeks the Society for the Promotion of German Colonisation received an Imperial charter of incorporation. Peters was appointed the first administrator of the colony.

But the annexations, owing to the trade obstruction set up, soon led to difficulties and complaints. In association with these differences the slave traffic between the coastal Sultanates and Arabia began to be heard of in Europe as a question of political interest. The traffic was old. Indeed, as the ownership of slaves was not looked upon either in these Mohammedan States or in Arabia as in any sense an immoral practice, and as slaves among the Arabs are with very rare exceptions well treated, the trade had gone on for centuries. But the horrors of slave catching and slave driving on the way down to the coast now formed the theme of indignant protest in German newspapers, and the outcry was echoed in the British Press.

Then, ostensibly to check the slave trade, though, it may be shrewdly inferred, for the safeguarding incidentally of British commercial interests, a British Protectorate was proclaimed over Zanzibar. What more immediately prompted this step was the discovery that the German Society had obtained on lease from Sayed Khalifa, the local potentate, an important concession of land south of the Umba River. The reply of the German Government to the British move was the proclamation of a German Protectorate over the Sultanate of Witu. As Witu was independent, and the Germans had neither interest nor footing there, the proclamation for the time meant nothing. But it added to the political complication. The outcome was a brisk correspondence between London and Berlin, and the upshot of this, in 1886, a Convention, which, defining the possessions of the *sultan* of Zanzibar as the islands along the coast, and a tract of the adjacent mainland ten miles from the sea, divided the hinterland into British and German spheres of influence.

In 1887 the rival association which had been formed by British and Indian traders was incorporated by Royal Charter as the Imperial British East Africa Company. The following year the German Government, whose nationals had had so far to trade through Zanzibar, or other ports in the British sphere, demanded from the Sultan of Witu a concession of Lamu, the chief port in his territory. The concession was refused. By this incident the question of East Africa was reo-pened. Certain German traders had meanwhile established themselves in Witu. Following upon the Lamu demand, feeling against them was strong, and in 1890, with a somewhat curious opportuneness, ten of them were attacked and killed. To the Government at Berlin the affair was diplomatically useful, for it brought matters to a head just when the business of determining European possessions in other parts of Africa was under consideration. In consequence, East Africa was com-prised in the delimitation agreement and German East Africa defi-nitely divided off from British East Africa.

Thus German authority over a vast tract of country was interna-tionally recognised. The limits inland were understood to be the line of the Great Lakes, but they were vague, and one of the first steps of the German administration was an attempt to extend them. The Ger-man administrator, Dr. Karl Peters, afterwards unenviably notorious, made his way in 1890 to Uganda, and opened negotiations with the king for a political treaty in the interests of Germany. Before the treaty was concluded, however, the British East Africa Company occupied Uganda, and it was held by a force of Soudanese troops. To follow the secret working of the matter is not easy, yet there is little reason to doubt that in repayment of this rebuff—Germany at that time had no armed forces at her disposal in East Africa—the new possession served as a base for anti-British intrigues, and for fomenting and covertly supplying with arms the movement in the Eastern Soudan headed by the *Mahdi*. In 1897, the Soudanese forces in Uganda mutinied, and the Mahdist movement, until finally put down in 1898 by the late Lord Kitchener's Expedition to Khartoum, was formidable.

The German administration of East Africa was planned on rather elaborate lines. There were fourteen principal and six subordinate de-partments. The delimited territory had a coast line of more than 400 miles, including the ports of Dar-es-Salem, Tanga, and Lindi, and the whole of it was to be governed directly from Dar-es-Salem with the exception of the Mohammedan States of Bukoba, Ruanda, and Urun-di. In each of them a German Resident was appointed. Another ex-ception was the territory of the Mazai, whom the German authorities thought it better not for the present to disturb. The lines on which the possession was governed were, first, a German commercial monopoly, which of course meant a marked swelling of profits, and, secondly, the exploitation of the natives as labourers in the interests of whites, and those whites German. To check other white immigration, a deposit of

£30 per head was exacted, and any white man, not a German, visiting the colony was required to report himself to the German police once a month, and obtain renewal of permission to remain. Trade overseas was confined to the German East African Line, a concern subsidised by the Imperial Government.

The obstacle in the way of development, as the German administration and Germans at home understood the term, was the difficulty of finding enough plantation labour. The country was divided up among communities of peasant cultivators, to whom the idea of labour for wages was entirely novel, and difficulty in carrying- out so sweeping a change as that determined upon would in the like circumstances present itself anywhere. Instead, however, of taking that view, German officialdom, both in Berlin and on the spot, looked, or professed to look, upon the native usages and economy as an obstinate adherence to African barbarism.

At first it was necessary to proceed with caution. As the white population were a mere handful, and never at any time more than 5,000, the first measure was the establishment of a native police, armed and trained under German instructors on military lines. For this purpose the directly governed part of the possession was mapped out into twenty-four administrative centres, and the peaceable areas entrusted to district officers, each with a police contingent. There remained the tracts, chiefly those on the southern border, those contiguous to the Mazai *steppe*, and the remote region to the north-west beyond the mountains, which it was judged preferable to govern on a purely military footing. A native standing army was therefore recruited in addition to the black police, and trained in the same manner.

These measures formed the core of German policy. In the northwest there were wild tribes lower in the scale of civilisation than the mass of the natives. The German administration enlisted them for its new force. The pay offered was, for a native, high—twenty to thirty German *rupees* a month, and to a native brigand wealth. This professional army, for such it was, and the police force was really part of it, did not, according to German official representations, exceed, police included, 5,000 men. In the course of time, however, it was steadily increased, the military charges being covered by a subvention from the German Government at home, until the strength of the force became more than three times that total.

Now a standing black army of that strength and character was an unpleasant portent, and it was the more unpleasant, not to say dangerous, because the men who entered the German service became detribalised. It was one of the conditions. To be detribalised, however, was among the natives of East Africa, as it always is in the tribal stage of society, to be an outcast, or pariah. By the natives at large, consequently, the German police and German soldiery were on that ground despised. But they were, according to native standards, highly paid, and were encouraged by the Germans to regard themselves, in view of their military instruction, as a superior caste. There was thus set up between them and the native population at large a chronic antagonism. The effect of it on the one hand was, completely dividing them off from the tribal communities, to make them willing and slavish tools of their employers and masters, and ready executants of the German orders, whatever the orders might prove to be.

The effect on the other hand was to turn them, as social outcasts, into keen informers, and nosers-out of offences. To give edge to this system the German administration, once its police and army had been established, promulgated an elaborate code of regulations containing numerous and to the natives strange prohibitions, each, however, a subject for severe punishment, and this code was applied red-hot to a population whose only idea of law was common custom. Further, there was imposed a hut- or house-tax of three *rupees* a year, and in the case of male adult natives not having a house of their own, a poll tax of the like amount. That these measures were deliberate, and by making the lot of the native cultivator miserable, intended to force him into the plantation labour market, is proved by their being most steadily and severely applied to the Yaos, and others of the native tribes who were physically finest, and most intelligent, and therefore the best labour material. The amount of the taxation may not appear large, but to a native who had never had need of money, and to raise it had either to sell his produce for just what the Germans chose to offer, or to work in earning it for just what the Germans chose to pay, it was a serious impost.

All these things were, needless to observe, causes of discontent, and the more so because as time went on there grew up not only the same abuse of the *sjambok* as in South-west Africa, and the like cruel repetition of the torture at intervals of a fortnight, but the practice on the part of the native police, since these floggings were inflicted at the discretion of the police, of taking bribes from terrified "delinquents," and of levying blackmail upon the villages. Nevertheless, in spite of this pressure, the labour difficulty showed no signs of being solved. In the mass the native population were set against the change, and their opposition was softened neither by German methods of administration nor by the practices of German planters. As this, in official opinion, kept back the development of the colony, which was slow, and as the officials on the spot knew that their jobs depended upon pushing that development, other devices were resorted to. The criminal code was so amended that on relatively trivial charges natives could be condemned to long terms of penal servitude.

By this means there was obtained a small army of so-called convicts, who were set to labour upon public undertakings, more especially at the ports. Dar-es-Salem and Tanga expanded into wide, straight streets and showy buildings, but the commonest of all sights were the gangs of prisoners working in the open in chains, and that too in the most trying climate in Africa. The mortality among these unhappy men was of course heavy, but by the same means the supply could always be kept up.

Again licensed recruiters were appointed, and accompanied by the police went round the villages enrolling men in labour contracts. How far these contracts were under the conditions really voluntary may be considered doubtful. Another proceeding was the opening of "labour markets." Planters reported to the German district officer the number of hands they wanted. The district officer set about the collection, ostensibly by arrangement with the native chiefs of his area. When rounded up, the "recruits "were gathered at some convenient centre, and the planters came and picked them out. Though nominally free labour, all this was obviously but separated by a tissue-paper partition from chattel slavery. The Mazai would never accept work on plantations under any circumstances.

The tendency of the German measures, it was seen by all impartial observers, could only in the end mean the creation of a wretched proletariat, morally degraded as well as materially impoverished. And the tendency had its dangers, for the increasing burden of oppressions led in 1904 to an armed rising in the southern and south-western area of the colony, so serious than von Trotha had to be sent out to put it down. And he did put it down, or was supposed to have done so, on the extermination principle, amid incidents on all fours with those in the campaign against the Hereros. The legend had been spread that the "*Wadachi,*" or Germans, were as strong as the Russians, Japanese and British put together, for the natives were not altogether uninformed as to outside affairs. It was thought advisable to afford a concrete example of "*Wadachi*" might. Von Trotha turned the formerly populous south-western region of the colony into a solitude.

And after this the German screw was tightened. The "lesson," it was thought, would suffice. The judgment proved an error. In 1905 the Wamwera and Wangoni in the south-eastern and southern parts of the colony rose in arms. Driven to desperation, they had, in their extremity, found two capable and intrepid leaders. Seliman Mamba, head of the Wamwera, was, as his name suggests, a Mussulman, and his followers, racially related to the Swahili, were partly of that faith. The Germans, very ill-advisedly for themselves, had by this time formed the opinion that Mohammedanism and the labour trouble were linked together, and, though its upholders in Turkey, had shown themselves hostile to that faith. Their action blew the smouldering discontent into a flame. Shabruma, the leader of the Wangoni, was, like his tribe, of Bantu origin. His tactics were those of guerilla warfare, and he carried them out with great skill.

The storm broke to all intents without warning. Before the German authorities could act, plantations, posts, and stations in this part of the country were swept over and destroyed. And the war, which lasted for more than a year, proved a very desperate business. The Wamwera fought with extraordinary valour, time and again, in one bitter battle after another, charging up to the machine-guns within spear's length, and stabbing the gunners. Nothing, in fact, but the mechanical superiority of their arms saved the Germans and their native auxiliaries. The reason, it was said, for this desperation was the propagation among the revolted natives of the legend that according to a divine revelation every man who drank of the hot springs at Kimembara would become endowed with strength and courage enough to drive the Germans into the sea, and at the same time invulnerable to their bullets.

On that account they called themselves the *Majimaji*, or "Magic-water men." To accept this version of the matter, German government had little to do with the revolt. But German government, or misgovernment, was in truth the substance of it. And the proof is that even after Seliman Mamba had at length fallen into the hands of his foes, the Wamwera refused to accept defeat. Those who survived betook themselves in a body to the bush. There the greater number perished of disease and starvation. Not until months afterwards did the last remnant, urged by the pangs of famine, come out in small parties into the open country. They were then living skeletons, coated with dirt, suffering from skin affections of a virulent type, and from inflamed eyes.

The treatment meted out to them was penal servitude. Seliman was executed, but before his execution, though so enfeebled by hardship and sickness that he could barely drag his chains, he was daily driven to labour in a chain gang. Such was German gallantry towards a brave man. Shabruma and his following proved to be more elusive. Finding refuge in the southern mountains, they descended upon German posts, and in various instances wiped them out. The Germans found themselves committed to a prolonged and costly campaign, the more difficult because the natives were in sympathy with the insurgents.

The facts just outlined will be found in many ways to throw light upon the campaigning in East Africa, which followed upon the outbreak of war in 1914, and they go to show why the continent was swept by war from Darfur in the north to Rhodesia and Nyassaland in the south, and to simplify what might otherwise appear a complicated narrative.

CHAPTER 5

East African Campaign 1914-1916

When war was declared in August, 1914, the Germans in East Africa were ready. Though construction had been kept back by native troubles, by administrative complications, and by engineering difficulties, the thousand miles of central railway from Dar-es-Salem to Ujiji had just been completed and opened for traffic, and, whether by design or by accident, there were in the colony a number of German officers who had come out to assist in the celebration of the event. They were, needless to say, extremely useful in increasing the native levies, and as a reserve. The German planters and settlers fit for active service, some 3,000 in number, were of course called out. Of guns, machine-guns, rifles, ammunition, and military stores of all kinds there had been a steady accumulation, for the chances of replenishment from oversea were at best uncertain.

But besides the forces actually in the territory, the German administration had not ceased to carry on a propaganda among the Arabs of the Eastern Soudan, and confidently, and as it proved correctly, reckoned upon raising an appreciable total of auxiliaries in that quarter. In contrast with their attitude towards the Mohammedans along the coast, the Germans in these remote inland districts gave themselves out as firm friends of Islam, had provided for distribution a stock of green flags decorated with a crescent and a star, and neglected no means to turn fanaticism to profit. Appreciating, too, the importance of the Great Lakes as a line of communication, they had been careful to ensure for themselves a superiority in armed vessels. On the lakes means for shipbuilding and ship repairing had been set up. Materials and parts of war craft, shipped from Germany and transported up from the coast at great labour and expense, were "assembled "on these lakeside slips. The result was that, Lake Nyassa excepted, Germany had command of these inland waters.

Not the least, however, of the German advantages was the fact that Colonel von Lettow-Vorbeck,[1] *commandant* of the forces in East Africa, was a military leader at once intrepid and resourceful. He had grasped the supreme value of sound administrative work in campaigning, and most of all in campaigning extended over so enormous an area, and he had very clearly realised the conditions under which the coming struggle must be fought. The one mistake into which he fell, a mistake common to all Germans at this date, was anticipation of a rapid German success in Europe. Calculating upon that and knowing that the British, his chief antagonists, were ill-prepared, his plan was an offensive against contiguous British possessions, so that when the war as a whole had been concluded there would be the accomplished fact of a German occupation of these regions. The plan, as it proved, was a mistake. It made an inroad upon his resources he could not, as was later discovered, afford.

Acting upon this plan, he disposed the troops under his command into three bodies: The first and strongest, under Major Kraut, was to operate across the northern frontier against British East Africa, occupy Mombasa, and Nairobi, and seize the Mombasa-Kisumu railway. The second, under General von Wehle, and with bases at Mwanza and Bukoba, was to attack northwards along both shores of the Victoria Nyanza, but, as its main purpose, to invade and occupy Uganda. The third, entrusted to Count von Falkenstein, was to operate to the south against Nyassaland and Northern Rhodesia, and seizing the frontier posts, to cut off communication between South Africa and the Lake region. Contrasted fortune attended these enterprises. The operations against British East Africa, to begin with, met with a measure of success. On the other hand, the offensive by von Wehle turned out a failure, and that of von Falkenstein suffered an even more complete check.

In August, 1914, the British had on the East African station only two light cruisers, *Astræa* and *Pegasus*, and some guard ships. The cruisers, and this was the first hostile act in the campaign, on August 8 bombarded Dar-es-Salem and sank a floating dock and the survey ship *Mowe*. Later, as already noted, *Astræa* was told off to escort transports from Capetown, and it was probably knowledge of that fact

1. *My Reminiscences of East Africa* by Paul Emil von Lettow-Vorbeck, *The East Africa Campaign of the First World War by the Most Notable German Commander* , also published by Leonaur.

which caused the German cruiser *Königsberg*, swifter and more powerful than either of the two British ships of the cruiser class, to appear at Zanzibar. *Pegasus*, at the moment undergoing refitment, was disabled by *Königsberg's* attack and the guard ships *Cupid* and *Khalifa* sent to the bottom. Owing partly to these losses, a blockade of the coast was not established until February, 1915, nearly six months after the outbreak of war. This delay, had they been ready to take advantage of it, was a great point in the Germans' favour.

Not, however, until later was blockade running seriously attempted, and the loophole left during the first six months cannot be said materially to have affected the course of the land struggle. What would have affected it, and decisively, would have been a German command of the coast such as would have prevented the landing of British reinforcements. In British East Africa the total of troops when war broke out was so slender that they barely sufficed for a defensive, and from the landward side the nearest British bases were El Obeid in the north, and Buluwayo in the south. Practically, then, the British campaign depended upon the sea. The Germans, however, were never able thus to command the coast, and apart from that command their preparations and efforts were in truth a gamble turning upon their fortunes in Europe.

In these circumstances the initial success which attended the German operations across the northern border is readily explained. Within the first fortnight the troops of Kraut had occupied Taveta, a frontier town on the Tanga trade route, and a road centre which gave them an excellent jumping-off position, either for operations against Mombasa, or for attacks upon the railway, the latter not more than eighty miles away. And Mombasa was the main point at which their movement was directed, because, failing command of the coast, the alternative was to seize its harbours, and particularly a place like Mombasa, having railway communication with the interior.

The risk of the adventure lay in a counter-attack across the pass between Kilimanjaro and Mount Longido, for a countermove of that kind, if it reached Moschi, would cut Kraut's communications, and get astride his line of retreat. To prevent such a development, the Germans laid out on Longido a strongly fortified position. Incidentally, it also served them as a base for raids, and, menacing Nairobi, was likely to check dispatch of reinforcements from that place to the British defending the Mombasa road.

There was skill in these German dispositions. And they were aided

UGANDA
Victoria Nyanza
Kisumu
Karungu
Nairobi
Bukoba
Kagera R.
Sherati
L. Kivu
Uherera I.
Muanza
Magadi
LONGIDO
KILIMANJARO
Lamu
URUNDI
Moschi
Taveta
Voi
Arusha
MOMBASA
Usambara Plateau
Kondoa Irangi
Vanga
CONGO
Kilgoma
Country
Tabora
Mazai Plateau
Pemba
Tanga
Lake
Albertville
Kilimatinde
NGURU MTS.
ZANZIBAR
FREE
Tanganyika
Open Upland
Morogoro
Dar es Salem
Kilossa
STATE
MAIN
Kissaki
Mafia
New Iringa
Ruaha R.
Rufigi R.
Bismarckburg
Kibata
Kituta
Kilwa
Kassaklawe
New Langenburg
Melangali
Mahenge
Abercorn
Ubena
Kiswere
Saisi
Mahungo
RHODESIA
Karonga
Lindi
Kasama
Wiedhafen
Southern Plateau
Livingstone
NYASALAND
Lake Nyasa
Lukuledi R.
Railways
Roads
SCALE
0 50 100 150 MILES

by a converging movement upon Mombasa from Tanga along the coast. The attack from landward, too, was to have been supported from the sea by *Königsberg*. The scheme, however, was upset by the arrival at Mombasa of a contingent of troops from India under the command of Brigadier-General J. M. Stewart. The disembarkation took place only in the nick of time. Had it been delayed even for a day or two the chances were that Mombasa would have fallen into the enemy's hands.

As it was, the Germans having occupied the small port of Vanga, halfway between Tanga and Mombasa, and pushed on, were held up merely by the gallant defence of a British fortified camp and block-house which commanded the route, and as it happened the only route, since at this point the road crossed a swamp. At the head of a com-pany of 130 Arabs, hastily recruited, Lieut. Wavell, placed in charge of this post, held out against all the efforts to rush the position. He was relieved eventually by a column made up of the Jind Infantry and the King's African Rifles. The enemy was compelled to retreat, and it proved to be the end of his Mombasa project. With the door at Mom-basa open the British held the means of, in time, turning the balance.

Meanwhile, on the British side the decision had been formed to pass to the offensive, and a plan had been adopted for squeezing the Germans out of their positions along the frontier by on the one flank attacking them at Longido, and on the other turning them by a land-ing in their right rear at Tanga. If successful, this latter operation would enable a move to be made inland along the railway to Wilhelmstal, and force evacuation of the Usambara plateau, a dominating rise it was desirable to seize.

In accordance with the decision, there was sent from India a fur-ther reinforcement of 6,000 troops under the command of Major-General Aitken. Tanga was their destination, and the transports arrived off that port on November 2. The British information was that the town was not defended. Likely enough, when that intelligence was gleaned the town was not, but either the enemy had got wind of the intended descent, or suspected it. At any rate, he had thrown a strong garrison into the place. Further, he had very carefully barricaded the streets and loopholed the houses, and the woods and cane bush by which Tanga was surrounded had been elaborately set with traps and entanglements.

On the arrival of the ships, General Aitken sent ashore a summons to the German commandant to surrender. The demand was refused.

As it soon became evident that the place was held in strength, the direct attempt to land was not persisted in. In face of the enemy's guns the attempt would have been impracticable. Not willing to give the project up, however, General Aitken two days later threw part of his force ashore at the south end of the bay. To reach the town the troops had to struggle through the bush. The infantry resistance met with was not serious, but the enemy batteries were turned upon the advance, their fire guided by a variety of ingenious devices. The cane bush grows to a height of eight feet or more, so that to detect movement through it by direct observation was not easy.

But the enemy had set traps which, when disturbed, signalled the range to his gunners. In spite of this, the attacking troops fought their way forward to and into Tanga. There the fighting became a succession of furious street combats, and the storming of barricades and houses. Possibly enough, if at this point the rest of the Expeditionary Force had been thrown ashore at the port, the place might have been won, but on the transports the situation seems to have been thought less favourable than it was. Hence the attacking column, instead of the support they had looked for, received the order to withdraw. Their losses, of course, were further increased during the retirement and they were sufficiently serious—nearly 800 officers and men.

Though it did not in any way shake the *morale* of the force, this was an unpleasant check, rendered none the less unpleasant by the lack of success which had also attended the Longido enterprise. The cause in that instance was a breakdown in the water transport. The troops fought well, but after hours of hard fighting in the tropics men parched with thirst which no means are found of relieving are in almost the most intolerable position it is possible to imagine. The defences won had to be evacuated. There was little use in retaining conquered positions when they could only be held at the risk of perishing from lack of water.

But though the grand scheme for a converging offensive had fallen through, another effort was made to relieve Mombasa from menace, for until that was done no important advance towards the interior could be undertaken. Accordingly, the enemy was attacked at Vanga and driven out, and the town garrisoned by a force of Indian infantry under the command of Colonel Ragbir Singh. Unwilling to sit down under this reverse, the Germans attempted a recapture, and with a powerful column. The defence was brilliant. The garrison fought until they had fired their last shot. Their gallant commander had fallen

86

beating off an assault. Happily, just at this critical juncture, the distant boom of guns and roll of rifle-fire announced that relief had arrived. The German forces were pressed back over the frontier. Substantially this was the situation when, in April, 1915, the command was transferred to Brigadier-General Tighe. The Germans still held Taveta. Beyond that, however, their plan had come to nothing.

It is here advisable to glance at operations in other parts of this vast theatre of hostilities. They include some of the most romantic episodes and adventures of the war.

In September, 1914, part of the force under the command of von Wehle had seized Karungu, a small port on the Victoria Nyanza just across the British East Africa boundary. The purpose of von Wehle's advance was occupation of the port and railway terminus at Kisumu, and the isolation of Uganda. Apparently it had been assumed, first, that the British, concerned for the defence of Mombasa, would have few troops at this inland end of the railway, and, secondly, that a German invasion and occupation of Uganda would prove fairly easy. Both assumptions turned out to be wrong.

With the arrival of reinforcements from India the British, instead of weakening their force at Kisumu, had strengthened it, and they reacted promptly. Two squadrons of the East African Mounted Rifles were sent from Kisumu to Karungu on the steamer *Winifred*. But the German attack on the latter place was supported by the German armed steamer *Mwanza*, and *Winifred*, chased off by her, was compelled to return. A mounted column, however, was sent south to Karungu overland, and the Germans fell back. The real reason for withdrawal was the resistance met with on the Uganda boundary from the native troops of the Protectorate. The resistance was stiff, so stiff that von Wehle could make no headway. In January, in fact, he found himself placed on the defensive. Not only had his invasion of Uganda been beaten off with a considerable loss on his side, but *Mwanza* had been attacked and disabled, and east of the Victoria Nyanza the British column from Karungu had crossed the German frontier and captured Shirati.

That, however, was by no means the worst. Sent up country with his brigade, General Stewart had made Karungu his headquarters, and in order once for all to cripple the German operations against Uganda, lost no time in organising an expedition across the Lake to Bukoba. Stewart's force, which included British as well as Indian troops and a detachment of Driscoll's Frontiersmen, who had joined as mounted scouts, was to co-operate with a Uganda column moving upon Bu-koba down the Kagera River. The enterprise proved entirely success-ful. While a demonstration was made from the water front a battalion of Lancashires, previously thrown ashore at daybreak some miles to the south, attacked from inland, entered the town and speedily mas-tered it. The munitions and military stores found were large. So far as time allowed these were seized and shipped. The remainder were destroyed, and to the Germans the loss was more serious than that of men. The destruction of their base at Bukoba meant that Uganda was henceforth safe from their attentions.

This stroke formed a shrewd reprisal for German proceedings in the south. On the outbreak of war each side there had striven to get its blow in first. In Nyassaland reserves of the King's African Rifles were called out, men on leave summoned back to quarters, volunteers en-rolled, and a staff formed of officers and civilian officials in the colony. The mobilisation at Livingstone, the capital, and the organisation of the whole force into double companies, were completed in little more than a week. Placed under the command of Captain Barton, D.S.O., of the Northampton Regiment, the troops were embarked on the Lake Nyassa flotilla, and by August 22 had reached and were concentrated at Karonga, some thirty miles south of the boundary, equipped and ready for the field.

Without command of the lake, such a move would, of course, have been impossible. On these waters the Germans had placed an armed steamer, *Hermann von Wissmann*. To ascertain her whereabouts, Com-mander E. L. Rhoades, in the British armed steamer *Gwendolen*, was sent to reconnoitre the German port of Sphinxhaven. Rhoades found *Hermann von Wissmann* on the stocks. Running in at dawn, he and his men boldly attacked and took possession of the dockyard, made prisoners of *Wissmann's* crew, and finding it impossible to tow her off, removed her guns and dismantled her machinery. This lively little af-fair took place on August 13, and it was the opening.

On land, however, the Germans were out first. Their concentration at New Langenburg, north of Lake Nyassa, was estimated at 700 rifles, with eight maxims and a battery of light field guns. Part of this force on August 20 crossed the Songwe River—the boundary—and seized Kapora, which they laid out as an advanced post. Barton, leaving a detachment at Karonga under the command of Lieut. P. D. Bishop, King's African Rifles, at once moved out to attack. *En route* a double company of the enemy were found barring the road at the crossing of the Lufira River. After a show of resistance they fell back, and the meaning of the manoeuvre was soon revealed by distant gunfire from the direction of Karonga. During the night, while Barton and his troops were on the way towards the Rufira, the main enemy column, following the shore of the lake, had made a dash towards Karonga, hoping to find that place but feebly held, and by its capture to isolate and at one stroke finish off the Nyassaland Protectorate force.

The opposition on the Rufira was a ruse to keep Barton occupied there meanwhile. Karonga had been reached at about seven in the morning, but fortunately Bishop put up a stout defence, and the attack had lasted for four hours and was still in progress when Captain A. H. Griffiths, sent back to its relief with a double company of the K.A.R. and a maxim, appeared on the scene. Thus entrapped, the Germans and their auxiliaries hastily retired, losing in the pursuit two of their machine-guns. They were not yet, however, out of their difficulties. Barton, with the remainder of his force, moving across country to intercept them, fell upon them as they were passing the Kasoa River. For this fresh onset they were unprepared, and, completely defeated and broken up by it, abandoned two field guns, numerous rifles, 10,000 rounds of ammunition, and a quantity of stores and explosives. In short, the incursion into Nyassaland had been a fiasco. The adventure was never renewed.

On the border of Rhodesia between Lake Nyassa and Lake Tanganyika, the British forces consisted of no more than the ordinary police patrols holding the frontier posts of Abercorn and Fife. The main body of the Rhodesian police had been moved up to occupy Schukmannburg in the Caprivi strip of German South-west Africa. To safeguard the border, a mobile column was sent from Livingstone to Kasama in Rhodesia, and placed under the command of Lieut.-Colonel Stennett. At the same time, a call was issued for European volunteers, who assembled at Kasama from all parts, many having trekked long distances across the *veldt* in ox-carts.

A battalion of Belgian native infantry opportunely came in from the Congo Free State, but as these defences on a frontier extending over 200 miles were slender, the 2nd Mobile Column of Rhodesian Mounted Police, sent into the Caprivi strip, was recalled. Under their commander, Major J. J. O'Sullevan, this column, to reach the border in time, executed, though it was the wet season, a march of 430 miles within twenty days. Their arrival enabled a fortified position to be established at Saisi, barring the route to Kasama.

It very soon became evident that these precautions were not un-called for. Repulsed in Nyassaland, von Falkenstein, leading an expe-dition from Bismarckburg, on September 6 laid siege to Abercorn. The latter place was twenty miles within the British boundary, and Bismarckburg, a port on Lake Tanganyika, about the same distance from the line on the German side. Stennett's column at the time was ninety-nine miles away. Put on their mettle, the men covered the road in seventy-six hours, and Stennett appeared before Abercorn on the morning of September 9. With the Karonga experience still fresh in mind, the enemy did not await an engagement. He was attacked in falling back by the Rhodesian police, and chased over the frontier.

In face of these repulses, the Germans now turned to account the command they had of Lake Tanganyika. Besides unarmed craft, their Tanganyika flotilla, with which at this time the Allies had nothing to compete, consisted of a lake cruiser of 500 tons, *Graf von Gotzen*, armed with one 4-inch and two smaller guns, and two gunboats, *Kingani* and *Hedwig von Wissmann*, each carrying one bow gun. The second stroke from Bismarckburg was therefore "amphibious" and directed against the stores of the African Lakes Corporation at Kituta, a port at the extreme south end of the Lake. Convoyed by the flotilla, and in two transports, the German troops landed at Kituta (November 17), sank a small steamer lying in the port, and sacked and burned the stores.

From Kituta the attack was moved, also by water, to Kasakalawe, where a large quantity of telegraph material was captured. While the looting was still going on an attack was delivered by Rhodesian police and Belgian troops, but the Germans, aided by the fire of their armed ships, were enabled to re-embark. As Tanganyika is a body of water 600 miles in length, and divides the Congo Free State from German East Africa, it was plain that so long as the Germans retained com-mand of it they could not only transfer forces with great facility from north to south or *vice versa*, but that substantial aid from the Congo Free State in the East African campaign was barred out.

And this was a matter of moment, because if two Allied forces could operate one to the east and one to the west of the main moun-tain chain, there was much more hope of some decision. Indeed, on any other lines the campaign could never be conclusive. A request, therefore, was sent to the British Admiralty in London for the dispatch of two motor launches of a speed and armament outclassing those of the German gunboats. The craft had to be forwarded to Capetown, railed from there by way of Buluwayo and Livingstone to Elizabethville in the Congo Free State, a distance of 2,300 miles; from Eliza-bethville hauled by tractors across 150 miles of mountainous country, transferred again to a short section of railway; floated 400 miles down the Lualaba River, partly on barrels and lighters, and through shoals and rapids; and finally railed to the Belgian port of Albertville.

This extraordinary adventure, accomplished by Commander G. Spicer Simson, R.N., and a small body of naval men, occupied five months.

The country over which the launches had to be "towed" from Elizabethville was held there to be totally impassable. There were passes to be climbed 6,000 feet above sea-level. Commander Simson was assured by advisers on the spot when his vessels and the tractor engines arrived that he would never do it. He was convinced that he could, and determined that he would. Critics voted him crazy. But he had not come to Elizabethville in order to leave his plant to rot there, and most assuredly he was not going to take it back again. Amid local official pity he set out. There were times when on the so-called road, amid the remotest solitudes of Africa, he and his expedition appeared to be stuck.

The gradients were some of them deterrent, and they were almost worse downhill than uphill. But the resolution not to be beaten, and the prospect of a brush with the Germans on Tanganyika, kept eve-rybody's morale high, so high that when water ran short, as on the loftiest part of the track, an arid wilderness of mountains, it did, they halved their scanty allowance of drinking water so that the tractors might not lack steam. At length from the heights the far off line of the inland sea broke upon their view, flashing in the tropical sunlight. They were dusty and unwashed; thirsty with an unholy and uncivi-lised thirst; scarecrows hardly to be recognised, but this was the prom-ise of the end.

And in due course *Mimi* and *Toutou*, as the boats had been called, were launched. They had not been three days afloat when *Kingani* was fallen in with. The German did not decline the fight. His surprise came when one of the pair, keeping well out of range of his gun, but still within the range of her own piece, lured him on, while the other manoeuvred astern where he had no armament, and with her first shell smashed his gun shield, and killed both the captain and two of the gun crew. The rest of the tale is brief. Two or three more shots which penetrated astern, and the crew of *Kingani* ran up the white flag. They were made prisoners, and their vessel taken in tow. She was sinking, but Simson managed to bring her into port in time, and, re-paired, she was added to the new British flotilla. For some time after this *Hedwig von Wissmann* kept out of the way, but finally was caught in the open.

The same tactics were followed, and the only difference was that, a shell happening to burst in the German's engine-room, he foundered. All the survivors were picked up. *Graf von Gotzen* then adopted the classic German manoeuvre of remaining in harbour—Kilgoma, on the German shore. Enticements to battle proving futile, she was attacked by aeroplane. At the finish the Germans themselves, fearing a "cutting out "enterprise, scuttled her. From that time Tanganyika became for them a closed book. All the members of this naval expedition, sixteen in number, were decorated for distinguished service. Never had the honour been better earned.

For some time after the raids upon Kituta and Kasakalawe events in Northern Rhodesia were limited to the attack and defence of small posts and scrimmages along the boundary, but while the Germans still had command of the lakes, part of von Wehle's force with a rein-forcement of Arab auxiliaries was transported south to Bismarckburg, joined there by a contingent of Falkenstein's troops from New Lan-genburg, and under the command of von Wehle, crossed the frontier and laid siege to Saisi. Relatively, this invasion was formidable. The Column comprised eight double companies of German native infan-try under European officers, 400 European mounted riflemen, and a corps of Arabs, and it was well equipped with field artillery and machine-guns.

The advance upon Saisi, indeed, could not be seriously opposed, and everything depended upon the defence of that position. Fortu-nately, in the interval the defences had been strengthened and ex-tended. Saisi at this time (July, 1915) was held by Major O'Sullevan's Column of Rhodesian Mounted Police, 470 all told. Some Belgian native troops were also hastily thrown into the place. Outnumbering the garrison five times over, the enemy drew a cordon round the posi-tion, and opened a hot bombardment, firing in more than 200 high explosive shells. This, combined with successive attempts to rush the defences at different points, chiefly in night attacks, went on for six days and nights.

The danger, however, lay not so much in the German superiority in numbers and artillery as in the shortage of supplies. So sudden had been the irruption that no chance of sending in extra stores had been allowed. The scanty rations had therefore to be doled out with the utmost parsimony. And to lack of food was added shortage of water. For its supply the camp depended partly upon wells, partly upon a neighbouring small river. One of the first steps of the besiegers, however, had been, by employment of their superiority of force, to seize the wells, and driving in the outposts of the defence on that side, to picket the stream. All that could be done was for men of the garrison to sally out by night, singly or in twos and threes, and surprising or evading the pickets, to fill the water bottles brought with them. It was risky work.

Nevertheless by this means the garrison managed to carry on. In the meantime, efforts at relief had been made by Belgian native troops, but had failed to break through, and on the seventh day von Wehle sent in a demand for surrender. It was emphatically refused. For four days longer the besiegers hung on, and O'Sullevan and his men having eaten their last carefully-husbanded biscuit, were face to face with the prospect of being starved out, when, after indications and sounds of activity during the darkness, it was found at daybreak that the Germans had decamped and were on their way back to the frontier. They themselves, it turned out, owing to the movement of the relief forces round the outside of their lines, had had their supplies cut off, and were in no better case than the besieged. Their movement had been an expensive failure, and they did not repeat it. For his services in this affair Major O'Sullevan was made a Companion of the D.S.O. Some idea of the labour involved in moving up supplies and stores to this remote region may be gathered from the fact that 20,000 native carriers had constantly to be employed.

Could von Lettow-Vorbeck have achieved, as he had intended, the conquest and occupation of Uganda, he would have been directly in touch with the Eastern Soudan. Failing that, he had to depend upon communication across the Victoria Nyanza, which line he knew was precarious. All the same, while it remained open, and notwithstanding the repulse of the German invasion of Uganda, he took full advantage of it. The effect speedily appeared in the attitude of Ali Dinar, Sultan of Darfur. Ali Dinar had in 1898 been a prisoner of the *Mahdi*, but escaping south after the battle of Omdurman, and professing loyalty to the restored British authority, had been confirmed on the throne of Darfur subject to the payment of a nominal tribute. His kingdom, covering 150,000 square miles, had a population of about a million, and he had a native standing army of, roundly, 10,000 men, for the most part well armed.

He was therefore a somewhat formidable potentate, and it was the more difficult to deal with him in the event of his disaffection because his capital, El Fasher, lies 950 miles to the south-west of Khartoum, which is itself 500 miles from the nearest point on the seaboard (Suakim) and more than 1,000 miles south of Cairo. From Khartoum a railway has in recent years been laid to El Obeid, the capital of Kardofan (435 miles), but to reach El Fasher from El Obeid 400 miles of country had to be crossed on foot, and in that distance there were two desert, and, save for far-spaced oases, waterless belts, each 100 miles wide.

Great, however, as were the obstacles presented by these distances and conditions, they had to be faced, since, seduced by German propagandists, and imbued with the belief both that Germany was the Greatest Power and the British Empire at the point of downfall, Ali Dinar had early in 1915 formally and openly renounced his allegiance. This meant at once a very serious movement in the Eastern Soudan, and a grave threat to Uganda.

Accordingly, a British Column of some 2,000 men was concentrated at Hahud in Kordofan, under the command of Lieut.-Colonel P.V. Kelly, 3rd Hussars, but serving attached in the Egyptian army. The main body of the force consisted of the 13th and 14th Soudanese Infantry, the 4th Egyptian Infantry, and a battalion of Arab riflemen. As a cavalry arm there were five companies of the Camel Corps and two companies of Mounted Infantry, as well as two batteries of light guns, and a mule battery of maxims. Darfur was invaded. The opposition immediately met with was limited to encounters with the hostile cavalry, who attempted to harass the transit.

After a march of two months, time being taken up by the necessity of assuring communications, the British Column reached Abiad. Scouts had brought in word that in the meantime the *sultan*, calling in his provincial garrisons, had massed his forces in the capital. For the British it was one of those situations in which failure could not be risked. A reverse at such a distance from railhead meant annihilation. The practical problem was the crossing of the sixty-eight miles of dry country between Abiad and Meleit, the position from which the final dash forward to El Fasher was to be made. The problem was solved by a skilful manoeuvre. Colonel Kelly sent his camelry and mounted troops forward to a point forty miles in advance, so that, his mobile troops clearing the country, the rest of his column might negotiate this expanse by a rapid and uninterrupted march. Not only was that done, but it was found out later that by the rounding up of enemy observers and patrols, information of the advance upon Meleit did not reach El Fasher until the British Column had arrived.

The *sultan's* best chance was thus lost. Nevertheless, Ali Dinar at once moved out to give battle, and his presence was disclosed by the large parties of his horsemen and camelry, who, as soon as the British force struck camp at Meleit, hung on to it. The *sultan's* army was found drawn up behind the village of Beringia, in a strong position, his left extending forward in a semi-circle, his right wing "refused," and its flank covered by a steep depression. The centre and left were entrenched. These were capable dispositions, and the task before Colonel Kelly's force looked no easy thing. The infantry were formed into a square, and advanced in that order.

Covering and screening the advance, part of the British camelry penetrated into Beringia, and some of them pushed through it, to a ridge on the farther side. Here they came under a concentrated hostile fire, and were compelled to retreat. On the part of the enemy this seems to have been taken as the beginning of a British defeat, for leaving their trenches they forthwith dashed out in pursuit. The British screen of mounted men then drew off, but disclosed the square. Ali Dinar's army charged down upon it, attempting to enclose on three sides. And the assault was desperate, for despite the fire of the machine-guns and the withering volleys of the riflemen, some of the enemy fell within ten yards.

Nor was one repulse enough. The attack was rallied, and after a brisk fusillade again thrown forward. This time, however, the ranks were seen to waver. Instantly the order was given for counter-attack. With great steadiness the troops formed into line and, the maxims keeping pace with them, swept forward with notable dash. The *sultan's* army was driven in disorder from the field. Just outside El Fasher there was another action—a hostile night assault, but the back of the resistance had been broken, and the capital was occupied without further fighting. Ali Dinar, now a fugitive, fled to the south-west. For some time he kept up a desultory opposition, but finally, at Guiba, was surprised in his camp at dawn. His body was found about a mile from the camp. While striving to escape he had been shot through the head.

CHAPTER 6

The Campaign of General Smuts: First Phase

General Smuts, at the request of the British Government at home, assumed command of the British forces in East Africa on February 12, 1916, and embarking at Capetown on the same day, reached the scene of operations in British East Africa on February 19. During the eighteen months which had now gone by since the outbreak of the war, the situation had materially changed. Though the Germans still remained in possession, so far undisputed, of the whole of their territory, the change had been against them. Their offensive enterprises north-west and south-west had alike failed, and the inroad thus made into their resources had brought no corresponding profit. They had lost, too, and this was even more important, the line of communication along the Great Lakes.

Definitely von Lettow-Vorbeek, who had expected the war by this time to be over, found himself placed upon the defensive, and with the prospect, not only of an inroad from the north, but of an attack across Tanganyika from the Congo Free State, and an incursion, the preparations for which were already in hand, from Rhodesia. His forces had from casualties and sickness suffered serious diminution, these losses amounting roughly to a third of the total, but he had yet in the field some 14,000 native and 2,000 European troops, and he had, it was reliably estimated, 60 guns and 80 machine-guns. Since, also, the native element of his army were, in fact, professional soldiers, they were by no means to be despised. He could rely besides implicitly upon their fidelity, for being detribalised, if the Germans were beaten in the war these men must lose their all.

It was all round a serious situation. At the same time, if von Lettow-

Vorbeck could hold off the main British attack from the north, there was the chance by guerilla tactics of wearing out the others. And the outlook on the north was from the German standpoint not altogether gloomy. For eighteen months the German forces had not only held Taveta, and defied every effort to oust them, but they had established and at this date occupied round that place a crescent of strong and strongly fortified positions.

Taveta lies just below the south-eastern spur of Kilimanjaro, and upon the little River Lumi, which rising high up on the great mountain, falls in the first place into a mountain lake or *tarn* called Chala, and then flows southwards through Taveta until lost in Lake Yipe some ten miles below the town. And through Taveta, east to west, crossing the Lumi, run both the high road and the branch railway from Voi (on the line to Mombasa), to Moschi. It was clear that so long as the Germans held Taveta no British advance to the south could take place. Taveta was the key position.

Why the Germans had held the place so long will be the more readily understood when it is added that they had fortified themselves on the high ground round Lake Chala, had seized, fortified, and connected up with the Chala position a bold bluff called the Salaita, some twenty miles to the east of Taveta and covering the town on that side; a position on and commanding the Voi-Moschi railway, Serengeti, where they had constructed a fortified camp; and a strong advanced post at Mbuyuni, another four miles along the railway to the east, and seventeen miles from Taveta.

And with this arc of positions they appeared secure, for Lake Yipe, surrounded by high hills, being in the way, an attack upon Taveta from the south was not practicable. From the west Taveta is overlooked by the outlying foothills of Kilimanjaro. Between two of these, Latema on the north, and Reata on the south, there is a pass over which the road and railway to Moschi are alike carried. The pass likewise had been fortified, but to assail the Taveta position on that side it was necessary to undertake a long detour across the main mountain range. Thus posted, the Germans during these eighteen months had not remained passive. They had used their lines round Taveta as a base for frequent raids and incursions, and near the coast, to arrest any invasion in that quarter, had maintained a considerable force on the River Umba.

On his side also, General Tighe had not been inactive. He had re-organised the forces under his command into two divisions. The 1st, under Major-General Stewart (promoted for his services at Bukoba), was told off to operate against the Longido position, held by the Germans in order to bar a turning movement. Stewart's base was the railhead of the branch line to Lake Magadi. The 2nd Division, under Brigadier-General Malleson, was to operate against Mbuyuni and the Serengeti camp. Malleson carried the advanced work on January 22, and captured the camp two days later.

The next intended stage was the seizure of Salaita. For that purpose a strong concentration at Mbuyuni was essential, but before it could be carried out the problem of water supply had to be taken in hand. The country to the east of Taveta is arid. Of the 100,000 gallons needed day by day for troops and transport, 40,000 had been obtained by laying a pipe-line across the dry belt. The other 60,000 gallons a day had to be brought up by rail, or by road in storage tanks. With all these difficulties the engineers, under the direction of Lieut.-Colonel Collins, R.E., had successfully grappled, notwithstanding the German efforts to destroy the reservoir which fed the pipe-line.

As for the general scheme of operations, assuming the attack upon Salaita to prosper, the proposal of General Tighe was an advance upon Taveta from the Salaita hill in conjunction with Stewart's turning movement across the mountains. It was hoped to drive the enemy from Taveta upon Kahe to the south-west, at which point the 2nd Division was to join up with the 1st. The Germans ought by these combined operations to be pushed coastwards towards Wilhelmstal.

Such was the position of the affairs when General Smuts reached the front. He had been preceded by an important reinforcement of South African troops, both mounted and foot, and his South African Staff included Generals Van Deventer and Beves, whose conspicuous services in South-west Africa have already been described. This accession of strength, of course, made a most substantial difference.

From the general plan of his predecessor General Smuts, on reviewing the situation, did not dissent, but in order to bring in the South African troops he modified it. Opposed to him there were, according to reliable intelligence, 6,000 enemy riflemen with 16 field pieces and 37 machine-guns. His decision was this:—

The 1st Division (Stewart) was to begin its movement from Longido, with the Moschi road as its immediate objective, on March 5.

On March 7, allowing Stewart two clear days' start, the South Africans (Van Deventer) were, setting out from Mbuyuni and Serengeti in the evening, to make a night march round and to the north of the German lines, and attacking east of Lake Chala, were from that point to strike to the west of Taveta across the Taveta-Moschi road. By this manoeuvre a direct attack through the thick bush between Salaita and Taveta could be avoided. The South Africans of Van Deventer's force were the 1st Mounted Brigade and the 3rd Infantry Brigade.

The 2nd Division (Tighe) was on the morning of March 8 to advance against Salaita, entrench on a line facing the ridge, and make preparations for an assault, supported by the massed artillery of the whole British force. By the time this demonstration was in progress, Van Deventer in all probability would have debouched to the west of Taveta.

Reserve (Beves) consisting of the 2nd South African Infantry Brigade, with two batteries of guns (one battery heavies) was to move up between Van Deventer and the 2nd Division, and taking up a position astride the Lumi, reinforce either as required.

By the 7th, Stewart's movement was well under way, and he had covered the worst part of the road. Also by six on the morning of the 8th, Van Deventer's force had reached the Lumi. His mounted men rode round by the north of the lake, while his infantry pushed east of it. Not expecting an onset here, the enemy, too thin successfully to resist, fell back upon Taveta. The attack cut off a German contingent on the extreme left of their line, and these troops, making for Taveta along the Lumi, encountered the British Reserve.

In a sharp bush battle they were beaten off. Pushing on, Van Deventer threw his Mounted Brigade astride the Taveta-Moschi road. The result was the enemy's speedy evacuation of Taveta. But this movement was apparently, when heard of there, countermanded from the German headquarters, and a large body of the retreating troops were turned back. They found themselves anticipated. Part of Van Deventer's mounted brigade had already ridden in, and the outcome was that the retreat had to be renewed but with the South Africans in hot pursuit. The Germans fell back towards the Latema-Reata pass.

In the meanwhile, Tighe had brought off his demonstration before Salaita, and the artillery had opened upon the position. In due course, the infantry advanced to the assault, but all they found to assault were empty trenches. Hearing of the operation at Chala and of its result, the enemy had decamped. The retirement had been expected, and a body of mounted men had been moved up from Taveta to bar the Salaita-Taveta road. To avoid them, the enemy from Salaita struck across country to the south-west. It was plain from these events that the Germans had been thrown into confusion. Not only had the

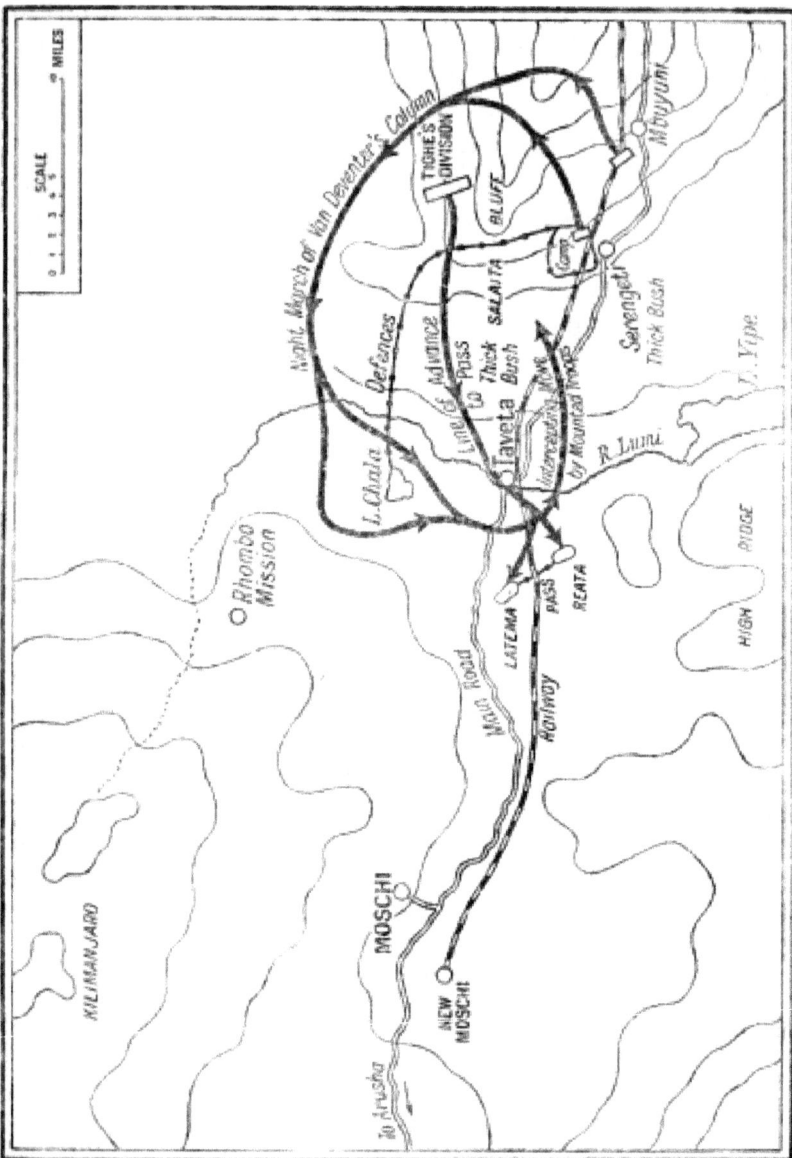

SCALE
0 1 2 3 4 5   10 MILES

KILIMANJARO

Rhombo
Mission

MOSCHI

NEW
MOSCHI

to Arusha

Main Road

Halfway

LATEMA

PASS

REATA

HIGH   RIDGE

L.Chala

Defences

Line of Advance
to Pass

Night March of Von Deventer's Column

TIGHE'S
DIVISION

BLUFF

SALAITA

Thick
Bush

Taveta

Intercepting March
by Mounted Troops

R. Lumi

Camp

Serengeti
Thick Bush

L. Vipe

Mbuyuni

whole of their carefully elaborated line from Salaita to Chala fallen down like a house of cards, but their force had been cut into two parts. And what mattered most of all, they were on the move. This striking triumph too had been gained by Smuts with trifling casualties. Von Lettow-Vorbeck must have realised that he had to deal with an opponent who was his match in resources.

But he was not disposed yet to yield the honours. To check a British advance from Taveta was vital. If it could not be checked the campaign was as good as lost. A rally therefore took place on the Latema-Reata pass, and evidently orders had been issued to hold there at all costs. Uncertain as to the line of retirement the main body of the enemy had taken, General Smuts decided to throw out feelers, and Malleson, with a mixed force of South African, British, and Indian troops, was ordered to push up the pass, and if possible seize it.

The first phase of the battle had been a succession of sweeping and admirably co-ordinated movements; this second phase was by contrast obstinate and deadly. Since to advance directly up the pass exposed to machine-gun and rifle fire from both sides was out of the question, Malleson determined upon the capture of the Latema ridge, the higher of the two and dominating the road and railway both on the ascent and descent. The sides of this ridge are steep, and clothed with dense bush. Amid the growth the enemy had posted machine- gunners, and a battery of pom-poms was brought into action. The result was that Malleson's men could make but little headway. The attack was now stiffened from the Reserve, and Tighe, who had in the meantime marched into Taveta with his division, took on the command, Malleson having fallen out ill. Tighe's Rhodesians and King's African Rifles were added to the reinforcement at the same time. The former pressed gallantly up the ridge, and gained the summit. Most, however, could not maintain their footing.

General Tighe, the battle having lasted all day, now resorted to the manoeuvre of a night attack, or rather an attack by moonlight. The idea was for two battalions of South African infantry to advance in file covered by the clumps of bush along each side of the main road. This operation was led by Lieut.-Colonel Byron, 5th South African Infantry. It was met with a sweeping fire. Byron fought his way up to the summit of the pass, but by that time many of his battalion having lost themselves, he had with him only twenty men. It was the intention when the summit had been reached for the force to wheel outward and push up on to the spurs. Lieut.-Colonel Freeth, 7th South

African Infantry, with one party of his own men went up the slope of the Latema ridge; Major Thompson, of the same corps, up the Reata slope.

The climb in each case was precipitous. Freeth got to the top, and joined there the Rhodesians and Africans who had held on. But though the summit of the pass had been gained further progress was impossible, for the enemy's main position was found to have been dug across it, and was defended by a fierce crossfire. At one in the morning, after moonset, the 130th Baluchis were ordered forward in support. While moving up they met Byron coming down. He told them he had directed a retirement. The Indian troops therefore dug in.

Looking at these events, though the total British losses in the action had not exceeded 270 men, a fact attributed to the high and rank growth and the cover afforded by it, General Smuts, convinced that evacuation of the pass would be an assured result of Stewart's movement, decided upon a withdrawal, and it was being carried out when the patrols sent to call in the parties who had climbed the ridges found them in undisputed possession. The enemy, whose losses, judging by the abandoned and unburied dead found on the ground, had been severe, was in full retreat. He had seemingly already heard that the column from Longido was menacing his rear. Stewart had found his road barred by the destruction of bridges, but had discovered another way out farther to the west, and to the Germans' surprise and discomfiture had debouched on to the road from Moschi. The Germans had consequently to fall back upon Kahe.

General Smuts was now about to begin his drive towards the south. As a preliminary Van Deventer pushed on to Moschi, and apart from brushes of his vanguard with parties of enemy riflemen, he entered the place unopposed. Moschi, the centre of the British-Dutch settlement round Kilimanjaro, is a town of some importance, and about thirty miles within the German boundary. Since it was both the terminus of the railway from Tanga *via* Wilhelmstal, and the meeting point of several main roads, it was a jumping-off position of the highest value. At New Moschi, on the road to the west, Stewart's Column joined up.

While his advance parties were reconnoitring the positions taken up by von Lettow-Vorbeck's forces at Kahe and along the Pangani (or Ruwu) River, the British commander, with Moschi as his new base, at once got to work upon preparations for his movement. The chase, if it was to be effective, must be a long-winded chase. Risk of breakdown could not be taken. The road from Taveta to Moschi had to be repaired and improved: transport overhauled and reorganised; supplies brought forward. Time was of consequence, because it was of no slight moment to drive the enemy across the Pangani before the coming of the rains. Unless that were done, the task of dislodging him would be difficult.

The key of the Pangani position was Kahe. Between Kilimanjaro and the Usambara plateau on the coast there is, running north to south, a long rib of rising land which at its highest point—the Pare Mountains—is more than 2,000 feet above sea-level. To the east of it lies the Umba valley and the dry country of Taveta; to the west, the Pangani valley. The main road from Moschi to Tanga had been constructed along the westward slope of this rib, and below the road in the valley, following an almost parallel track, ran the railway. Kahe, on the main road at the upper end of the Pangani valley, occupied a hump jutting out from the ridge, and terminating in a bold, and apparently isolated, summit. The place was a natural fortress, and the enemy had turned it to the best account. To attack it in the ordinary way would have been a costly and uncertain operation.

In the attack, however, General Smuts followed his characteristic South African tactics. There was a frontal advance from Moschi initiated on the 18th under the command of General Sheppard with the mounted troops of the 1st Division, supported by mountain guns and some field pieces. The advance was sharply resisted, and three battalions of the 2nd South African Brigade were detailed to stiffen it. On the 18th and 19th this action went on, and to all appearances the attack made very little impression. But on March 20, the enemy being thus busily occupied, and probably pluming himself on his defence, Van Deventer moved out of Moschi with the 1st South African Mounted Brigade, the 4th South African Horse, and two batteries of guns; struck south-west, wheeled to the east; crossed the river; and while the enemy was busy with a night attack upon Sheppard's camp got astride the railway and the road. Then, moving up the valley, he boldly made for Kahe hill, driving in the rear and flank guards opposed to him. By this time, however, the enemy had taken the alarm, and Kahe had been hastily evacuated. Thus by skilful manoeuvring the Germans had in rapid succession been squeezed out of two important and naturally strong positions.

Here appeared a counter-stratagem on the part of the German general which more than once turned up in the course of the campaign. It might have been supposed that his force would have fallen back towards the east across the rise, or moved along it towards the south. Either of those moves, however, would have entrapped them. What they in fact did was to strike to the west, slipping out through the gap between Van Deventer's force and that of Sheppard. To cover this movement and give their main body a better start, they sent back a contingent ostensibly to retake Kahe, as though its abandonment had been a mistake.

Farther down the Pangani valley they took up a strong position between the Soko Nassai and Defu Rivers, two of the Pangani's tributaries. Those streams covered the enemy's flanks. Along the front of his line there was a clearing in the bush varying in breadth from 600 to 1,200 yards. To attack him at close quarters this space had to be crossed. But as his forces were hidden in the high thick undergrowth on the farther side, the crossing was a ticklish proposition. Moving out on March 21 to clear the valley, Sheppard was brought up against this obstruction. His plan was to turn the right of the German line. It was found, however, that the bush there was too dense to traverse, and with the exception of two companies of the 129th Baluchis who crossed the Soko Nassai, the troops told off for this part of the work never got into the fight at all.

In the circumstances a frontal attack was essayed. The effort was gallantly made, and it was well supported by the artillery, but it failed. Proofs were afterwards forthcoming that the enemy's losses had been severe, but those on the British side were 288, more than in the fight for the Latema-Reata pass. That night Sheppard's men dug in. At dawn it was intended to renew the assault, and patrols stole forward to reconnoitre. They found the German lines and trenches deserted. In the night von Lettow-Vorbeck had crossed the Pangani moving towards Lembeni. Of two 4.1-inch naval guns he had used in the battle, one mounted on a railway truck manoeuvred up and down the line, and the other in a fixed position, the latter had been left behind. It was evident from this action that European tactics were little suited to operations in a country where the wild growth is six to ten feet in height. At the same time, the important work of driving the enemy across the Pangani had been rapidly accomplished, and the price paid cannot be considered high. A chain of British posts was established along the river, and the preparations pushed on for continuing the campaign.

April and May are in this part of Africa the rainy months, and in this season of 1916 the rains happened to be above the average heavy. They are heaviest in any season in the mountain area round Kilimanjaro. For nearly six weeks, once the weather broke, the downpour continued day after day, the fall within twenty-four hours sometimes equalling four inches. When that occurs the country is flooded out; roads waist deep in water; the rivers and streams roaring and impassable torrents.

Under these conditions nothing could be done. All the same, General Smuts wasted no time. His force was increased by the 2nd South African Mounted Brigade, and he now took advantage of the rainy interval to reorganise. As he has himself stated, he was in command of a most heterogeneous army, got together from all quarters, contingent by contingent, and speaking a Babel of languages. By comparison, the enemy troops, though fewer in number, presented a unity alike in composition and in training. To tighten up the structure of the British field force was not merely advisable; it was essential.

In the meantime, too, there had arrived from Capetown Generals Brits, Manie Botha, and Berrangé. With those experienced officers also at his disposition, the commander-in-chief was able to form a striking force of three divisions, consisting in part of South Africans, mounted and foot, in part of native regiments recruited in British East Africa. These troops were the most acclimatised. None others, it was clear, could long stand the strain of swift campaigning in such a region. Accordingly, the British and Indian units were held in reserve. They had already gone through more than a year of the war, some a year and a half. The climate of East Africa exacts a heavier toll than battles. As re-shaped, the new divisions of manoeuvre were:—

1st Division (Major-General A. R. Hoskins) comprising the 1st East African Brigade (Sheppard) and the 2nd East African Brigade (Brigadier-General J. A. Hannyngton).

2nd Division (Van Deventer) comprising the 1st South African Mounted Brigade (Manie Botha), and the 3rd South African Infantry Brigade (Berrangé).

3rd Division (Brits) comprising the 2nd South African Mounted Brigade (Brigadier-General B. Enslin), and the 2nd South African Infantry Brigade (Beves).

The main body of the enemy had by this time fallen back south upon and were passing the wet season in the Pare Mountains, and that fact had a certain influence on the decision of General Smuts as to the strategy to be followed. The German recruiting ground lay west of the main mountain range, for in other parts of the colony the natives were at best passively hostile, and von Lettow-Vorbeck drew the larger part of his supplies from the same inland area, through Tabora, a place west of the mountains and on the Dar-es-Salem-Ujiji railway. If, then, the German commander, while keeping open his communications with Tabora, could retain his hold on the Pare Mountains and the Usambara plateau, a most difficult triangle of country, he had a chance of carrying on the campaign in a manner calculated at once to conserve his own resources and to waste those of the attack. Further, if to cripple him the British detached any considerable force to seize Tabora, moving it up to Kisumu, and across the Victoria Nyanza, to avoid the mountain barrier, he had the reply of a threat against Mombasa.

General Smuts inferred that the retreat of the hostile main body upon the Pare range had been made with these ideas in view. Weighing, therefore, and rejecting possible alternatives, he decided first to strike at the Tabora line of communication directly across country from Moschi. That move on his part, he had no doubt, would have the effect of detaching a strong contingent from the German main force, and, assuming that it had, he could then, with very slight risk, thrust south along the lower course of the Pangani, cut in between the two enemy bodies, and either isolate those on the Usambara heights or squeeze them out. It was a simple, bold, and practicable plan, and at the earliest moment after the rains, and on the first indication that the country was again becoming traversable, he put it into execution.

Before the wet season Arusha, seventy miles west of Moschi, had fallen into his hands, and Van Deventer with the 2nd Division was now there. The Germans had at the beginning of April a force at Lokissale, thirty- five miles south-west of Arusha. Their position commanding the road into the centre of the colony from Arusha was a mountain nearly 7,000 feet high, and it was important, because on it were the only springs of water in the area. The road from Arusha here runs with the mountains on one side, and the Masai tableland on the other, and it is a lonely upland region.

Likely enough, the Germans at Lokissale did not think they would be disturbed until after the rains, but on the evening of April 3, Van Deventer, with three regiments of his mounted men, dashed out of Arusha, and, after a night ride, was next morning before the enemy stronghold. Covered by the mists, he surrounded it. The Germans and their auxiliaries resisted with determination, for the position was vital. All that day and the next they held out. On the 6th, however, the whole force, 17 white and 404 *askari* combatants, with their commander, Kaempf, laid down their arms. Their stores, ammunition, pack animals and machine-guns fell into Van Deventer's hands, and a body of native porters and camp followers were obtained at the same time.

But not less valuable than the captures was the information gleaned from Kaempf's papers. It was learned that von Lettow-Vorbeck, in order to close this route, was taking steps to reinforce his garrisons at Ufiome, Kandoa Irangi, and other places on the western edge of the Masai *steppe*, and that meanwhile these garrisons had received orders, which were also the orders of Kaempf, to hold out, if attacked, as long as possible. This information at once confirmed the British commander-in-chief's inference, and his instant resolution was to seize Ufiome, Umbulu, and Kandoa Irangi before the enemy could reinforce. On April 7, accordingly, Van Deventer pushed on to the first of these three places. The enemy, 20 whites and 200 *askaris*, were found occupying a ridge. They were defeated and driven west into the mountains.

All the supplies at Ufiome, and they were large, were secured. In the interim the infantry of Van Deventer's Division had been following up, and a contingent took over the captured position. Some slight delay now arose owing to the exhaustion of the horses, but the move was as soon as possible resumed, and on April 11 Umbulu was taken. At Kandoa Irangi, one of the most important road centres in the colony, the Germans had a powerful wireless installation. On the approach of Van Deventer's mounted men, on April 17, the garrison, a considerable force, came out into the open and advanced four miles to the north. The fight went on for two days. By the end of that time Van Deventer had so manoeuvred as to thrust part of his force between the defence lines and the town, and having edged the garrison out of it and beaten them, he took it without further opposition. The captures here included 800 head of cattle.

How remarkable a feat this dash was may be inferred from the fact that Kandoa Irangi is distant from Arusha 120 miles, and the daring of the move may be gathered from the further fact that, owing to the rains, Van Deventer and his men were for several weeks entirely cut off from communication with Moschi, and had to live on supplies collected on the spot, supplemented by such provisions as could be carried across the country from Arusha by native porters.

On the campaign, however, the move had an influence beyond estimate. No sooner had the news of it reached him than von Lettow-Vorbeck, realising what it implied, hurried from Usambara at the head of 4,000 men. He had already, in the defeat and dispersal of his garrisons, had his total strength lessened by some 2,000 combatants. Rain or no rain therefore, partly by road, partly by railway, he pressed on, collecting another 1,000 men *en route*. From Kilimatinde, the nearest point on the central railway, Kandoa Irangi is distant about eighty miles. That final lap was covered by rapid marches, and on May 7 he arrived. Whether he still hoped to find Kandoa Irangi holding out is uncertain, but what is quite certain is that he had resolved to attack before Van Deventer's division could be reinforced, and inflict a crushing defeat upon it.

Owing to sickness and fatigue, the South African commander could not now muster more than 3,000 effectives fit for duty. In the circumstances, and looking at his isolated position, he stood upon the defensive. Von Lettow-Vorbeck gave his own troops, twenty-five double companies, two days' rest. Then he attacked, and the attack was desperate. Four times the *askaris*, urged on by their German officers, stormed up to the South African trenches, and four times they were beaten off. The enemy's bravery was almost fanatical. But against the shooting of the defending force it was of no avail.

While by no means indifferent shots, for their German instructors had taken every pains to make them efficient, the *askaris* were not a match for troops who, as marksmen, have no superiors in the world. Their losses, which were heavy, included von Kornatsky, a battalion commander, killed, and another battalion commander, von Bock, wounded. Nothing could better indicate the character of this struggle. The battle continued all day and far into the night. In the early hours of the morning, and well before daybreak, von Lettow-Vorbeck and his shattered force withdrew. His next move was to try to starve Van Deventer out by ranging, before the heaviest rains came on, over the surrounding country, one of the most fertile and healthy parts of East Africa. That procedure, however, did not succeed, and before long he had serious events elsewhere to claim his attention.

The moment he had news of the enemy's defeat at Kandoa Irangi, General Smuts hurried forward the movement which on his side was to form its sequel. There was the possibility that von Lettow-Vorbeck might, to save time, march back to Handeni, across the Masai *steppe* by the old caravan route, and if the intended British movement down the Pangani were thus forestalled it would find itself confronted by the reunited German main body. To cross the *steppe* to Handeni is, for infantry, a twelve days' march. It was imperative, therefore, that the British divisions at Kahe should move out on the earliest date on which transport became feasible. The rains continued to fall until nearly the middle of May, but as usual towards the end of the wet season, they became lighter, and by degrees the sun re-asserted its power. From Kahe to Handeni is, roughly, the same distance as from Kandoa Irangi, but the British forces had by far the more difficult stretch of country to negotiate. Besides, there were still in the Pare and Usambara area enough enemy troops to put up a serious delaying opposition. Everything, then, turned upon the length of time at the start.

The advance began on May 18. The main column (Sheppard and Beves) followed the road from Kahe southwards. With it was most of the artillery and the transport. Slightly to the rear of its leading formation marched, on the parallel route along the railway, a smaller flanking column (Hannyngton). A second flanking column (Colonel T. O. Fitzgerald) set out from Mbuyuni, and crossing the ridge south of Kilimanjaro by the Ngulu pass, joined the main column at the Pare Mountains. The main column thus went forward covered on both flanks, a disposition which contributed to rapid movement. General Smuts was himself in command, Hoskins assisting.

The enemy had taken up a position at Lembeni, chosen because at that point the railway runs close under the hills. But General Smuts had no intention of wasting time and men in a frontal attack upon fortified lines, much less upon lines affording every advantage to the defence and none to the assault. He was aware that even should Fitzgerald's movement not have the effect of compelling an evacuation, the movement of Hannyngton, who had turned off and was moving down the Pangani west of the railway, assuredly would. And the calculation proved exact. The enemy, finding that his retreat was threatened, abandoned Lembeni without waiting for the firing of a shot. To cut him off from the Usambara plateau, Hannyngton was sent across the hills with orders to double back through the Gonja Gap, a broad defile dividing off the Pare Mountains from the plateau. This move entirely succeeded. Hannyngton reached the Gap—it was a fine marching feat—and seized the bridge over the Mkomasi River, barring hostile retirement in that direction.

The gap closed, the German force, headed off the Usambara plateau, had no choice save to go on falling back down the Pangani valley, and their next stand was at Mikotscheni, a position very like that at Lembeni. On this occasion they waited for a fight, and the frontal assault they had expected was duly delivered by the 2nd Rhodesians. Is it necessary to add that it was *not* the real thing? The real thing was a movement by Sheppard's Brigade. Turning to the left a slight way up the Gonja Gap, the brigade swarmed up on to and carried the bluff overlooking and commanding the enemy's lines. To have retired now would have been disastrous, and rather shrewdly the German commander fought on, though outflanked, until past nightfall. Then as quietly as possible, he moved once more. The move was to Mombo station, connected with Handeni by a trolley line. Along this line the enemy marched to Mkalamo, where they entrenched.

So far they had been unmercifully hustled, for the distance from Lembeni to Handeni is a good hundred miles, and it had had to be covered in little more than a week, the fight at Mikotscheni included. In fact, in ten days the British force had advanced 130 miles, and that, too, in face of opposition and over a country which, with the exception of the route along the Pangani, was roadless. In bridge building and bridge repairing the engineers surpassed themselves.

Handeni, when reconnoitred, was found to be strongly fortified. Upon that position, after a sharp action in which they had been driven from their entrenchments at Mkalami by the 1st East African Brigade and had suffered serious loss, the enemy force had concentrated. In the meantime, having occupied Wilhelmstal and secured that place, Hannyngton had marched south through Mombo. His arrival made it practicable to detach Sheppard's Brigade for a characteristic manoeuvre. On the east side, that is, between the plateau and the coastal belt, the Masai *steppe* is fringed by mountains just as it is on the west. The light railway from Mombo to Handeni ran along the inner, or highland side of the hills, and the Handeni position was close to and commanded a gorge through which flows seaward the Msangasi River.

The Handeni position itself was a bold, and nearly isolated bluff, over 2,000 feet high. Its slopes had been scored into tiers of trenches. Here, therefore, the enemy not only obstructed the way south, but was safe against any attempt to turn him by a movement along and from the coast. But that was not the British commander's intention. What he did was to send Sheppard to the west. Crossing the Msangasi higher up, Sheppard struck south, and next day was at Pongwe, on the German line of retreat. A strong detachment with quick-firing guns were found holding the place. Sheppard attacked, drove them out, and scattered them through the bush, where one of their pom-poms, left behind, was picked up. This done, he doubled back towards Handeni. The hostile force there had, however, already evacuated the stronghold. They had split up, some retreating through the gorge, some across the hills, the rest westward over the plateau.

As it was certain that they meant to reassemble farther to the south, Fitzgerald with the 5th South Africans was sent in pursuit by way of Pongwe. He was to occupy Kangata, eight miles beyond that place. And at Kangata he butted into the new concentration. It had taken place there because Kangata was at the northern end of a main road which the Germans had recently constructed from Morogoro on their Central Railway. This road, though still unfinished, had been completed for eighty miles to the north from Morogoro, cutting transversely across the Nguru mountains. Round Kangata the bush is thick, and the enemy was entirely hidden in it, and but for the vigilance of the South African scouting Fitzgerald would have been ambushed. Greatly outnumbered, he lost heavily, but the effort to drive him off proved futile, and he held on until the main British Column came up.

The next obstacle was the Lukigura River. There the enemy held the bridge on which the new road had been carried over the stream, and as the Lukigura is rapid, tumbling seaward from the *steppe* through the mountains, and between precipitous banks, this was again a tough little problem. Round the north end of the bridge there was laid out an arc of defences. General Smuts, however, had again thought out his turning tactics. In the night Hoskins set out with two battalions of South Africans, and a composite battalion made up of Kashmiri Imperial Service Infantry, and companies of the 25th Royal Fusiliers, and a body of mounted scouts; followed the course of the Lukigura upstream; found a crossing; passed over; and was next morning, after a rough march through the hills, on the new road to the rear of the hostile position.

Preconcerted signals having shown that the manoeuvre had been brought off, Sheppard with both East African Brigades began a frontal attack, and it was in progress when Hoskins debouched on the enemy's rear. The enemy was now surrounded on three sides, and but for the bluffs, densely overgrown with scrub, would have been surrounded altogether. He no longer stood on ceremony, but breaking up, his now usual resource when in a tight place, made his way in parties through the jungle of grass and giant weeds. Much of his ammunition, and machine-gun and other equipment had, however, to be left behind, and a good proportion of his force was captured.

In every sense the drive south from Kahe had been extraordinary, and the more it is studied in detail the more remarkable it appears. There were not only the actual difficulties of such an advance in such a country; there was the necessity of dealing with guerilla tactics in the rear. When the Germans found that direct effective resistance was out of the question, they laid themselves out to hamper the transit of supplies, remounts, and munitions. Bands of snipers infested the country, and skirmishes with convoys were of daily occurrence. All this had to be systematically dealt with and put down, and apparently innocent non-combatants of German nationality rounded up. On the coast, from Tanga as far south as Bagamoyo, the occupation of the ports was effected by landing parties from the ships of the blockading squadron.

Meanwhile, in view of the distance to Moschi, the Lukigura represented for the present the limit of the advance. The problem of supply had been stretched to its utmost. The advanced base must be moved from Moschi farther to the south and the line of communication thoroughly secured. So far indeed had the supply problem been stretched, added to guerilla obstruction, that on the march from the Pangani the troops had lived upon half-rations. Not infrequently, also, they had had to face shortage of water. All this was wearing, and the percentage of sickness had become high. Had it not been for the wise prevision which had reserved ample force to deal with irregular attacks in the rear, the movement would have been held up. In any event, the time had come before going farther to reorganise, rest, and refit. Hence just south of the Lukigura, General Smuts laid out a standing camp sufficient for his whole force, and proceeded to overhaul his arrangements.

During the advance from Kahe, and belonging to this phase of the campaign, there had taken place, in the north-west, the invasion of Ruanda by Belgian forces from the Congo Free State, and the capture by the British of Mwanza, the German base in that area, where there had been erected another powerful wireless apparatus. In this region east and west of the Victoria Nyanza, co-operating with the Uganda units, Lieut.-Colonel D. R. Adye had under his command a Lake Detachment, four battalions of native regulars, and auxiliaries. For some months his Detachment could act only upon the defensive, but when the Belgian Column of General Tombeur crossed the frontier of Ruanda, and moved upon the capital Kigali, the most effective British support became a co-ordinated attack.

The first objective was Ukerewe Island, about fifty miles in length, near the south end of the lake. Its capture was important because from it, by way of Tabora, the Germans chiefly drew the supply of rice forming the staple ration of their *askaris*. Adye's force, transported by the British naval flotilla under Commander Thornley, R.N., landed by surprise and took the German garrison prisoners. After that stroke the way was open for a move against Mwanza. Under General Sir Charles Crewe, who had been meanwhile sent by General Smuts to take over the Lake command, the British troops there were formed into an Expeditionary Force, mustering some 1,800 rifles. Crewe to begin with occupied Bukoba, to check a hostile movement from that side. Mwanza, at the extreme south end of the Victoria Nyanza, lies on the eastern shore of a great inlet, and on the western side of a hilly promontory.

Assembling his main body on Ukerewe Island, General Crewe embarked them and crossed to the Mwanza peninsula by night, threw part of his force ashore at Kongoro, on its eastern side, and another part at its northern end. The two columns converged upon the town, and the need for these precautions was that Mwanza, the base of their operations in all this north-western tract, had been converted by the Germans into a fortress. It was now held by 500 *askaris* under German officers.

After a four days' blockade the British got in. The Germans in the place took to the ships in the harbour, and on two of these, the armed steamer *Mwanza*, and *Heinrich Otto*, together with a steam pinnace *Schwaben*, made a dash up the gulf inland. At the same time the natives of the garrison broke out along the Tabora road, and in the running fight which followed many got away. Abandoned steamers and lighters, and a great quantity of stores, baggage, and ammunition, were among the captures, but much more significant was the uprooting of German power in this part of the country, and the acquisition of a new and valuable base for an advance upon Tabora.

CHAPTER 7

East African Campaign: The Closing Phases

The second phase of the campaign of General Smuts opened towards the end of June, 1916. In this far-extended struggle in East Africa and in the interior, difficulties arising from transport, and it is by transport that civilised armies live, were enormous. At the same time, the character of the German forces and their leadership must not be lost sight of. That these troops were, with the exception of their European officers, black, implied no military inferiority. They were, in view of their training, a body of first class fighting men, imbued with a professional and caste spirit, and, as already pointed out, devoted to their service body and soul. The fact that they were natives was indeed an advantage. Inured to the climate, they were able to face long and fatiguing marches on very simple, often scanty, fare. In equipment, again, they lacked nothing, and so long as the German administration in East Africa had credit or authority, and retained control of the area west of the greater mountains, enrolment of recruits could be depended upon to fill gaps left by casualties.

In the opening phase of this campaign von Lettow–Vorbeck, beaten in his attempt to retake Kandoa Irangi, had not only lost his hold on the Usambara highlands, but had observed the British main force advancing irresistibly to the south until on the Lukigura it occupied a position threatening his flank on that side. Smuts was now not more than seventy miles from Morogoro and the Central Railway, and von Lettow–Vorbeck in the area of Kandoa Irangi was not only as far off the line himself, but actually farther to the north. Had he won in the battle at Kandoa Irangi he could, of course, have crossed the Masai *steppe* and thrown himself upon the flank of the British column, but to do that with a victorious opponent, Van Deventer, in his rear, was not to be thought of. He would find himself cut off from the south of the colony, where he had his chief remaining depots of ammunition and stores, and cut off, too from the west and from the railway and deprived therefore of his main means of supply.

The situation was one that might well have given rise to hesitation, and it had developed with startling rapidity. When, however, Smuts had reached and passed the Lukigura, hesitation was no longer possible. Van Deventer notwithstanding, the further advance of the British main column had to be barred. The German commander accordingly, leaving a rearguard to watch and oppose Van Deventer, moved his force across country by forced marches, and threw himself into the Nguru mountains. He there rejoined the remnant of his troops who from Lembeni had been righting an almost unbroken succession of rearguard actions. Their strength had been heavily reduced, and not least by the last and disastrous attempted stand upon the Lukigura. On the other hand, the Nguru mountains form a very rugged knot of country, and von Lettow-Vorbeck had there not merely a good road behind him, but was within easy distance of the railway, and in touch with his bases in the south. In the circumstances it was the best move he could have made.

Because it was that General Smuts had foreseen its probability and was ready for it. While his own force was being reorganised and recuperated, he had been in communication with Van Deventer, and as soon as evidence appeared of the enemy concentration in the Nguru area Van Deventer, re-equipped, was again on the move. A detachment of his Division (under the command of Lieut.-Colonel A. T. Taylor) moved west to and captured Ssingidia. Another detachment (under the command of Lieut.-Colonel H. J. Fitzpatrick) struck south-west to Saranda on the Central Railway. There was opposition on the way at Mpondi, but Fitzpatrick in a dashing attack swept it aside. Van Deventer's main body at the same time moved south, its destination the town of Dodoma, also on the railway, but 100 miles east of Saranda.

At Tschenene on the route the enemy had a well-fortified position, wired in, and covered by the well-known devices. To Van Deventer's equipment, however, there had now been added a battery of armoured motors, and they helped materially to make short work of the defence and defenders. Working up to and along the hostile line, they machine-gunned the occupants of the trenches at short range. From this point, to anticipate the moving up of enemy troops to Dodoma, Berrangé was sent on ahead with two battalions of infantry, a motor cycle corps, and a strong detachment of mounted scouts. He was in Dodoma four days later (July 29). By this prompt seizure of the railway one of the chief advantages of von Lettow-Vorbeck's move into the Nguru district was nullified. The move of Van Deventer besides was a necessary aid to the operations now developing against Tabora. In the west, Belgian troops transported across Tanganyika had taken both Ujiji and Kilgoma, and in the south-west General Northey, at the head of the Expeditionary Force from Rhodesia, had both driven the Germans out of Bismarckburg, and New Langenburg, and pushed them 150 miles into the interior.

Northey's force was made up of the 1st and 2nd South African Rifles; the British South Africa Police; the Northern Rhodesia Police, natives under white commissioned officers; and the 1st King's African Rifles. Arriving at Karonga from the Cape in February, 1916, General Northey had until the middle of May been hard at work setting on foot the organisation for an offensive and forward movement. His difficulties were not light. Supplies, munitions and stores had to be brought up either from the Cape to railhead in Rhodesia, 600 miles from the German boundary, or up the Zambesi, and then overland to Lake Nyassa. From Chinde on the Zambesi to the Karonga the distance was 700 miles. Besides the combatants more than 20,000 native carriers had to be provided for.

The country, too, over which prospective operations were to be carried on—the South-Western area of German East Africa—was crossed by lofty mountains, between them now desolate and depopulated valleys covered by dense tropical bush. And save for native tracks, some of them over passes 8,000 feet above sea level, it was without roads. Hardly is it possible to imagine a more formidable wilderness. This had been the scene of the long drawn out native struggle against German rule, and its solitudes still testified to the desperation on the one side, and mercilessness on the other. But of the solid work of General Northey the convincing proof is that during the many months of this campaign his troops never once found themselves short of supplies.

As soon as the further move on the part of Van Deventer had been carried out, and the enemy's main supply line from the west cut, General Smuts, at the beginning of August, 1916, struck his camp at Msiha, south of the Lukigura, and proceeded to deal with the hostile concentration confronting him. His road lay in the first instance over a

116

pass through the hills which divide the valley of the Lukigura from that of the Mdonga. The latter river cuts the block of mountains into two parts. To the east is the Kanga mountain and a tumble of foothills; to the west the main mass of the Nguru range. Across the pass to the south-west, and then along the valley of the Mdonga to the south, the new road to Morogoro had been constructed.

The enemy, of course, had obstructed the pass, and to force it by direct attack would have been tedious and costly. But there is a break in the main chain to the north-west by way of Kimbe, and this defile led to the valley of the Kisseru, a tributary of the Mdonga. Following the rough track along the Kisseru a movement might be made which would come out into the Mdonga valley at Mhonda mission station, and so get astride of the German line of retreat. General Smuts seized upon this opening. Informed that the mountain tracks were practicable for wheeled transport, his plan was to send the division of Brits round by Kimbe to Mhonda, the Mounted Brigade of Enslin leading, and Beves's Infantry Brigade in support.

On the other (left) wing to the east, the brigade of Sheppard, while part of his force feinted, to begin with, at the enemy defences of the pass, was to work round by Mount Kanga, cross the foothills, and strike the Mdonga valley nearly opposite to Mhonda. Hannyngton, in the centre, was to move out of Msiha camp and work up the pass along the foothills. It was a well-planned scheme, and assuming that it was carried out as designed, von Lettow-Vorbeck would find the main British force massed on his right flank and in his rear, and his own troops pinned against the Nguru mountains.

But it happened that the scheme was not carried out as designed. Enslin, on reaching the valley of the Kisseru, sent back word that the tracks to Mhonda were not practicable for wheeled transport. The brigade of Beves was therefore diverted to Mahasi, at the lower or south-western outlet of the pass, and Enslin not only pushed on to Mhonda without infantry support, but with only two out of his three mounted corps. The third, losing its way in the hills, followed the track of the infantry brigade to Mahasi. Further, Sheppard's men also were delayed owing to difficulties in cutting through the bush.

The result of all this was that the enemy, falling back before Hannyngton, on discovering the danger in the rear, encountered on endeavouring to debouch from the pass the troops of Beves, and at Matamondo, with the force of Beves in front and that of Hannyngton on the rear, was brought to action. The fight lasted two days (August

117

10 and 11) and the troops of von Lettow-Vorbeck were severely handled. Nevertheless he managed in the end to break out. At Mhonda he came across the two corps of Enslin's brigade holding positions across the main road. Here, being in superior strength, he attacked and with resolution, for he was in a hurry. Enslin held on, but was not strong enough to bar the exit. Badly damaged therefore though they were, the German force contrived once more to get away.

In the meantime (August 11), Sheppard had reached the point at which he was to touch the route, the Russongo River. By that time, however, the quarry had flown. South of Mhonda there is a junction of roads and the routes run to Morogoro due south, and to Kilossa south-west. At this junction, alike to confuse the pursuit and speed up the retreat, the German troops divided, the smaller body making for Kilossa, the larger for Morogoro. Hannyngton now moved in pursuit to Kilossa, and Sheppard again to the left, while Enslin followed up along the main route. The latter at Dakava crosses the Wami, and as the Wami is both wide and deep there was here a large modern bridge. The British intention was, if possible, to seize this crossing.

Sheppard, having those orders, struck the Wami lower down at Kipera, and in time to prevent the destruction of a light footbridge at that place; crossed with his brigade to the south bank, and pushed westward for Dakava. But the enemy had got over in strength just before, and were (August 16) able some miles downstream to hold him off. Coincidently Enslin had followed them up and was on the north bank. The German rearguard, however, there defended the bridgehead with determination, and Enslin's brigade had to find a fordable crossing up stream. When they were discovered to have passed the river von Lettow-Vorbeck resumed his march south (August 18).

His extrication of himself and his forces out of the Nguru entanglement, the severity of the fighting and marching involved, and his serious losses both of men and of equipment, proved in truth to be one of the determining points of the campaign. Immediately south of the Central Railway at Morogoro lies another knot of rugged country—the area of the Uluguru mountains, and it had formed part of von Lettow-Vorbeck's plan to hold on to this tract. It commanded the railway, and so long as he remained in possession the line could not be used. Behind him he had his southern depots, for a notable feature of the German preparations, intended alike to reduce transport and to. minimise the risks of capture, had been the storage of reserves of arms and ammunition at various centres, any one of which could readily

Legend:
① British Camp
② Enemy defences across the pass
③ Route of Britz's Column
④ Route of Shepherd's Column
⑤ Direction of Hanyngton's attack
= Roads

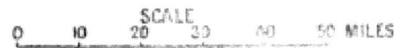

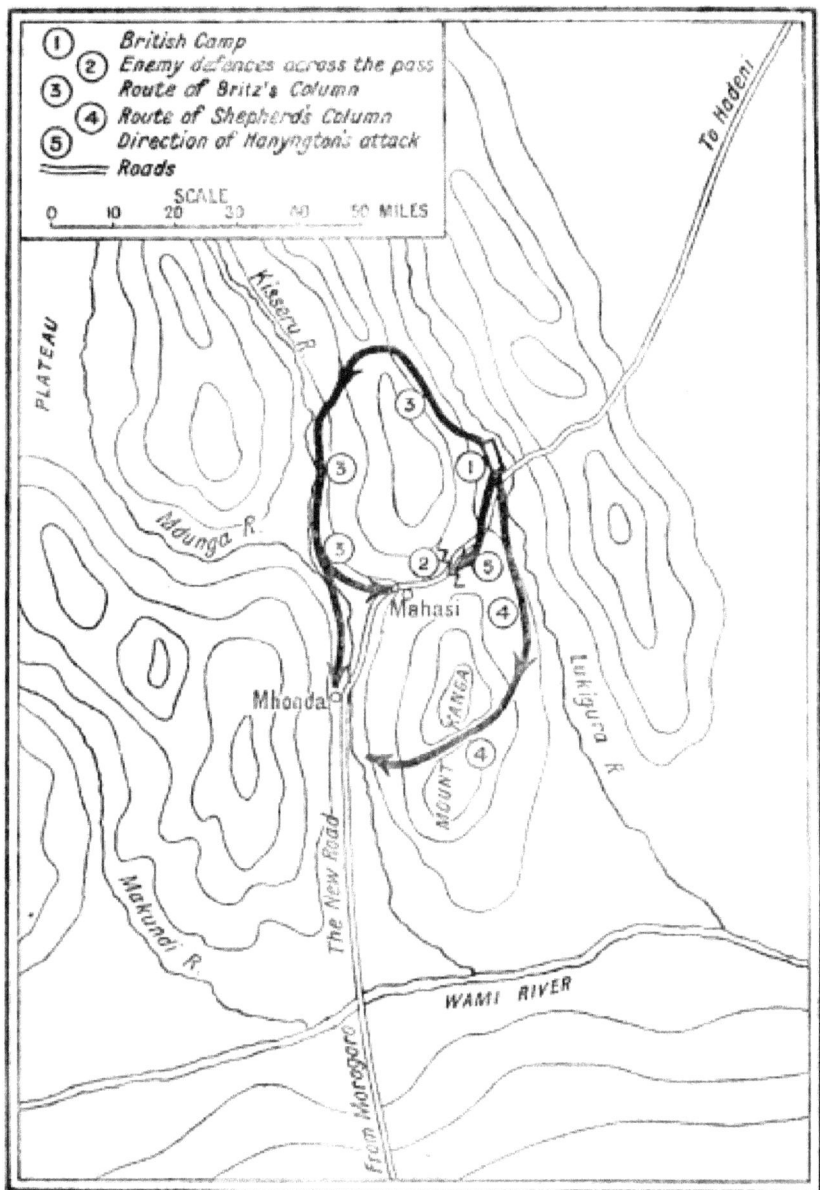

SCALE
0   10   20   30   40   50 MILES

To Hadeni

PLATEAU

Kissera R.

Mounga R.

Mahasi

Mhonda

MOUNT KANGA

Lukigura R.

The New Road

Makundi R.

From Morogoro

WAMI RIVER

be converted into a base. The measures adopted for the defence of the Uluguru area had been, it was evident, carefully thought out. Military roads had been cut, and in one instance carried over a defile along the face of a sheer cliff upon a gallery of massive beams; naval 4.1 inch guns emplaced at commanding points, and large reserves of heavy munitions accumulated.

But a combination of circumstances now went to render these German preparations futile. The first was the state of von Lettow-Vorbeck's forces. They were showing unmistakable signs of wear. Their *morale*, shaken by the defeat at Kandoa Irangi, where they had fairly measured themselves in the open with their opponents, was falling. Since then they had experienced nothing save reverses. Mechanical preparations are of little avail if there are not resolute men behind them. The German officers were doubtless still resolute, but their men in the mass were discouraged, and fought on from a habit of obedience. It was not enough. Secondly, the developments in the west were gloomy.

On a review of events not the slightest doubt can be entertained that the German scheme for the defence of East Africa, seeing that attack depended upon the sea, assumed as a condition precedent command of the Great Lakes, and ability to safeguard themselves on that side. And, safe on that side and their chief recruiting and supply ground assured, to hold in succession from north to south such knots of country as the Usambara plateau, the Nguru mountains, the Uluguru mountains, and the Upogoro hills near Mahenge, should have enabled them to confront an attack with a series of almost insoluble problems.

But command of the lakes, which is in effect the mastery of the interior of Africa, had been lost, and there had come to pass what had never been reckoned probable—an attack from north to south parallel with the coast, combined with a converging onset west of the main mountains. At this very time while Northey was moving in from the south-west, and Crewe pushing south from the Victoria Nyanza, three columns of Belgian native troops were in a swift and remarkably timed co-ordination closing upon Tabora. Von Wehle, who had fallen back on that place, was striving to head off his opponents, but he was out-weighted, and his retreat with such of his troops as he could keep together was imminent. Not less serious, von Falkenstein in the south-west was equally outmatched, and had been uniformly unsuccessful.

From Dakava, looking at his proceedings from the British standpoint, the German commander-in-chief, having the option of retiring either upon Kilossa or upon Morogoro, was as likely as not to choose the former alternative, since Kilossa lay on the direct route to Mahenge. The defences in the Uluguru mountains were not then known. It appeared therefore desirable to deprive him of this option, and to leave Morogoro his only choice. According to the calculations of General Smuts, there was a good chance of there rounding him up. On these grounds Van Deventer had been asked to advance with his Division east along the railway and occupy Kilossa before the main German force, then in the Nguru mountains, could fall back to that point. Van Deventer's advanced troops were then at Gulwe, and the distance of Gulwe from Kilossa is seventy miles. But it is seventy miles of most difficult country. Its character may be inferred from the fact that on this section of the railway there were some forty bridges. The country was a succession of ridges, and they were only to be crossed through defiles, often narrow.

It is hardly necessary to say that von Lettow-Vorbeck had not neglected to cover his flank in this direction. The force Van Deventer had against him was ten double companies, mustering at full strength 2,000 rifles; a feeble total, of course, measured by the standard of operations in Europe, but in such a country, and falling back from ridge to ridge, capable of offering a serious opposition. The South African commander set out on this march on August 9, and it was one of the most remarkable in the whole East African campaign. In their advance from Kandoa Irangi his men had had an arduous time, and owing to the distance and the difficulty of provisioning from Moschi they had had to go very often upon short commons.

They responded, however, to this new call with spirit, and faced its fatigues cheerfully. And the fatigues were far from light. Van Deventer found himself obstinately opposed, not merely every mile, but every yard of the way. All the bridges on the railway had been mined, and where not wholly destroyed—some were massive—were left unfit for traffic. Had it not been for the industry and ingenuity of the engineers, who with local material rigged them up and adapted them for motor trolley transport, Van Deventer's Division could not have got on at all. But from one position after another, usually by skilful turning tactics, the enemy was hunted. The hostile positions were well prepared; every place suitable for an ambuscade taken advantage of Ruse, however, was met with ruse, and steadily the advance rolled on.

The last stage of the march was the worst. It lay through the Usugara mountains, along the defile twenty-five miles in length worn in the hills by the Mkondokwa River. The defile is narrow, a canon having on either hand steep wooded bluffs rising to nearly 2,000 feet above sea level, and the river winding from side to side across the nearly flat floor. Here was a position lending itself to every artifice of defence, and one of the enemy's means of defence was a bombardment along the valley with naval guns outranging any pieces Van Deventer had or could move. Nevertheless, he fought his way through, and he got through with very slight casualties, for in ambuscades he bettered the Germans at their own game. On August 22 he was in Kilossa.

He arrived there four days after the Germans left Dakava. But Dakava is sixty miles away, and therefore he had arrived just in time. And von Lettow-Vorbeck, having, as was supposed, thus been headed off to Morogoro, the next thing was to fasten him there. That, on the information then available, could be done by blocking the outlets of the Uluguru mountains in his rear. There were, it was believed, two of these outlets; one on the west through Mlali; the other to the south-east through Kiroka. Enslin, reinforced by Van Deventer's 1st Mounted Brigade under the command of General Nussey, was sent round to Mlali; Sheppard to Kiroka, and both places were occupied. In the meantime the British main column, crossing the Wami—the bridge at Dakava having been repaired—moved upon Morogoro by a slightly roundabout route and approached from the north-east.

The reason for this manoeuvre was that, informed of Enslin's move, and believing it to be the prelude of an attack from the west, the German General had disposed the main strength of his troops in that direction. It was important to attack him before he could change front. The last part of the British march was therefore made at the best speed, but twenty-five miles of the way lay across a waterless belt, and in other places through bush, and where the sun at noonday is without shadow in a weary land, this was trying. It was, indeed, the most trying march the troops had been called upon so far to face. They faced it cheerfully, because there was at last the prospect of a decisive stroke.

Unfortunately, the great stroke—the stroke which was to have wound up the campaign—missed fire. When they arrived at Morogoro von Lettow-Vorbeck was not there. East Africa, of course, was not a country which had then been systematically surveyed, and much of the detail of its geography was guesswork. Unknown to General Smuts or to his Intelligence Service, there was a road from Morogoro out of the Uluguru tangle to the south through Kissaki. The elusive von Lettow-Vorbeck had taken it. He had had to leave behind him his heavy guns and a mass of ammunition, but all that was a detail compared with slipping past the pincers.

As usual when in a corner, he had, for the sake of speed in movement, and in part also to ensure the escape of his main body, sent detachments along the side tracks to Mlali and Kiroka on the chance of finding those doors still open. Enslin and Sheppard, being already there, these detachments were broken up. General Smuts found out what the situation was on arriving at Mlali just after the fight. Forthwith Brits, with Enslin's and Beves's Brigades made a dash for Kissaki, while Nussey, striking from Mlali eastward into the hills, was to get on to the road from Morogoro to Kissaki and hustle the enemy's rear. Nussey was guided by the abandoned ammunition which he found everywhere strewn along the line of flight.

And now ensued one of the most peculiar actions of the campaign. At Kissaki von Lettow-Vorbeck, encumbered with sick, found it imperative at last to allow his harried troops a slight pause, and he was at Kissaki when, on September 5, Brits appeared. On the way, however, Brits had had to pass the Mssongossi River, and he found it too deep to take over either his wagons or his artillery. Nor were there any means of constructing bridges strong enough for such a purpose. Nevertheless, though without guns, he decided to go on. Arriving before Kissaki, he opened an attack. This native town is on the north bank of the Mgeta River, and the attack by the British infantry (Beves's Brigade) was from the north, conjoined by an attack from the west and south-west by Enslin's troopers.

But, his manoeuvre covered by the bush, von Lettow-Vorbeck dexterously thrust a strong contingent in between the attacking infantry and the attacking horse, and wedged them apart. The result was that neither operation prospered, for having effected that disposition he threw his main body against Enslin, and compelled his retirement. In the circumstances, Brits decided to entrench six miles north of Kissaki and await the arrival of Nussey. Next morning Nussey rode down from the mountains. During his move his wireless had been put out of action by an accident, and he was not aware that Brits was in the neighbourhood. Finding the enemy in Kissaki, he also attacked, but he speedily discovered that he had to confront the whole German force. The battle lasted all day, Nussey gallantly holding his ground against greatly superior numbers, and it was heard from Whigu Hill, where the troops of Brits had dug in. It was a case, however, of so near and yet so far. To move through the interlying bush was not possible. All that could be done was to warn Nussey of the situation, and direct him to retire.

Not slow to perceive the advantage which had thus unexpectedly fallen to him, von Lettow-Vorbeck sat tight at Kissaki for another week, a pause which to him and his tired forces was beyond estimate. But, of course, he was aware that the squeeze would soon be renewed, so that when Hannyngton's Brigade moved upon him from the east, having come down from Kiroka, and Enslin began to encircle him from the north-east, he made up his mind that Kissaki was too hot to remain in, and resumed his wanderings, leaving to his foes his sick, who included seventy-two Germans.

So far as manoeuvring was concerned, von Lettow-Vorbeck had been at Kissaki brought definitely to bay, and could the British forces then and there have closed in upon him the campaign to all intents would have been at an end. He could not have avoided surrender. But if his troops were tired the British were not less so. In this last, and as it was hoped final, effort they had put forth their last ounce of energy. The advance round the eastern spurs of the Uluguru block had been an extraordinary feat. Besides marching with their kit under a scorching and pitiless sun, the men of Sheppard's Brigade had been engaged in road-cutting and road-making.

In one instance, where the route to the south was found to lead to a perpendicular cliff, a way down had been blasted through the rock. Sheppard was a military engineer, and his skill in the direction of all this work was invaluable. At the same time, while it alone made the moving up of supplies practicable, it involved fatigue. Shortage of rations, economised to permit of rapidity of manoeuvre, and rapidity could be achieved in no other way, had, too, added to the climate, caused a high percentage of sickness. Again, in crossing the belts of the country infested by the *tsetse* fly, the horses had perished by hundreds. Means of moving the guns and supply wagons became uncertain or were crippled; mounted corps were mounted for the most part only in name, and nine-tenths of the men left fit fought on foot. In short, the Divisions of Smuts which closed round Kissaki were threadbare.

It is true that the force of von Lettow-Vorbeck was in the matter of effectives in no better case. The German General had through disease and casualties lost half his men. In particular, the European element of his force had been reduced to a remnant, and that remnant was itself fast disappearing. His equipment and supplies, besides, had gone to wreck. But in one vital respect affairs had altered in his favour. His force now possessed superior mobility, where before it had been inferior. And in Kissaki, owing to the accidents which had frustrated the British co-ordination, and enabled him to check the British attacks in detail, his men had had a respite which at this juncture it had been of the utmost consequence to deny. On the other hand, their efforts having missed fire, the troops of General Smuts had had no such advantage. When, therefore, von Lettow-Vorbeck moved out of Kissaki, it was in face of an enemy unable to follow him up.

The motive for his move was not only the desire to slip away while opportunity, a piece of unlooked-for good fortune, offered, but the necessity which had now arisen for stiffening the German resistance round Mahenge. The British had a column, mustering 1,800 rifles, under the command of General Edwards, who was safe-guarding the lines of communication, moving down the coastal zone, and led by an energetic officer, Colonel Price, a swift march had been made towards Dar-es-Salem. The port itself had been seized by a landing party from the British squadron, and having the railway from that place now in their hands, the reorganising elements of the attack were hard at work adapting the line for transport.

In the west, Tombeur had pinched von Wehle out of Tabora (September 19) and Crewe was east of that place at Igalulu. With such troops as he could still keep together, von Wehle was in retreat through the Itumba mountains, and his lieutenant, Wintgens, covering his flank from the south, on the move with a smaller column by way of Sikonge. Both bodies were making for New Iringa, 120 miles or thereabouts north-west of Mahenge. It was of consequence for what was left of the German forces to gather at Mahenge. Northey, however, was pushing towards that place, and one column of his force was now south-west of it on the Ruhuje River, while another was already on the Ruanga to the north-west. It was no longer certain that von Wehle and Wintgens could dodge him. Finally, the Portuguese, having joined with the other Allies, had crossed the southern frontier.

In the circumstances, the one course open to von Lettow-Vorbeck was, while safeguarding the line of the Rufigi, to march as rapidly as possible towards Mahenge, and before the British main force could again get on the move, and in conjunction with his western lieutenants, defeat Northey in detail. But the tide of fortune, which had for a moment seemed favourable, once more turned against him. Northey, on hearing of the move of von Wehle upon New Iringa, directed his Ruanga column towards the same point. South of New Iringa, on October 19, the two bodies met, and the Germans, though assisted by a diversion from Mahenge, were defeated. Having thus disposed for the time of von Wehle, Northey turned to deal with the column from Mahenge, encountered it on the Ruhuje, and in a desperate little battle in which the enemy's loss in killed, wounded, and prisoners was nearly 300 men, threw it back across the river. In the meantime, also from Mahenge, the Germans had moved out to attack the southwestern column.

This was a well-devised counter-stroke, for while one part of their force marched rapidly west to Northey's advanced base at Lupembe, and laid siege to it, the other manoeuvred to place itself between Lupembe and New Iringa so as to cut off relief. But Northey acted with promptitude and energy. Reuniting his troops, he shepherded the intercepting enemy off the route to Lupembe into the hilly country to the north-west, and pushed them to Itembule Mission, sixty miles off Lupembe. There, isolated in the hills, after an attempt to cut their way out in which they lost seventy-one German officers, with proportionate native casualties, the rest, with fifty-three German officers, laid down their arms. The prisoners totalled over 500. After this Northey turned to the relief of Lupembe, and on his approach the siege was raised. While he was thus engaged, von Wehle had got through to Mahenge, but the march of 500 miles from Tabora, added to the losses in and desertions following his reverse, had left his contingent a skeleton. The blows the Germans had suffered had been among the heaviest they had yet experienced. All that remained to them of East Africa, and of the once enormous sphere of influence, was the territory south of the Rufigi.

The campaign now entered upon its final phase, and the features which marked that phase were first a further reorganisation of the forces on the British side; secondly, and with a view to hindering that reorganisation, a German counter-offensive; thirdly, the renewed British advance.

All the white combatants in General Smuts's forces declared to be medically unfit were sent home. They were replaced by African infantry, partly raised and trained in East Africa, and enrolled as fresh battalions of the King's African Rifles, partly by a Nigerian Brigade, excellent Hausa regiments, under the command of Brigadier-General F. H. B. Cunliffe. Towards the enrolment of troops on the spot the work of the British Political Officers in the part of the country already occupied had contributed most materially. These experienced and capable men were in touch with the native chiefs and communities, and in view of the general odium of German rule, naturally warlike recruits were readily forthcoming.

The chief change in the forces was the reduction in the proportion of mounted men, owing to the heavy wastage of horses. Some indication of the loss will be gathered from the fact that in the course of this campaign there were sent from South Africa more than 23,000 horses, upwards of 24,000 mules, and 7,500 and more donkeys. But even with that huge importation it was impossible to keep pace with the ravages of disease set up by the *tsetse* pest. The Mounted Brigade of Enslin was therefore rolled into that of Nussey, and both placed under the latter's command. As re-formed the main force was made up of two divisions and a Reserve on this basis:—

1st Division (Hoskins) consisting of the 3rd East African Brigade (assigned to Hannyngton) and Hannyngton's old command, the 2nd East African Brigade (transferred to Brigadier-General H. de C. O'Grady).

2nd Division (Van Deventer) with the native regulars of Crewe's Lake force added to it.

Reserve, 1st East African Brigade (Sheppard), South African Infantry Brigade (Beves), the Nigerians, and a contingent of Indian troops.

As regards the disposition of forces there had been made at the end of October, the important move of sending the 3rd East African Brigade, then a new formation, by sea from Dar-es-Salem to Kilwa, 150 miles farther south on the coast, and sixty miles south of the Rufigi estuary. North of the Rufigi the enemy still held towards the coast a triangle of country from which he made thrusts towards Dar-es-Salem and the railway. His chief point of support here was at Kisseranga, a strong position at the end of a range of rugged hills. An attempt had been made to turn him out of it, but it had not been successful. Beginning at Kilwa on the east, going round by Kisseranga, through Kidatu, and New Iringa (now Van Deventer's headquarters) to Northey's main position on the Ruhuje, the British forces were disposed roughly along two-thirds of a circle. Northey was being reinforced by a battalion of South African Infantry sent north by rail and then across Lake Nyassa.

The Rufigi is the main trunk of a great system of rivers, and streams which, like the branches and twigs of a tree, converge into it from the interior plateaux. Everywhere the plateaux have been scored into ridges, divided by valleys which in the wet season are swamps, and in the dry a rank growth of tangled tropical bush. Manifestly it was an ideal country in which to play a game of hide-and-seek, as the Germans had themselves found in the native wars, and it was conversely a very unideal terrain over which to hunt a slim and elusive foe. Von Lettow-Vorbeck, therefore, was long-headed in selecting this as the stage for the last act of his drama.

Because of the character of the country and its opportunities, he was not disposed to remain passive while Smuts worked out preparations for crushing him. What those preparations were was disclosed to some extent by the trace of the British line. It probably appeared to von Lettow-Vorbeck that the two-thirds of a circle were meant shortly to become a whole one. His counter-plan was to wall up the force at Kilwa, which had fastened dangerously upon his flank, and in the weeks which must elapse before the British main force was on its legs again, to strike with all his weight at Northey. If that troublesome opponent could be disposed of, and the force at Kilwa held, then as likely as not the British thrust when it took place might be turned into a failure.

But von Lettow-Vorbeck disguised these intentions with characteristic finesse. The first move was an attempt to wedge Northey off from Van Deventer—they were acting in co-operation. It was thought on the British side that this was an effort to break through, and there was a good deal of miscellaneous fighting and skirmishing, with the result that for a time Northey was cut off from communication with New Iringa. Whether he saw the true character of the manoeuvre or not, Northey had prudently concentrated his forces at Lupembe, holding Malangali with an advanced detachment. To Malangali the Germans laid siege (November 8-12), and being somewhat in haste to get on, tried to carry the defences by storm.

In that kind of operation, however, they had had very poor fortune, and this was no exception. Three times their storming parties came on, and each time they were dogged enough to get to close quarters, but they were not dogged enough to get in, and they were still sitting before the place when Lieut.-Colonel R. E. Murray advanced with a column to its relief. A week later (November 17) Lupembe was attacked. Though on a small scale, it was a fierce battle, and the German losses may be judged from the circumstance that here and at Malangali, besides the wounded, who must have been at least thrice the number, those found dead and abandoned on the field, and the prisoners, totalled 125 Europeans and 619 *askaris*. Northey had again proved a hard nut to crack, and he was still at Lupembe, and a nasty threat to Mahenge; a threat which, if the walling up operations at Kilwa were to come to anything, ought to be got rid of. But the last straw of ill-luck came when Murray surrounded the contingent of Lieut.-Colonel Heubner, who had been scouring the country towards New Iringa and had made himself very unpleasant. Heubner's column was 500 strong. The survivors who surrendered were 54 Germans and 303 natives.

North-west of Kilwa on the coast, the British had seized among other positions a bold spur of the Matumbi hills, and the native town of Kibata sited upon it. If they were to be blockaded at Kilwa, this Kibata position, which was on the way to the Rufigi, must be retaken, and there was a determined effort to retake it. The loss of Kibata, however, would have left the British move on Kilwa stranded, and the defence was as determined as the attack. On and around the spur were various outlying positions. In the fighting they were taken and retaken. On December 10 the enemy essayed to carry the position by storm in a night attack, supported by naval guns as well as by field pieces. The British guns were unable to get up owing to the state of the roads—the wet season had now set in—but in spite of that the garrison beat off the assault. The next step was an effort to encircle the place and starve out the defence by a close blockade. Hannyngton's Brigade, however, moving up from Kilwa, worked west and, acting in conjunction with that of O'Grady, cut the German communication. It was now they who were likely to be starved out. Without further delay they raised the siege.

Both in the coastal area and in the south-west the German counter-offensive had met with a check.

Between the operations at Kissali and the renewed advance of General Smuts there was an interval of three months. In part the pause arose from reorganisation difficulties; in part from the weather. But by the end of December, 1916, everything was ready for another move. This time, since the main force still commanded by von Lettow-Vorbeck was now on the Rufigi, safeguarding—it is a wide and deep river—the practicable crossings, and especially that at Kibambwe, south-east of Kissaki, the plan of General Smuts was, passing over the river, to advance to the south-east, in conjunction with an advance of Hoskins's Division from Kilwa to the north-west. The two approaching lines of advance would thus trace, as it were, the base of a triangle of which the Rufigi was one side and the coast the other, and within that triangle the force of the enemy, if not bottled up, should in breaking out be heavily trounced. At the same time communication between these hostile troops on the Rufigi and those at Mahenge should be cut.

In order, however, that the scheme might not become too soon apparent, it was essential to throw the manoeuvring force over the Rufigi *before* the enemy's suspicions were aroused, to secure, therefore, an unopposed crossing, and until that had been done, to disguise the intention.

The procedure of disguise was in the first instance to set Van Deventer in movement, and marching out from New Iringa towards Mahenge, he fought (December 25-27) a three days' battle with hostile forces entrenched in the Lukegeta pass. Northey also started to move upon Mahenge by way of Mfirika. So far the main British force gave no sign of activity, except that some little time before Beves's Brigade had marched south from Morogoro. The troops in line were the brigades of Sheppard, Beves, and Cunliffe, with the Indian contingent in reserve.

The enemy still held north of the Rufigi the three-corner-shaped area marked off by the little river Mgeta, and the line of hills beyond Kissangire, and with that area, to which von Lettow-Vorbeck had tenaciously hung, their main communication was by the bridge at Kibambwe. Near this line of front was Dutumi, held by the British, and Tulo. On their side of the line the Germans held Behobeho.

The brigades of Sheppard and Cunliffe were massed at Dutumi and Tulo for an attack upon this part of the enemy front, the manifest object of the move being to cut him off from the Kibambwe crossing and isolate his troops north of the big river. And that there might be no mistake that the move was seriously meant, it was supported by a flanking manoeuvre to the east by a column made up of the 2nd Kashmiris, and a Nigerian battalion, under the command of Lieut.-Colonel R. A. Lyall, whose instructions were to work round to a point on the road north of Behobeho.

At the same time, Sheppard was dispatched on a movement round the enemy's western flank, and in association with this manoeuvre Lieut.-Colonel Dyke, with a double company of the 130th Baluchis, was, moving on an outer but nearly parallel line, to work round by the west and reach the same point as Lyall, but from the opposite direction.

All these tactics, needless to say, were designed to mask the real purpose of the whole operation, which was to secure a crossing of the Rufigi unopposed and before the enemy suspected it. And that, the vital part of the affair, was entrusted to Beves. The point Beves made for, setting out from Kirengwe as secretly as possible, was Mkalinso, at the confluence of the Rufigi and its principal tributary, the Ruaha. This point lay twenty miles above Kibambwe. Beves had before him a march of thirty miles, and part of the way a road had to be cut. Before the operations round Behobeho, though they were no more than a holding attack, the enemy showed signs of giving way. Of this Beves was duly warned, and his South Africans, to save time, covered the last stage in a continuous march of thirty hours, a feat which has rarely had a parallel and is in tropical campaigning a record. They arrived a day in advance of the time table; crossed the Rufigi unopposed, and established a bridgehead on the farther bank.

The main object of the operations thus made good, the attack north of Behobeho became a serious business designed to push the enemy eastward and delay his retirement over the Kibambwe bridge. Striving to elude Sheppard, the retreating force came across Dyke, who with his Baluchis had put himself astride the road. He was attacked, but held on. Four charges were made, and there was hand-to-hand fighting with the bayonet. Still the road could not be cleared, and the enemy had at length to find a way round to the east. South of Behobeho, the road was again obstructed by the 25th Fusiliers, and there was another bitter little battle. Here Capt. F. C. Selous, the famous hunter, explorer, and naturalist, who had joined the regiment as a volunteer, was killed at the head of his company.

With the exception of their garrison at Kissangire, and some other detachments, the Germans had by January 5, though in some disorder and with no slight loss, got across the river at Kibambwe. By that time, of course, information of the bridgehead at Mkalinso was common knowledge, and consequently, while watching the crossing at Kibambwe, part of them were at once hurried to Mkalinso, where they proceeded to throw up an entrenched line. This gave Sheppard his chance, and on January 6 he got part of his force over at Kibambwe, notwithstanding that the Germans had damaged the bridge. The enemy had now two bridge-heads to blockade. In these circumstances, the Nigerians were transferred to Mkalinso, and from that place on January 17 the drive to the south-east was begun.

Such was the state of affairs when, on January 17, 1917, General Smuts, summoned to London to take part in an Imperial Conference, laid down the command.

Previously to this, indeed since the cutting of his communications with Tabora, von Lettow-Vorbeck had been in the military sense living upon his fat. There were not only no means of filling the gaps left by his losses, and sickness and fatigue continued also to exact a heavy toll, but he was severely pinched for supplies. And that state of things with a rainy season of unusual severity which turned all the lower area of the Rufigi into an inundation, found him at length unable to feed even his reduced force, though everything consumable within his reach was ruthlessly seized. Kraut crossed the Portuguese frontier on a food raid, and that not yielding enough, Wintgens at the head of some 600 men broke out towards Tabora. He was finally rounded up and surrendered to a Belgian force.

The British command had been assigned to General Hoskins. Owing to the state of the country, however, little could be done beyond rounding up the enemy still north of the Rufigi. At the end of May the command-in-chief devolved upon General Van Deventer, and his plan was, in conjunction with a combined advance upon Mahenge by Northey and the Belgians, to push westward from the coast both from Kilwa and from Lindi. This was again an encircling scheme starting from opposite directions. The substance of the plan, however, lay in the fact that von Lettow-Vorbeck's chief remaining depots of ammunition were along the section of coast lying between the columns advancing westward. Either then the German General, in falling back, would have to abandon them or he would have to give battle. He chose the latter alternative, and at Narongombe, south-west of Kilwa, on July 19 there took place one of the stubbornest actions of the campaign.

The Germans were forced back, and retired upon Mahungo, the most important of these supply places. Later (September 28) that place was captured. Von Lettow-Vorbeck now found himself driven south towards the Lukuledi River, and though just dodging the column from Lindi, he managed to cross into the mountainous area contiguous to the Portuguese frontier, nearly 1,000 of his men, among them 241 Germans, surrendered. His casualties, too, had been severe. In the west, covering Mahenge, he had under the command of Colonel Tafel a force of some 2,000 rifles, but Tafel, attacked by the Belgians, was driven east from his defences, and Mahenge with its munitions and stores, now precious beyond estimate, fell into their hands. At the same time, Van Deventer was pressing von Lettow-Vorbeck westwards along the Lukuledi valley. The South African General's strategy was to force the enemy to accept battle, and with his back this time to the wall von Lettow-Vorbeck had no other choice.

After a severe battle at Mahiwa (Oct. 15-18), he made his last stand on the Lukuledi on November 15 and he fought on for four days. The action broke him. Nearly 1,500 of his force, surrounded, laid down their aims. Henceforth he was a fugitive. With Tafel he had lost touch. At the head of 1,400 men, Tafel, dexterously avoiding contact with British troops, marched from Mahenge across country towards the Portuguese border, and he had got to Nevala, within twenty miles of it, when he found himself in an unlooked for difficulty.

It had been the intention of von Lettow-Vorbeck and Tafel, joining forces, to cross the Rovuma into Portuguese East Africa. On the other hand, to prevent the German commanders from combining, and to bar their way over the Rovuma, had now become General Van Deventer's main aim. Nevala had been the appointed German rendezvous, and von Lettow-Vorbeck had fought at Masasi on the Lukaledi in November because for one thing Masasi is on the road to Nevala from Mahenge. When the action at Masasi proved for him disastrous he was headed off this route towards the south-west. His lieutenant, retreating from Mahenge, was not aware of these events. Hurrying towards Nevala Tafel unwittingly marched across the rear of the British forces who had followed up the enemy's main body.

At Nevala, therefore, his men, fatigued by their long and trying retreat, and without supplies, found themselves between the British and the coast. So far as Tafel could tell von Lettow-Vorbeck had left him to his fate. The German commander-in-chief was somewhere to the west, but where was uncertain. In an attempt to rejoin him Tafel made a move out of Nevala. He was opposed by the 129th Baluchis. They were but a feeble contingent, not more than 120 strong, but behind them was a British mounted brigade made up in part of Indian cavalry, in part of South African burghers, and twenty miles to the west, though in touch with the mounted men, was the Number 1 Column of the British posted at the confluence of the Rovuma and the Bangalla River, a tributary flowing T in from the north. Judging these obstacles to be insurmountable, aware that the British, now informed of his whereabouts, would speedily close in upon him, and believing the end of the campaign to be at hand, Tafel sent out a flag of truce.

On November 28 he surrendered with his entire force.

Von Lettow-Vorbeck, it was estimated, had with him 320 whites and 2,500 blacks, about 1,500 of the latter veteran combatants. To prevent him from breaking away to the south over the Rovuma, a body of Portuguese native troops, 900 strong, under the command of Major Pinto, had been moved up to Ngomani where the main river is joined from the south by the Lugendi. Unfortunately Pinto does not appear to have been a very energetic officer, and while he was laying out his camp at Ngomani, von Lettow-Vorbeck, unopposed, crossed the Rovuma higher up stream; carried out a swift encircling march; and fell unexpectedly upon the Portuguese position. Pinto's camp at Ngomani was on the south bank of the Rovuma, and he was looking for attack from the farther side of the river. Instead he found himself assailed from the rear. In the defence he lost his life, and the casualties of his corps, outnumbered by two to one, were heavy.

The 700 or so who survived capitulated. Von Lettow-Vorbeck thus obtained a valuable haul of arms, and what had become of even greater moment, a supply of ammunition, and a great quantity of stores. He was without either, and his men were in rags. Re-clothing them in the uniforms of the Portuguese, whom he impressed as carriers, he at the same time rearmed them with the Portuguese rifles and cartridges, and, his commissariat for the present again assured, set out for the south. It was two days before the British, when news of this disaster reached them, could get well on the move in pursuit. Those two days the German commander had as a clear start. Once more, then, and just when he seemed to have been brought to the last extremity, he was on his legs. And he meant to keep on them, for he moved rapidly south towards Fort Nanguri.

Portuguese East Africa is traversed by the chain of the Ukula mountains, and Fort Nanguri was a military post and depot commanding the chief pass over the range on the road from Mozambique to the Great Lakes. The garrison of the fort moved out to obstruct the pass. This, in the circumstances, was a blunder. They were completely defeated. The result was that von Lettow-Vorbeck seized the fort and in it rations enough to keep his men on full supplies for six weeks, besides a huge reserve of ammunition. All the probabilities are that he had learned all about Fort Nanguri and its contents from his prisoners. Evidently, too, the defeated garrison, misled by the Portuguese uniforms of the hostile force, had allowed themselves to be attacked suddenly and at short range. Hence, by what appeared to be singular good fortune, though it was in fact resourcefulness combined with decision, von Lettow-Vorbeck had established himself in a strong position in the very heart of Portuguese East Africa, and had made a hash of the resistance.

The rainy season also was now again at hand. To move up forces against him from the coast was, he knew, during the rains next to impossible. Next to impossible, too, was it in the wet months to pursue him from across the Rovuma. The wet season had been relied upon to destroy him. But he was living, and living well on the spoils of the foe; he was in a country undevastated by war; and he had a following who had reduced the squeezing of supplies out of the natives to a fine art. All the anxieties were with the enemy.

Under the conditions the chase for the time hung fire. The British, however, or rather the not less resourceful brain of Van Deventer, had thought out another move. This was the transport of troops down and across Lake Nyassa. From the south end of the lake to the Ukula mountains the distance, as distances go in Africa, is short, and on Lake Nyassa the British had available four steamers. As soon therefore as the season made the movement practicable, the flotilla was made use of for this purpose. It was now von Lettow-Vorbeck's turn to be surprised. He was dislodged, driven to the south-east; but doubled back across the mountains, and headed for the Upper Rovuma.

Hard on his heels came a column of the King's African Rifles under the command of Colonel Giffard, while ahead of him in the Ssongea area, north-east of Lake Nyassa, were other Allied troops all eager to entrap him. The movements of the fugitive were swift. For many days together he kept up an average march of 18 miles a day, notwithstanding that, compelled to exist on the country, he had to collect food and cattle en route. The uncertainties of campaigning in this wild and little known part of Africa may be illustrated by one well authenticated episode. Following up at top speed along what was thought to be the hostile track, but was in truth a parallel route, Giffard passed by and outpaced the retreating Germans. Not less in the dark as to Giffard's movements, the latter, thinking it the safer, had diverted themselves on to Giffard's route.

The consequence was that the German advance guard came into contact with the British rearguard. Giffard forthwith faced about. But the time needed for him to change his dispositions, was time enough for von Lettow-Vorbeck to plan how to elude him. Just as Giffard's column had swung into position, and the battle had begun, night came on with tropical suddenness. In the darkness the Germans slipped away. They had, however, to leave behind a large part of their baggage, and much of their stock of ammunition.

So the chase went on. It had opened in May; it continued throughout the dry season. In September, 1918, von Lettow-Vorbeck recrossed the Upper Rovuma into German East Africa. Then, in the tumbled region round Ssongea, his exact whereabouts remained unknown for nearly a month. With him secrecy had become safety. What he might do was guesswork. He might make towards Mahenge and New Iringa, in which wilderness he might dodge about until the next rains, when once more pursuit would have to be suspended. In view of the possibility the British garrisons of Mahenge and of New Iringa were increased. But equally he might adopt any one of half a dozen possible alternatives.

To bottle him up in the Ssongea area General Edwards at Tabora had orders to move troops to the south, and General Hawthorn transported a brigade across Lake Nyassa to Wiedhaven. In the meantime General Van Deventer had made up his mind that if there was an attempt to break out of the country round Ssongea, which had to be looked for as soon as it was no longer possible to exist there, and all the food to be had had been picked up, the break out would be to the north-west following the track past Lake Rukwa.

That body of water, a kind of connecting link between Nyassa and Tanganyika, is surrounded by extensive swamps. But to the west of it is a pastoral district where the natives possessed cattle, and in the opinion of General Van Deventer the cattle would be an attraction. This inference turned out correct. Early in October the whereabouts of the fugitives had been picked up by a contingent of the Northern Rhodesian Police. They were encountered at Fuses, fifteen miles south-west of Ssongea, and were moving as had been expected. The business now was if possible to trap them in the district west of Lake Rukwa. So far as a break out to the north was concerned the way had been barred by the transport of a brigade down Tanganyika to Bismarckburg. Northern Rhodesia, however, was bare of armed forces.

All had been transferred across Lake Nyassa. To bring them back again, land them at the head of the Lake and move them up to New Langenburg should have been a much quicker proceeding than even the quickest march von Lettow-Vorbeck might make by land, and if that could be done he was at last caught. But as it turned out it could not be done, at all events not in time. Of the four steamers on the lake three were out of commission. They had been heavily worked, and were under repair. With one only the transfer was not completed before October 18. By that date the enemy column had got past the intended obstruction.

Finding the road north barred by General Edwards at Bismarck-burg, and not venturing to attack, von Lettow-Vorbeck turned south and crossed the Rhodesian boundary. In Rhodesia his prospects of picking up a living were poor. The country was open *veldt*, farms few, and at long distances from each other; villages even fewer. At the same time he had for the moment no opposition to fear. In the hope of plunder he first appeared before Abercorn, but as a precaution two companies had been sent south from Bismarckburg to occupy the place, and confronted with their carefully made entrenchments his attack failed. The German general then moved south towards Kasama, the Bismarckburg force shadowing him. By this time he was plainly in any event near the end of his tether. The wandering fugitive life, and its unrelieved hardships; the successive defeats, and the hopelessness of the struggle, had begun to tell even on the fidelity of his *askaris*. They had served him with rare devotion, for as already pointed out he was their all, and like all black righting men they worshipped the heroic. But on the other hand they were vagabonds and outlaws, once more in rags, and wandering they knew not whither.

After a brush with the pursuing forces at Kayambi—it was the last combat of the campaign—von Lettow-Vorbeck arrived on November 8 at Kasama. But he had, on the approach of his pursuers, speedily to evacuate it, and when the armistice was entered into on November 11 he was out somewhere on the *veldt*. By clause 17 of the armistice, which related to him exclusively, he was allowed a month in which to give himself up. He was encountered once more a few days later, and informed of these conditions. In compliance with them he, on November 25, 1918, formally, with his following, surrendered to General Edwards, at Abercorn. There were then with him 155 Europeans, and 1,168 natives. Recognising the gallantry of his struggle, for independently of its motives it had been remarkably intrepid, he as well as his remaining officers were allowed by General Van Deventer to retain their swords, and his men to carry their arms as far as Dar-es-Salem.

So closed this protracted conflict. On both sides it had involved hardships beyond example. But out of the evil there had arisen incidentally a certain degree of good. To move the supplies on which they were dependent the British had had perforce to lay down thousands of miles of motor roads. These were of permanent benefit to the country and its primary need. Again the struggle had lifted from this vast region of Africa the dark menace of chattel slavery, and put an end to the reign of cruelty and violence. The country had been ravaged, but for the first time in its history it was to know the meaning of a settled peace. The injury was transient; the advantage enduring.

CHAPTER 8

The Campaign in Togoland

As in the case of South-west Africa, Togoland was handed over to Germany by the British Imperial Government in opposition alike to the opinion of the Gold Coast Colony administration and to the protests of the natives. On the coast at Togo German traders had established a factory. Later, by agreement with local chiefs there were added some 500 square miles of adjacent territory. The hinterland was, or was presumed to be, within the sphere of the Gold Coast administration. At all events the natives, though little interfered with, understood themselves to be under British protection, and that protection was of value, since after the subjugation of the warlike Ashantis who had long terrorised this region of Africa, British authority had brought about a settled peace. But in 1890 the Togo hinterland, about 30,000 square miles in area, was acknowledged to be a possession of the German Government. To the representations of the Gold Coast Colony Council on behalf of the natives, the reply of the British Imperial Government was that if Germany wished to acquire colonies, her co-operation in the work of civilisation would be welcomed.

The co-operation of Germany in the work of civilisation proved to be in Togoland what it was in South-west Africa.

Owning their respective lands in common, the native tribal communities had under settled conditions made some progress in agriculture. They grew in rotation each year a crop of yams, and a crop of corn, and on suitable soil, when trade in that commodity had been opened through Lome and the Gold Coast territory, cultivated cotton. By the Germans this new possession was exploited purely for profit. From the lands best adapted for cotton growing the natives were expropriated on a "compensation" fixed by the Germans themselves, and, it is hardly necessary to say, derisive.

To ensure native labour for these estates the natives were subjected to a poll tax of 6s. per head annually. In order to pay it, and with rare exceptions they had no other means, they were obliged to sell themselves for a part of the year. This made the cultivation of their own farms difficult. To add to the difficulty they were subjected to annual *corvees*. In large gangs they were transported from one part of the country to another, and, under conditions which caused a high rate of mortality, forced to labour on the making of roads and other works. Almost always these demands coincided with their own seed-time. Through the resultant losses of their crops they were brought down to a state of abject penury.

Since, too, their cotton could now only be sold to Germans, it became no uncommon practice for a German official, when the crop was ripe, to come along, inspect it, and "purchase" it for one shilling, or two shillings. But the grievances of the natives were not economic merely. There were the same punishments without inquiry and the same abuse of the lash for infringements of a code of which the natives remained totally ignorant. And in regard to native women, there was the same disregard of honour and decency. In a word, Togoland became in West Africa an area of misery from which all who could escaped across its boundaries.

To arrest this loss of the most able-bodied of the population, aged parents were lashed for complicity. Such were the scenes enacted in these villages, and the share in advancing the work of civilisation. It happened that the western boundary of Togoland north of the Daka River had been drawn by European diplomatists right through the middle of the territories of several native tribes, so that while one half in the Gold Coast Colony was tranquil, the other half, so far as it could not be deserted, presented all the features of German rule. Naturally such contrasts added to the bitterness of the native lot. If no revolt took place in Togoland as elsewhere it was because the population were too few. There was nothing for it save to endure.

With a breadth from west to east of 150 miles on the average, and a length of 500 miles from north to south, Togoland lay like a long wedge between the British Gold Coast territory on the one side and the French possession of Dahomey on the other. On the north it was limitrophic with the French colony of Upper Senegal. The possession was thus readily open to invasion from all sides, and as the Germans dared not trust the natives with arms, and had only a force of some 500 native police, and those not wholly to be relied upon, the resistance they could offer was but feeble.

Their power had in fact been undermined by their own methods of government. The real obstacle to attack lay both in the distances to be covered, and the character of the country, for despite its development by forced labour, roads in the ordinary sense of the word were still few. The only practicable means of traversing it was with a multitude of native porters from three to four times as numerous as the combatant element. Much therefore depended upon the goodwill of the population, and of that the invaders were assured.

On the other hand, the Germans were very anxious to keep their footing in this part of Africa. Togoland was looked upon as the nucleus of a much larger possession. Assuming German success in the war, the probabilities were judged to be that the African dependencies of the German Empire would stretch across the Continent from the Atlantic to the Indian Ocean, and from the Mediterranean to the northern boundary of the South African Union. In brief, the Union would become the only non-German part of Africa, and even that an appanage.

In 1914 these ambitions were no secret. That Germany aspired to found in Africa a vast consolidated dominion was a project which had reached the stage of public discussion. Later and during the African campaigns, official reserve being now judged of little value, it was debated by Paul Leutwein, Hans Delbrück, Paul Rohrbach, Davis Trietsch, Emil Zimmermann and others regarded in Germany as authorities, and written up in detail both military and economic. The German Tropical Empire was to comprise not only both German and British East Africa, but the Congo Free State and French Equatorial Africa, thus linking East Africa up with the Cameroons. And on the north it was to comprise Uganda and the Soudan, with Egypt and Tripoli, again become nominally Turkish but really German dependencies.

There was even in view a German express route from Berlin *via* the Mediterranean to Timbuctu. On the south the possession was to be linked up with German South-west Africa by the annexation of Portuguese Angola, and Rhodesia as well as Nyassaland, and Portuguese East Africa. The capability of these African territories of supplying raw materials for German industry at a cheap rate had been carefully gone into, and the easiest means of economical control by an apparent alliance for the time being with Mohammedanism in the north schemed out. On the military side, the value of this great consolidated dominion was held to lie in the fact that it could be rendered not merely sufficient for its own defence, but a sensible addition to Germany's armed power.

Assuming the Turkish Empire to be maintained—which would follow from a German success, even though it would be a German possession in everything save the name—then the German African Empire could only be attacked by sea from east or west. Those attacks, however, could have in any event but slight hope of prevailing. In the face of a native army of from 60,000 to 80,000 men, trained on European methods, and scientifically equipped, the probability might with perfect safety be dismissed, and a native army of that strength could, it was computed, be maintained without costing the German Imperial Treasury a cent. Already in German East Africa the beginnings of such an army had been set on foot, and it will be seen when the campaign in the Cameroons is narrated how German military measures there as well as in East Africa had been shaped to fit in with this larger project.

In 1914 the mask of deceptive professions about the work of civilisation had been cast aside. They were useful in the day of preparation before Germany had a powerful fleet, and when her military system had not yet reached its full stature; they had become superfluous now that the powerful fleet was in being, and the military machine ready to act as soon as the German Staff pulled the lever. The future of Togoland in German estimation had been disclosed besides by the installation at Kamina, the inland terminus of the railway from the coast, of a powerful wireless installation complementary of those at Mwanza and Windhuk. Such a work, completed at great labour and expense, and it may be added at the cost of many native lives, formed no part of the development of the Togoland colony.

It was a link in the chain which was being forged to bind the world. On these grounds the Allies were as desirous of ousting the Germans from West Africa as the Germans themselves were to remain, and the Allies were the more resolved to act because here as elsewhere German dealings with the natives were a disturbing influence spreading far beyond their own boundaries. It can therefore readily be understood why, acting upon instructions from Berlin, Colonel von Doring, then in charge of the colony, should have proposed to the authorities both of the Gold Coast and of Dahomey that pending the issue of the war in Europe Togoland should be treated as neutral territory. Properly, had it been entered into, an agreement of that kind would have involved the disuse of the wireless installation for war purposes.

But that was not the intention of the Government at Berlin. They wanted all the benefit of an armistice where it was a benefit, yet meant to evade its obligations. Their instructions to von Doring left the point beyond doubt. It is hardly likely in any event that the proposition would have been entertained, but on this discovery it could not so much as be considered. Accordingly within a week from the outbreak of war Togoland was invaded by the Allies from both sides.

While from the west Captain Barker, with a small mobile column of Gold Coast troops, crossed the frontier and occupied Lome, the administrative capital, the French crossed from Dahomey, and occupied Anecho and Togo. The Allies had thus the whole of the coast line in their hands.

So far they met with no resistance. The Germans with their native auxiliaries had removed themselves inland, and announced that they had surrendered the territory up to 120 kilometres from the seaboard. That, however, was no more than a military move in their own favour. In retiring they had dismantled the railway, and they were well aware that, apart from the railway, this coastal belt, densely overgrown with tropical bush, would be far from easy to penetrate. What the move in fact covered was preparation for defence inland, where their own limited force would be on terms of equality with the attacking troops. The position selected was on the Chra River.

On the way inland to Kamina the railway crosses that stream which here flows through the jungle, its banks a mass of rank reeds and undergrowth. To all intents, the bridge over the Chra having been wrecked, such a crossing in the face of a hostile force was impregnable. It had been picked out with an eye to its defensive value, and here the German force sat down, hoping it may be that the Allies, advancing north from Lome, and expecting in view of the reported surrender little opposition, would blunder into this deadly ambuscade.

In the meantime, on the side of the Allies the decision had been arrived at to push into the interior. For that purpose the British and French columns which had moved in along the coast were united under the command of Colonel Bryant. He landed at Lome on August 12 with a reinforcement of the Gold Coast Regiment, and a body of native porters, and to anticipate hostile obstacles, began his march inland without delay. In eight days he had covered 80 miles to Nuatya. Up to that time there had been no sign of the enemy though it was known that all the Germans inland had been hurrying south.

On August 22, however, the crossing of the Chra was reached. Reconnaissance disclosed the formidable character of the position. Across the river lay the wreck of the railway bridge, destroyed by dynamite. There were various efforts to get over at various points, but none were successful. Securely hidden amid the undergrowth on the farther bank the hostile force had matters pretty well their own way and the attack was completely held up. But it had after all not been futile. While von Doring had thus been occupied on the Chra, a French column, setting out from Abomé, had crossed the frontier, and meeting with no opposition, had made a swift march across country towards Kamina. The German commander now found his chance of moving inland menaced.

If the French arrived at Kamina before he did he would be entrapped, and the wireless installation would fall into their hands. That above all had to be prevented. Accordingly on the night of August 22 von Doring evacuated the Chra position and hurried north. Colonel Bryant pushed on after him. On August 24 the advanced guard of the Allied column came in sight of the tall skeleton tower, the landmark of the Kamina installation. But soon afterwards there was a succession of heavy explosions. The tower swayed, and heeling over disappeared from view. When Bryant's main body reached Kamina next day they were met by a German *parlementaire*, sent forward to negotiate terms of surrender. The reply was that the surrender must be unconditional. Since in the interval the French had been closing in on the north and von Doring's already meagre force had been thinned by desertions during his retreat, he had no choice left save compliance. On August 26 therefore his troops laid down their arms. The campaign, the shortest in the war, had lasted just three weeks, and German dominion in West Africa was dead.

CHAPTER 9

The Campaign in the Cameroons

In the German Cameroons the Allied forces were called upon to face some of the hardest military problems of the War, and the manner in which those problems were overcome renders the Cameroons campaign one of the most instructive. It is a mark of these campaigns in Africa that no one of them was in its features a repetition of another. Each was distinct. That already has been strikingly evident in the operations in South-west Africa and in East Africa. When the struggle in the Cameroons is told the observation will be found equally to apply.

Covering 306,000 square miles, this possession was one and a half times as large as the German Empire in Europe. By itself probably such a statement conveys little, for little-known countries are commonly studied on small maps, and this vast equatorial land was before the War and outside the German Colonial Office, one of the least known parts of the world. Even the Germans themselves had over great tracts of it but slight dealings with the natives. Their first concern, having regard to their ultimate aims, had been to ensure their retention of the country in case of attack, and to that matter they had given careful attention. Running north-east and inland from the Bight of Biafra there is a great mountain chain, which extends almost all the way—1,000 miles—to Lake Chad in the Western Soudan.

A feature of this mass of mountains, the natural boundary between Nigeria and the Cameroons, is the breadth of their area. The area is 100 miles across. They constituted therefore a military obstacle of the first class. And to the south-east of the mountains spreads a vast plateau, having a rugged northern rim. From this plateau the land falls northwards towards the lower levels of the Western Soudan; east and south towards the wide basin of the Congo. Notwithstanding that it

145

lies nearly under the equator, the tableland has a relatively temperate climate. There are expanses of open grasslands, and in the hollows belts of wood. It is only along the lower-lying coastal belt, and in the lower levels of the Congo basin that the tropical jungle is met with. Earlier European explorers appear to have judged the country as a whole from those characteristics, and to have concluded that it was uninhabitable by white men. But the lower levels are comparatively a small part of it—its mere outer fringe. The Germans saw that it had capacities for development.

Their Cameroons military scheme, which alone need be touched upon here, consisted in the first place of the enrolment and training of a native army. With the offer of attractive pay that was not difficult, and in 1914 this force numbered roundly 20,000 men. Its equipment had not been stinted; indeed, was on a European scale. Above all, it had been amply provided with machine-guns, weapons especially formidable in bush fighting. Neither in Nigeria on the one side nor in French Equatorial Africa on the other were there forces of anything like this same magnitude. The troops of both possessions united would not reach the total of this German standing army. Even if they should act together, however, they would be nearly as distant from each other as the armies on the Western and Eastern main fronts in Europe.

Under the conditions efficient co-operation would be far from easy, and it was reasonable enough to suppose that the German force would be fully capable of defeating each in turn. Beyond doubt it was to impede such a possible co-operation that the Germans in 1911, in return for relinquishment of their claims in Morocco, had exacted from France the concession of 100,000 square miles of Equatorial Africa, which carried the boundary of the German Cameroons at one point to the Congo, and at another point to the Ubangi, its great northern tributary. All the same, still further to economise their military resources, and to make assurance doubly sure, they had established in and along the mountain chain—the boundary of Nigeria having been drawn along its north-western foot, leaving the area therefore wholly within German jurisdiction—a system of fortresses, which barred the main passes.

Thus in any event an attack from the side of Nigeria would be difficult, while the distances from the French side imposed hardly less grave impediments. On the other hand, as German columns might readily descend into Nigeria from the mountains, a counter-offensive, or if necessary a set attack, might with advantage be carried out.

146

Looking at it as a whole, few schemes have been more complete. The Cameroons, in fact, had been converted into a tropical Prussia, and it is manifest that the task of pulling this system up by the roots could be no easy affair. Another point relied upon in the German scheme was the difficulty of penetrating inland across the tropical jungle along the coast. As a military operation an advance from the coast presented so many deterrents that the Germans did not believe it could succeed, even if attempted.

And the first operations of the campaign corresponded fully with their forecasts. The British attacked from Nigeria. At suitable jump-ing-off places along the frontier—Maidugari, Yola, and Ikum on the Cross River—columns of Nigerian troops were rapidly assembled, and sent forward into the hills. Unsuspectingly they bumped into the strongest German line of defence. They were on the move early in August, 1914, and two of them, that from Maidugari, and that from Yola, set out on the same day, August 25. It was supposed that this alac-rity would find the Germans in the mountain region not yet prepared. The Germans had been prepared for years. The Maidugari Column, under the command of Major (then Captain) R. W. Fox, of the Royal Warwickshires, was to march by the route leading past Mora and over the northern spurs of the Mandara mountains.

As to whether or not the enterprise was practicable it is enough to observe that at Mora the Germans had established one of their for-tresses. The position was an almost flat-topped mountain mass, nearly thirty miles round the base, and 1,700 feet high. What made it a natu-ral stronghold were its sides, sheer cliffs, their wall broken here and there at long distances only by steep gullies. In the rainy season the beds of roaring torrents, these breaks or chimneys were full of great boulders, for sharpshooters a readymade but perfect cover.

And the position, its flat top miles in diameter, was capable of be-ing provisioned for a siege of indefinite duration, to say nothing of the fact that only a large force could effectually blockade it. That a small mobile column could dislodge from such a fastness a garrison as numerous as itself was of course out of the question. Seeing that it *was* out of the question, Captain Fox did what he judged the next best thing. He took up a position on the road from Mora to Garua, and held on there until joined (October 13) by a column of French troops who, under the command of Lieut.-Colonel Brisset, were moving south from the district of Lake Chad.

The march of the Yola Column, commanded by Lieut.- Colonel P.

Maclear, Royal Dublin Fusiliers, was upon Garua. On the way at Tepe, the column was opposed, and obliged to drive the enemy out of the village. The fight, however, was stiff and the casualties considerable. On August 30 Garua was reached, but Garua had also been converted into a fortress. The place was a precipitous bluff on the north bank of the Benue River, which circles round it on three sides. The only means of access, save for an attempt to cross the river, in face of the artillery the Germans had mounted, was from the rear.

In the rear, however, there had been constructed three forts with linked defences, enclosing an area large enough for an entrenched camp. The column of Colonel Maclear had marched and climbed nearly 100 miles, and to that gallant officer, who later lost his life, it hardly seemed the thing to turn back without a fight. In view of the natural strength of the Garua position his plan was a night attack. The attack failed, and this column had to retread the weary miles, beating off assaults most of the way. Only a remnant returned.

The Cross River Column, Lieut.-Colonel G. T. Mair, R. A., in command, was directed upon Ossidinge. Its advance guard had reached Nsanakang, ten miles across the border, when a much more powerful hostile force, hurriedly sent north from Duala by rail, fell upon it. Outnumbered, these gallant men, 200 strong, could not avoid being surrounded. With the exception of two British officers and ninety native rank and file, who cut their way through with the bayonet, took refuge in the bush, and reached safety after a series of hairbreadth escapes, and after undergoing the extreme of hardships, the advance guard was wiped out. It had exacted a heavy toll from the enemy, heavier than its own numbers, for it fought till the last man, and the struggle was bitter. Nevertheless this was a serious check, and looking at the experiences and losses of the Yola Column the campaign could hardly have opened more unfortunately.

In these circumstances affairs were placed in the hands of Major-General C. M. Dobell, who left England early in September. Though not then definitely formed, his plan was to seize Duala, the chief port of the Cameroons, and the seat of the German administration, and from that place as a base to push inland. Inquiries at the ports of call on the West Coast of Africa during his passage out went, General Dobell has stated, to confirm his view. The news of the reverses which had overtaken the Nigeria columns was now on the coast common knowledge, and gave the aspect of affairs a gloomy cast. It was advisable to act with promptitude and energy. Otherwise, despite distances and the lack of railways, the check experienced on the British side might very well be followed by misfortune to the French operations set on foot at the same time from French Equatorial Africa.

In part it was the French attack which after the British reverses kept the Germans still on the defensive. For the most part the colonists in the region of the Cameroons added in 1911 were Frenchmen. They not only detested this transference to German authority: they were on good terms with the natives. When, consequently, war broke out they instantly rose in arms. Bonga on the Congo, and Zinga on the Ubangi, fell at once into the hands of these bodies of volunteers, whose knowledge of the country was to the French troops moving in under the command of General Aymerich invaluable. It was necessary for Colonel Zimmermann, the German commander-in-chief, to detach no unimportant part of his army to deal with the menace, and as his nearest railhead was 450 miles from these frontier posts, his defensive on the east was a heavy obligation.

Already one column of French troops was marching from Bonga up the Sanga River, and another from Zinga pushing west to Bania and Carnot. Zimmermann had won the first round, but he was much too prudent to presume on that preliminary success. He confined himself therefore on the Nigerian boundary to frontier raids, designed to pin there as many British troops as possible. And in order further to free his hand for dealing with his French antagonists, he took measures in the event of attack for transferring the German administration from Duala to Jaunde, 150 miles inland, and on the edge of the plateau overlooking the coastal zone.

Nor had any precautions likely to obstruct attack upon Duala from the sea been omitted. The town stands on the southern shore of a large inlet. Less than five miles across at its entrance this body of water expands into a wide, tranquil, and deep lagoon, one of the best natural harbours in Africa and navigable inland by ships of large tonnage for thirty miles from the seaboard. The entrance, the channels, and the Cameroon river had all been skilfully mined, for into Duala on the outbreak of war a number of German craft, including eight liners, had run for safety, and this shipping was now at Bonaberi, the secondary port on the opposite shore of the gulf.

But not relying merely upon mines, the Germans had provided themselves with torpedoes, some designed to be fired from shore, others adapted for being towed out, and launched against an attacking warship at short range. The Cameroon River had also been blocked by sinking craft loaded with stones and ballast.

On the coast at this time the British had H.M.S. *Challenger*, H.M.S. *Cumberland*, and the gunboat *Dwarf*, and by them business of dealing with the obstructions had been taken in hand. *Cumberland*, in charge of the mine-sweeping operations, cleared the entrance and the lower main channels, while *Dwarf*, owing to her lighter draft, was put on to the Cameroon river obstacles. She had the work of blowing up and removing the wrecks, and it was work which had to be done in the face of constant attacks. Three times she narrowly missed being torpedoed. When those efforts failed the Germans sent down a steamer for the purpose of ramming her, but this craft crashed into one of the sunken obstructions and was wrecked. *Challenger* supported these activities. By incessant work, joined to bulldog tenacity and pluck, the approaches had been so far cleared in the latter half of September as to allow transports to enter into the lagoon, and approach near enough to Duala to admit both of a bombardment by the warships and of a landing.

General Dobell had in the meantime been pushing forward his preparations. He found that the native troops at his disposal totalled 4,300, and adding Europeans less than 5,000 in all. Not a large force, and not one with which anything ambitious in the way of inland operations could be essayed, but enough, it was hoped, for the seizure of Duala. The success of the operation must in part at any rate be attributed to its promptitude. The descent took place on September 26, and there is little doubt this rapidity took the Germans by surprise. An attack of course they had looked for, but they had not looked for an attack on this scale within a fortnight of the British commander's arrival. They had not been given time to remove either their guns or their stores, and the German civilian population of Duala was still in the place.

A little later, doubtless, the port would have been left an empty shell. As it was, it was an egg full of meat. Knowing that if he afforded the chance what there was of value would be forthwith destroyed, General Dobell on arrival sent ashore a summons to surrender. The demand was refused. It had been intimated that in the event of refusal a bombardment would be opened, and the enemy soon found that the threat was no empty one. Immediately the negative was learned, the guns of the warships opened. All that day while the ships poured in shell, a strong detachment, thrown ashore, was drawing a cordon round the town. Next morning the German *commandant* ran up the white flag. Duala, Bonaberi, with an area contiguous were formally surrendered. In the two towns 400 Germans of military age were rounded up, the captures of guns, stores, and munitions were large; and the shipping at Bonaberi formed a prize of the utmost usefulness.

Beyond doubt this sudden and severe blow, which more than counterbalanced the British losses, exercised a very adverse effect on German prospects all through the campaign. And Zimmermann, his attention directed towards the French invasion, was not ready with a reply. His main strength had been thrown far into the interior, nor was it until three months had gone by that he found himself able to react with vigour. General Dobell did not neglect the opportunity. When it was said that the Germans discounted the probability of a successful attack from Duala they assumed a sufficient and effective defence, and on that assumption the justice of the conclusion cannot be questioned, for, given such a defence, a British force in Duala and Bonaberi, if not entirely bottled up, would find it difficult and costly to get out. This was a risk General Dobell had to face, and his venture and its result offer another illustration of the effect of boldness in war. The sufficient defence was for the time being not there.

Near Duala, their lower courses converging towards that point, the coastal flats are traversed by three rivers—the Wuri, the Sanaga, and the Njong, and they are all of them deep enough and wide enough to be bad military obstacles. The Sanaga is a great stream. More than that these rivers flowed here through the tropical forest, growing down to their banks, and even encroaching on their beds. By far the best routes inland lay along the railways. The line from Duala ran inland through Edea, crossing the Sanaga. From Bonaberi there was also a line northwards to Bare (80 miles), where the higher land is reached. To convert Duala into a suitable base it was essential to command these routes, and to seize them without loss of time.

The clearance of the area between Duala and the Sanaga having been effected, a move was made up the Wuri River upon Jabassi, for down the Wuri a counter-attack might be delivered, and until Jabassi was occupied a move upon Edea would not be safe. There had been added to the Expedition a flotilla of armed river craft, and these were now employed to cover the transport of the Wuri attacking force up stream. The first attempt, on October 8, failed. Coming under machine gun fire for the first time, always a trying experience, the native troops got out of hand. There had been here a defect in their training. But as nothing could be done until this move had been carried out,

Railways
Roads
SCALE
0 50 100 150 MILES
Lake Chad
Maidugari
Kusseri
Mora
NIGERIA
Garua
YOLA
Benue River
Frontier
Gashaka
Ngaundere
Banyo
Ikum
Bagam
Fumban
Central
Plateau
Dschang
Bare
Nkongsamba
Sanaga
Bertua
Baturi
Carnot
Nachtigall Falls
BUEA
Victoria
Duala
Edea
Jaunde
Dume
Bania
Zinga
Eseka
Lome
Campo
Campo R.
Ebolowa
RIO MUNI
N'Zimu
Sanga R.
Ubangi R.
Ogowe River
FRENCH
EQUATORIAL
AFRICA
Bangi
Congo River

the column was reorganised, and in the second try Jabassi was taken, and the district cleared.

The operation against Edea was a larger affair. While the armed flotilla was sent up the Sanaga, a dangerous feat in view of the sandbanks, but carried out under the direction of Commander L. W. Braithwaite, R.N., with conspicuous skill, two columns were to converge upon Edea by land—one, a French contingent under Colonel Mayer, from Japoma; the other by way of the Njong River, and then by a track through the forest. The Japoma bridge over the Dibamba Creek, 900 yards long, had been broken by the enemy in two places, but though opposed by a brisk rifle and machine-gun fusillade, the French troops, with support from the naval guns, gallantly made good these gaps.

All along the line of railway there was stiff fighting, for there the enemy had disposed his chief force. The attack by the flotilla and the turning movement by way of the Njong possibly enough took him by surprise. At any rate the operation was brilliantly successful. Edea was occupied (October 26) and the column pushed forward along the railway to Kopongo, nearly twenty miles farther inland.

After this General Dobell turned to the clearing of the line north from Bonaberi. The preliminaries here had been entrusted to Lieut.-Colonel Haywood, and in continuous minor scrimmages he had pushed the enemy steadily back. That opened the way for a move against the port of Victoria, which the Germans still occupied, and against their summer resort, Buea, on the slopes of the Cameroon mountain. In conjunction with the ships of the squadron both places were seized. Naval activity had been in evidence all along the coast which was now securely held and patrolled. One result was to bring up the bag of Germans of military age to 968, a heavy loss to the enemy's defence.

The completing step in this preparation of a secure base and jumping-off position was now undertaken—a movement along the northern railway to the railhead, Nkongsamba. With a strong column Colonel Gorges, taking up the work of Haywood, fought his way to Nkongsamba, and pushed fifty miles farther on into the mountains to Dschang, where the Germans had built one of their fortified positions. Dschang was taken and its defences destroyed. For the time, however, it was the judgment of General Dobell that Dschang was too distant from Duala to be occupied. His small force had had already to be disposed over a territory as large as Wales, and for such a purpose and until reinforcements arrived it was no easy matter to make it go round.

Sickness, and the effects of the tropical rains had also to be provided for.

His operations had been completed none too soon. Dschang was taken on January 3, 1915. On January 5 the German reaction set in. Probably enough because British activity was the most evident round Dschang, the counter-attack came from the opposite quarter. The first intimation of it at Duala was a severing of the wires to Edea. That place lies on the south bank of the Sanaga, and to reach it from Duala the river had to be crossed. It is in the forest zone, and is a scattered settlement in the midst of a large clearing, but the ground is uneven and ridged, and the position plainly lent itself to surprise. As well as the advanced post at Kopongo, where a blockhouse had been built, it was occupied by the Senegalese troops of Mayer, who, seeing the possibilities of surprise, had prudently laid out a ring of defences, skil-fully concealed, traps in fact in which the enemy, if and when he reappeared, was intended to be caught in his own toils. And caught he was.

The attack was delivered by a column of German troops 1,000 strong, and it was obstinate. The Senegalese, however, are first class shots, and one attempt to break in after another was beaten off in con-fusion. Finally, after losing a good proportion of their force—about a fourth were found and buried or picked up wounded—the Germans drew off. It attests the character of the defence and of the defences that the casualties of Mayer's force were only 15, 4 killed and 11 wounded. Coincidently another part of the German expedition had attacked Kopongo. But the garrison there had been put by natives on the alert, and that assault also was a fiasco.

And very likely believing that these attacks, their success being counted upon, would draw the Allies towards Edea, the enemy became active round Nkongsamba. The fighting here was heavy, for by barring communication along the northern railway the Germans aimed at isolating the British force in Duala from the troops on the frontier of Nigeria, well aware that sooner or later the two forces were meant to co-operate. The purpose of Zimmermann, and from a military point of view it was quite sound, was to keep the various Allied bodies in the Cameroons isolated from each other. He evidently still had hopes that Dobell might be contained.

In that case he could hope, too, with his strong points in the moun-tains, to hold off any inroads from that quarter. And if enabled to do this then he had a fair chance against the French. Pursuant to this scheme, he pushed Dobell's contingent in the north back upon Bare, the outpost of railhead, and he entrenched in a commanding position. An attempt was made to oust him, and unfortunately it did not succeed. In this fighting the losses on both sides were heavy.

Apart from the limited advantage thus won, the German reaction had fallen flat, and it had been an expensive venture. What had in part prompted it and made it feasible had been a certain measure of success against the French. The French forces were penetrating into the Cameroons in three converging columns—that of Colonel Brisset moving from the north; that of Colonel Morrison, advancing from Zinga on the east; and that of Colonel Hutin following the course of the Sanga from the south. The plan was to converge upon Jaunde in conjunction with a British advance from the west and north-west.

The marches of both Morrison and Hutin had been rapid. At Bania, on the Upper Sanga, they had joined, had taken Carnot, and moved upon Bertua, halfway from Carnot to Jaunde. Affairs from the German point of view now began to look serious, for at Bertua the united French force was distant from Jaunde only 175 miles. But Zimmermann was able in time to collect a larger body of troops, and at Dumé there was fought one of the most considerable battles of the campaign. The French were compelled to fall back. Having brought off that stroke, the German commander dispatched a swift moving column south-east to N'Zimu on the Sanga, there got astride of Hutin's communications, and laid out a fortified position. Nor was the enemy dislodged until a column of Belgian troops from the Congo, under the command of General Aymerich, was pushed north and retook N'Zimu after a three days' battle.

On the face of affairs it now looked as though the Allied operations had been brought to a halt. Zimmermann, in order to fight the battle at Dumé had risked and incurred the Duala surprise, yet it cannot be said that so far he had come off badly. To General Dobell, considering the situation at the beginning of February, 1915, the sound course appeared to be a resumption of the Allied advance from the north. An advance from the north should enable the advance from the east and south-east—Aymerich had begun a move from N'Zimu upon Lome—also to be resumed, and in conjunction with these movements, if his reinforcements which were coming in slowly arrived, he could himself co-operate from the west. It was in accordance with these views that at his request Brigadier-General F. J. Cunliffe undertook the command of the troops in Nigeria.

But on the French side other ideas prevailed. There was at Paris, if not in London, some impatience at the delay and the turn the campaign had taken. A very natural desire existed to retrieve as soon as possible the check at Dumé, and there was the political value of a swift success. These views were put before General Dobell at Duala in March, 1915, by an official deputation from French Equatorial Africa, headed by M. Fourneau, Lieut.-Governor of the Middle Congo. General Dobell had his doubts. The dry season was nearing its end, and the difficulties of forcing his way at the worst time of the year through such a country as he had in face of him and with the forces then at his disposal were not to be ignored.

The difficulties could hardly have been ignored had the opposition to be looked for not been too serious. It was certain, however, that the opposition would be serious. In his opinion such an advance, to be successful under the conditions, should take place in association with a French pressure close to Jaunde, for in that case the German main forces would be drawn to defend the place. But while the French were still at a distance from Jaunde, the Germans would for the time being be comparatively free to resist the western advance. Nevertheless, looking at "the advantage which would follow upon an early occupation of Jaunde," he agreed to fall in with the plan. The plan proved another of the instances in which more haste is less speed, for it both prolonged the campaign and caused the Allies their heaviest losses.

So far as the force of General Dobell was concerned, the first stage in the advance thus initiated was to the Kele River, and it was opened conjointly by a British column commanded by Lieut.-Colonel Haywood and by the Senegalese troops of Colonel Mayer. As expected, the resistance met with was stiff. Indeed it soon became evident that the enemy was concentrating on this front. On May 1, preparations for an attack in strength having been completed, the column of Haywood was directed upon Wum Biagas, and the column of Mayer upon Eseka, the terminus of the Duala railway.

Both Wum Biagas and Eseka are about 100 miles inland, and 50 miles from Jaunde. Though impeded by broken bridges, and by difficulties of supply, through and across many miles of dense tropical jungle, Mayer's column reached and occupied Eseka on May 11. The enemy's position at Wum Biagas, a formidable one, was on May 4 carried by storm, but the losses incurred were heavy. Mayer and his force from Eseka then moved across to Wum Biagas, and there joined the British contingent. From this time Mayer was to command the advance.

But now came news that the troops of Aymerich, who were to have taken Dumé and Lome, and from those places marched upon Jaunde, had not on May 11 arrived at either. What with the beginning of the rainy season, and the resistance encountered they had not scored the progress looked for. On the other hand, for General Dobell to put off at this juncture the projected push from Wum Biagas meant that nothing more could be done until after the rains, and that in the meantime sickness would play havoc. The sickness rate was rising. It was one of those situations in which to go back, remain or go on offered no more than a choice of evils. The decision of General Dobell was to go on.

Accordingly, on May 25, at the head of about 2,000 effectives Mayer set out. Fifty miles to Jaunde may not seem a great distance, but it was fifty miles through the dense bush of the Sanaga valley, in places impenetrable without cutting a way through. The advance was slow, and the work of pushing up supplies to Wum Biagas and beyond, arduous in any event, became more difficult with every mile of the march. Not merely was the resistance obstinate, and backed by machine-guns at every turn, but the enemy resorted to stampeding the convoys of native carriers. As General Dobell at this time had only at his disposal three motor vehicles, the supplies had to be moved by man-transport, or not at all. This was the enemy's chance.

To stampede the porterage columns by machine-gun ambuscades was to leave Mayer's force without supplies. Hardships, shortage of food and exposure to the rains caused an outbreak of dysentery. Mayer asked for reinforcements. Up to June 5, though an energetic and resourceful commander, he had been able to advance only twelve miles, for in the latter part of the distance he had been impeded by a swamp, and as there was no way round, it had, in face of hostile fire, taken five days to make good a crossing. There are circumstances in which resolution conflicts with reason, and that was now the position. Mayer therefore sent back word that in his opinion a further advance was impracticable. Before deciding General Dobell asked for news regarding the Allied forces on the east. The answer came that there was no news.

Instructions were consequently sent up to Mayer to fall back. Mayer, however, had already been compelled to take the matter in his own hands. The loss of the supplies which were being brought to the front by a column of 500 carriers, just cut up and stampeded, had left his force foodless, and he had to get out as best he could. As soon as his retreat was observed the enemy rushed in upon his rearguards, and the last reinforcements General Dobell had at his command in Duala had to be sent forward to the relief by forced marches. They arrived on June 16, and they arrived in the nick of time, for the harassed rearguard were then beating off a heavy assault. The retreat was continued to the Kele River. Not until the end of June, and notwithstanding the losses involved, did the hostile attacks die down. Of Mayer's force one-fourth were killed or wounded.

Possibly enough, it was this German concentration against the Allied advance from the west which about the same time enabled the Allied forces on the east to retake Bertua, and to advance and establish themselves both in Dumé and in Lome. But in the absence of further western co-operation those advances were for the time without result. The scheme of March, undertaken in the defiance of sound military considerations, had broken down.

The one bright spot for the Allies in this phase of the campaign was in the north. In Nigeria, General Cunliffe had prudently decided to focus his force upon Garua, and to attack that place in conjunction with Brisset. Since the effort of Maclear the fortifications of Garua had, however, been elaborated, and it was afterwards found out that 2,000 native labourers had been employed upon them. They were also armed with ordnance outranging field pieces. It was evident therefore that if the place was to be successfully besieged, the guns of the defences must at least be matched. This problem was solved by the landing of the 12-pounder guns of *Challenger,* which were sent up country together with a head of 500 shell, and a French 95 mm. naval gun. Whether or not he had heard of these preparations, the enemy's trans-frontier raids showed increasing boldness.

The investment of Garua began on April 18, 1915, and it lasted until June 10. At the outset, the investing lines were drawn round the place to the south and south-west, but early in the siege an enemy force of some 300 men, mounted and afoot, broke out, and under the command of Hauptmann von Crailsheim, who was defending the fortress, made a dash for the Nigerian frontier post of Gurin, possibly for the seizure of stores. The post was bravely and successfully defended. The discomfited raiders had then somehow to make their way back for fifty miles through the mountains.

By dodging round the hills, and by finally marching twenty-eight hours without a break, they eluded the pursuit, got back, and reentered Garua. Further reconnaissance had now convinced General Cunliffe that the best point of attack was from the north. A line of trenches was cut there, and night by night steadily advanced against Fort "A," marked out for seizure. The naval artillery of the Allies was meanwhile giving evidence of its effect. So affairs went on until June 9, when in the night there were two attempts on the part of the garrison to break out. One was driven back by rifle fire. In the second, a body of the German native troops tried to swim the Benue. As usual at this season, the river was in flood, and in the darkness, battling with the swirling current, most were drowned. Seventy bodies were cast up by or recovered from the water. Only some forty-five of the adventurers got over and escaped.

What these events in fact reflected was a mutiny of part of the black troops of the garrison. They had had enough. Next day, after a futile attempt to parley, the commandant capitulated. His garrison had been reduced to 37 Germans and 212 natives. Captures of matériel included 10 maxims, and nearly 115,000 rounds of small arms ammunition, besides guns and shells, and stores and equipment of various kinds.

General Cunliffe's next move was a dash south-east in order to surprise the enemy posts holding the tracks leading up to the great plateau. For that purpose a column was detached under the command of Lieut.-Colonel Webb-Bowen. The paths leading to the northern rim of the uplands are rugged and steep, and if not taken by surprise the enemy there might offer a costly opposition. On the way, the advance troops, led by Capt. C. H. Fowle, of the Hampshires, found themselves overtaken by an unusually severe tropical tornado. The wild solitudes, fantastically lit at one moment by a dazzling glare, were the next blotted out in impenetrable gloom, and while the thunder crashed and echoed and re-echoed through the hills, the rain came down as only it can come down in those latitudes.

Notwithstanding this, the advance guard held on. The enemy posts, sheltering from the storm, were rounded up to all intents without resistance. Ngaundere, on the main road over these hills, was thus attacked and captured by the main body before an attack had been expected. The German barrier across the north of the colony was broken.

Further immediate advance south, however, could not be undertaken because of the rains. In a country where the roads were still for the most part no more than tracks, and supplies and baggage had to be moved stage by stage on the backs of mules or on the heads of porters, the wet season is a bar to movement, and over the distances in the Cameroons an absolute bar. The base of these northern British operations was Yola on the Benue, and about thirty miles beyond the frontier. Garua lay on this line of communication, and had therefore first to be dealt with. But to the north the German garrison at Mora still held out.

True, there lay between Garua and Mora 120 miles as the crow flies of rugged mountains, but there was a track round the eastern spurs of the heights, and to move south, stretching still further his line of communications while leaving this menace in the rear, appeared to General Cunliffe inadvisable. As a general advance could not be resumed before the end of October, he proposed in the interval to reduce the Mora fastness. Returning to Yola, he began his preparations. Early in August they were finished. In a march of fourteen days the 170 miles between Yola and Mora were covered, and on August 23 his force was before the stronghold.

North of the Mora mountain rises a similar flat-topped mass called Ouatchke, of the same elevation, but less in perimeter. On Ouatchke the British troops were already established. The two mountains are divided from one another by a deep valley 600 yards wide. In the judgment of General Cunliffe the best chance of carrying the hostile position by assault, and it could be taken in no other way, was an attack across this valley, for the storming troops could then be supported by fire from Ouatchke. Two attacks were undertaken and both failed. A third reached the summit. There, however, commanding the debouchment from the main gully, the enemy had constructed a redoubt.

Arriving at the summit, the forlorn hope, part of the 1st Nigeria Regiment, made a dash for this work with the bayonet. But they had to cover exposed ground, and sixty yards from the redoubt were brought to a halt. There was, taking advantage of such cover as existed, nothing for it but to dig in and hold on, in the hope of reinforcement. And for two days and two nights, despite all the efforts of the enemy to dislodge them, they did hold on, though for the whole of that time they were without food or water. In the rear efforts were being made to send up relief and supplies, and they were brave and determined efforts. None, however, succeeded. The attack had got in by sheer desperate valour.

One of its leaders, Captain R. N. Pike, a Political Officer of the Nigerian Government, had displayed fearless gallantry. But the garrison, taken aback by the feat, which had been thought impossible, had rallied, and Pike had fallen. Reluctantly therefore, seeing there was no help for it, General Cunliffe ordered a withdrawal. And the attack had to be given up, for both the supply of shell for the guns and time had alike run out. All that could be done was to leave an investing force to watch the position and check raids. Mora held out all through the campaign.

Time had run out because at Duala towards the end of August there had been another conference between General Dobell and his French allies, attended this time by General Aymerich. Conditions had materially changed. If the Allies had suffered losses they could be made good. The Germans had sustained losses at least equal; losses of resources and equipment decidedly heavier, and they could not be made good. The way, too, was now open for an Allied advance from the north, which, besides being on a sure footing, would by sweeping the enemy off the central plateau deprive him of his best source of supply. In brief, the breach of the German barrier in the north had altered the outlook altogether. As General Dobell had considered all along, it was the hinge of the Allied campaign.

But the Duala conference decided upon an additional movement—an advance upon Jaunde from the south across the Campo River and through Ebolowa, conjointly with the march of a column from Campo on the coast to the same point. Jaunde was thus to be approached from all the four points of the compass. This convergence was to be set on foot early in October.

It was a useful preliminary that the force of General Cunliffe, though part was occupied before Mora, had been moving steadily south through the mountains, and in a dashing little operation had taken another fortified post—Gashaka. The position was turned by a twelve hours' march through extremely rugged country, as the reward of which adventure Captain C. G. Bowyer-Smijth of the Gloucesters, seized a hill which cut off the retreat of the garrison. Finding themselves entrapped, they dispersed in twos and threes, leaving their equipment behind them.

The reinforcements of which General Dobell was so much in need were now—including a contingent of Indian troops—beginning to arrive, and a further result of the advance from the north was that a British column at Ossidinge, under the command of Major Crookenden, was enabled to push forward to Dschang. This closed the gap between the forces of Dobell and those of Cunliffe. The point towards which Cunliffe's troops were to converge was Nachtigall Falls on the Sanaga, thirty miles due north of Jaunde.

The final moves of the campaign were now entered upon. Since the retreat in June, the forces of Dobell had remained on the line of the Kele River. They had again to push forward to Wum Biagas and Eseka. But this time the advance was designed to take place by two parallel columns, one French the other British, and each having its own line of supply. On October 9 Wum Biagas was in a dashing attack retaken by troops from the Gold Coast Colony. The track cut from Edea for fifty miles through the bush was made into a good motor road, and in the last week of November everything was ready for the concluding spring. It began on November 23. The enemy put up a stiff fight, and one of the severest engagements of the campaign took place at Lesogs, but the Northern Nigerian troops, skilfully handled by Lieut.-Colonel Cockburn, crushed the opposition. Though the enemy had contested every yard of the way, the British column on November 30 was at Ngung, with Jaunde only twenty miles distant.

In the meantime, Cunliffe, in the north-west, had uprooted the last important German stronghold. This was at Banyo. From amidst surrounding foothills the Banyo mountain, another of the steep-sided, flat-topped eminences peculiar to the country, rises in majestic isolation. Under its slopes at one side was a native town, the mountain being a natural place of refuge. The isolated mass had been fortified by the Germans with every resource of military art. On the precipitous slopes lay great boulders and masses of fallen cliff. These had been linked up by walls of rough stone, loopholed for rifles and machine-guns. There were nearly three hundred such walls. At every point of approach a fort had been built.

On the summit, as provision against a siege, there were reservoirs made watertight by the free use of cement, byres for cattle, fowl-houses, granaries, stores, and quarters for the garrison. And to ensure the position against being starved out, there were the agricultural and other implements for cultivating the area on the top. The enemy's confidence in the impregnability of the fortress was, in fact, absolute, and here the German contingents driven in from west and north had rallied, for that was one purpose of the fastness.

The British attack was timed to open at daybreak on November 4. The sides of the mountain were then veiled in a dense mist, but if this embarrassed the attack, it to a yet greater extent baffled the defence. When, some hours later, the fog cleared off the attacking troops were seen to be well up. The company of Captain Bowyer-Smijth, a dashing leader, and not less resourceful, climbed to the top. There, however, in striving to make good they were enfiladed from both sides. Captain Bowyer-Smijth unhappily fell. The rest had to beat a retreat. To dislodge the assailants from positions they had gained, the enemy hurled down from the top of the heights bombs filled with dynamite.

But in spite of that the attack turned one *sangar* after another, and at sunset on November 5 were generally one hundred yards only below the summit. That night there was a violent thunderstorm. In the midst of it the last climb was resumed, and at daybreak the assault got home. It was then found that, breaking up into small parties, the garrison, during the night and under cover of the storm, had climbed down remoter parts of the mountain by avenues of escape already selected. The majority were rounded up. Besides ammunition, stores, arms and implements, the takings included 226 head of cattle.

While this siege of Banyo had been going on, a combined move had been carried out by Major Crookenden and Lieut.-Colonel Cotton upon Bagam, followed up by a movement of Cotton and Major Uniake on Fumban. These were the last German posts in the hills. Brisset also had (December 3) pushed south to Yoko on the direct route to Nachtigall Falls.

In advance from the west, General Dobell's force had from Ngung reached and taken Dschang Mangas, and were now out of the forest tract into open country. The column of Mayer, operating through thick bush, and hotly opposed, had got to Mangales. From the south and east also the Allies were closing in, and it was perceived that before the British advance from Ngung the resistance had been visibly weakening. Under these circumstances, the column of Colonel Gorges was ordered to push on. He entered Jaunde on January 1, 1916.

The town had been evacuated. At the head of the remnant of his forces, now reduced to a few thousands, Zimmermann was on the way to Rio Muni, the small Spanish possession which forms an enclave in the south-west corner of the Cameroons territory. Following him up, Lieut.-Colonel Haywood at Kol Maka released the European and other combatants and native carriers whom the enemy had taken prisoners. Zimmermann finally was shepherded over the Spanish border by the French troops, and there with his following interned. The French forces had converged on Jaunde a few days after Gorges.

Save for the German garrison at Mora the campaign was now at an end. Hauptmann von Raben, in command at Mora, held out until

February 18, but, offered honourable terms, he capitulated. His native rank and file was released and given safe passages to their homes, the officers, sent to England as prisoners of war, retained their swords.

CHAPTER 10

The War in the Pacific and the Siege of Kiao-Chau

In the schemes of the Government at Berlin the possession of Kiao-Chau and the colonies of the Pacific Ocean fell into one category; for, in fact, German imperial policy had two co-related aspects. The first and older of the two was concerned with the establishment of the German Empire as the leading military Power on the Continent of Europe. Towards that end the initial step had been the welding of the Germanic Confederation into a military unity under the headship of Prussia, and the purpose was achieved by the victory over Austria in the war of 1866. The next step was by utilising and developing these unified resources to raise the new Hohenzollern Empire to the place of the leading military State, and in turn that aim was accomplished by the successes in the war of 1870-71 against France.

But between leadership and dominance there is a distinction, and after 1870-71 dominance, not leadership, became the ambition. The struggle for dominance, for which after the war of 1870-71 the rulers of the remodelled German Empire set themselves without delay to prepare, must, as they foresaw, arouse a wider and more formidable opposition. In the contest for leadership, and while their aims were not yet clearly perceived abroad, they had been able to deal with obstacles one by one. But in the contest for dominance it was not less certain that they would have to meet a combined resistance. One feature of their preparations was the steady improvement and enlargement of their military machine. That, in order to allay suspicions and misgivings, had to be carried out gradually, and covered meanwhile by reiterated and emphatic professions of pacificism.

Since, however, though improved and enlarged, their military machine and their own resources would not, unaided, suffice for a conflict against a combination, they set about creating a counter-combination; its core the offensive and defensive alliance with Austria-Hungary. As distinct from leadership—the position of *primus inter pares*—dominance involved, even on its lowest footing, the diplomatic and commercial dependence of other States on the continent of Europe. On its highest footing, and the lowest would assuredly and in time shade into the highest, it meant the conversion of Europe into a German possession.

But precisely because in the ambition of dominance all that was implied, there comes into view the second aspect of German policy— the dispersal or division of probable resistance. In the possible combination against this vast scheme, the most formidable antagonist to be reckoned with was Britain and to divide the potential combination, the active hostility of Britain had if possible to be fended off. With the Continental antagonists alone—France and Russia—the rulers of the German Empire believed confidently they could deal. They were the more confident since, by the alliance of 1883 the neutrality of Italy had apparently been assured. The feasible procedure was clearly to crush the continental opposition in the first place; to fight with Great Britain in the second; and finally to overthrow the resistance of the United States which the break-up of the British federation would undoubtedly arouse.

If, then, German diplomacy is to be understood and followed through its mazes, this purpose of realising ambitions by successive steps has always to be kept in mind as the inspiration at the back of it, and its guiding thread. And to begin with, we may say up to the year 1900, and during the whole of the thirty years which elapsed between 1870 and that date, German diplomacy, so far as Britain was concerned, seemed to be in every respect successful. German diplomacy—it was an obvious precaution—had not neglected to establish in high places in Great Britain an influence which on the surface worked towards a good understanding.

Though the old British suspicion against France had died away, it had not then yet given place to cordiality. During the transition the tendency of British opinion was to look upon affairs on the continent of Europe as of no more than indirect interest. This attitude of "splendid isolation," congenial to the British public as to that of the United States, fitted in with German aims. No means were neglected to foster it. Hence, in Great Britain, the beginnings of the German navy were regarded with indifference. It was not understood that command of the inland seas of Europe—the Baltic and the Black Sea—was essential to the first part of the German programme. It was not seen that, apart from secure German command of the Baltic, a formidable attack upon France could hardly be risked. It was not perceived that German command of the Baltic and of the Black Sea meant, while safeguarding a great German attack upon France, the isolation of Russia. Had these things been apprehended, it is at least highly doubtful if British opinion would during the thirty years between 1870 and 1900 have remained quiescent.

British indifference, however, to the earlier upgrowth of a German navy was not, in the judgment of the wire-pullers at Berlin, assurance enough. British indifference might suddenly change to mistrust. The assurance had to be increased by creating in various parts of the world German interests and footholds which, in the event of war, would have the effect of dispersing British naval resources. On the one hand, Great Britain was to be confronted in the North Sea by a naval concentration strong enough to impose circumspection; on the other, she was to be manoeuvred into a position which would make that concentration difficult to be dealt with. In these circumstances, her neutrality might be counted upon until France and Russia had been struck down. After that her attitude would not signify.

Probably the most remarkable of all the events of the period from 1870 to 1900 was the British-German Agreement, which not only enabled Germany in 1890 to annex great territories in Africa, and to round off her until then petty possessions in the Pacific, but gave her Heligoland as a place deemed of no value. The assumed equivalent, for what it was worth, was German goodwill. For German diplomacy, its aims and programme being what they were, the compact was a signal triumph, and on the face of matters the success may well have seemed at Berlin to be as dazzling as it was facile. British statesmanship appeared to have been hoodwinked.

Before the agreement the professions from Berlin were as smooth as oil. The words were fair. Germany's only motive was to guarantee the settled peace of the world, and the world was large enough for everybody. The value of German goodwill, however, was disclosed by the outbreak of the Boer War. It was then assumed that the mask might in part at any rate be dropped. The role of hypocrisy had been played so long that to the restive temperament of William II. it was becoming monotonous. He sent off his famous Kruger telegram, he gave the word for the long projected strategical railways to the frontiers of Holland and Belgium to go ahead, and he openly advertised that the future of Germany was upon the sea.

British statesmanship, waking up to the fact that it had been misled, set about repairing mistakes. The change led to friction. Once, when the Entente with France was on the eve of being concluded in 1904, affairs came within an ace of war. The rulers of Germany threatened and protested. Great Britain's reply was to mobilise her Fleet, and on reflection William II. and his advisers backed down. They were not yet sufficiently ready. The Anglo-French Entente, disagreeable bolus though it was, had to be swallowed. But they remained in an evil temper and the race of armaments was speeded up. The hope of British neutrality was not relinquished, though William II. had queered it.

German ambitions in Africa have already been touched upon. If a map of the world be consulted, and German possessions in the western Pacific—nearly all comprised in a great ring fence—be looked at, it will be seen that with a German Africa on one side, these Pacific possessions—enlarged—on the other; and a German dominance in Europe, Asia Minor, Persia, and Arabia, the British position in India, the route through the Mediterranean being held at best on sufferance, would become extremely difficult. And if the British position in India resolved itself eventually into a German position, then the exploitation of the Far East should be the sequel. Hence the steps towards "exercising a decisive influence" in the Far East—the feigned support of Russia as against Japan; the war with China; and the acquisition of Kiao-Chau.

The move countering these Far Eastern projects was the British alliance with Japan. It was for the rulers of Germany a disagreeable move, and it was the more disagreeable because Australian opposition to Mongolian immigration had been counted upon to keep Great Britain and Japan apart. So far as in that quarter of the world it carried weight, German influence, working by the usual methods of suggestion, and repeated *innuendo*, was employed to fan the belief in a white and yellow—that is to say a British and Japanese—contest for the Pacific. But by 1914 the trend of German activity had grown so plain that only the grossest deceit acting upon the grossest ignorance could disguise it.

Actually there was in the pigeon-holes of the Foreign Office at Berlin a plan, cut and dried, for the German government of Australia. When war broke out German activities and encroachments had assured not merely the prompt participation of Japan, but action not less prompt on the part of Australia and New Zealand. The three were equally determined to eliminate the Germans from the Pacific once for all.

Very briefly, for it has a bearing upon later events, the course of German associations with the Pacific may here be traced. Previously to 1870 German trade with this part of the world was mainly represented to the transactions of a mercantile house in Hamburg, the firm of Godeffroy and Co., its founder a French Huguenot. This house had opened a trade with the natives of Samoa, exporting cotton goods and arms, which were bartered for copra and cocoanut oil. By degrees this business was extended from the Samoan Islands to other archipelagos.

In the meantime more German firms had entered into the trade, and about the year 1875, to resist further competition, Godeffroy and Co. and two other German houses pooled their Pacific business into a company with a capital of some £60,000. The trade was now carried on on a larger footing. At this point the German Government came into the matter. In 1877, following the familiar practice, the German Government negotiated with the native chiefs of Samoa, a "most-favoured-nation" agreement. Under the terms of that concession the Germans occupied the ports, while to protect their interests a German Consul-General was appointed. Two years later the Native Council of Samoa was induced to enter into a treaty of mutual friendship with the German Empire. It was, in fact, a protection agreement of the type already noted in German dealings in Africa.

How far all this was useful may be inferred from the fact that by now the Germans had acquired in the Samoan Islands very extensive plantations, and in Upolu owned all the best lands. The privately floated one-horse company was wound up, but was succeeded by a concern having a capital of £500,000, and the interest of the German Government in the scheme was evidenced by its guarantee of a 3 per cent, dividend for twenty years. It happened, owing to opposition from rivals—the Cartel or Trust system being of German origin—that the Government guarantee was negatived in the Reichstag.

The project, however, was put through in a slightly modified form, and was associated with a Pacific bank having branches in various islands. There now, however, arose complications of an international character. Both the British and Americans had a footing in Samoa, and were not disposed to be ousted. Under the protection agreement when differences broke out between King Malietoa and Mataafa, a leading chief and rival, the Germans deposed the king, and evicted him to the Marshall Islands. He was, however, re-proclaimed through the action and protests of the American and British consuls. Finally in 1899 affairs were settled by a division of the Samoan Islands between the three Powers. Germany obtained Upolu and Savaii; the United States Tutuila; Great Britain the Tonga Archipelago.

Previously, however, to this, in 1885, Germany had in Oceania systematically annexed everything which any other European Power did not definitely claim. In New Guinea she picked up 70,000 square miles of territory, thereupon named Kaiser Wilhelm Land, and she annexed New Britain and New Ireland, and the Admiralty Islands, the whole group being renamed the Bismarck Archipelago. New Britain became New Pomerania, and New Ireland New Mecklenburg. She took possession also of the Marshall Islands, a profitable acquisition, since, besides defraying the costs of the administration, the German Chartered Company, to which they were farmed out, was able to pay its shareholders 12 *per cent.*

The rounding off of these Pacific possessions occurred in 1899. For £1,000,000 sterling, the German Government in that year bought from Spain the Pelew Islands, the Ladrone Islands, and the Carolines. The latter comprise 670 islands extending across the Pacific, from west to east for 1,500 miles and disposed into forty-seven groups. Germany's Pacific sphere of influence, nearly 3,000 miles from west to east and nearly 2,000 from south to north, was thus constituted, and the only speck upon it was the island of Guam, a possession of the United States.

Two developments which went to discount and disconcert these projects, so far as they in turn might not be offset by a possible German military success in Europe, were the rapid growth of the Japanese navy and the formation of an Australian naval squadron. In 1895 the Japanese navy was not strong enough to risk a conflict single-handed with the fleets of the three Powers who presented the ultimatum of that year which had obliged Japan to evacuate Port Arthur. But in 1904 the Japanese navy was sufficiently strong to fight and win the battle of Tschushima, and then disclosed itself as marvellously efficient.

The Australian squadron, too, was a sensible counter-poise. In view of these developments, Germany maintained at Kiao-Chau a powerful squadron, and the Austrian navy was represented by one of its battleships. But the squadron was not so powerful as to resist being blockaded by the Japanese Navy. Consequently on the outbreak of war in Europe, and, doubtless instructed that hostilities with Japan were impending, Admiral von Spee took out the five fastest ships, leaving the others to assist in the defence of the port. The three routes of communication from Europe with the Pacific, apart from that opened through the Panama canal are round Cape Horn, round the Cape of Good Hope, and through the Red Sea.

Possibly in other circumstances the Germans might have made an effort to cut those communications. But with Japan in the rear and the Australian squadron in the south the attempt could not in the Pacific seriously be made, and it is enough to say, though his proceedings do not enter into the scope of this narrative, that von Spee, recognising the situation, made for Port Stanley, the coaling station and base at the Falkland Islands, a position which, could he have seized it, might for a time have enabled him, while sufficiently distant from the Japanese, to have operated against both the Cape route and that round the Horn. Off the Falkland Islands, however, he met his doom.

Save for the depredations of *Emden*[1] the Pacific was then clear of naval opposition, and that was the state of affairs in the Western Pacific from the outset. It was this circumstance which rendered the seizure of Germany's island possessions one of the most rapid of the allied operations.

The plan was that the German Islands of the Samoan group were to be attacked from New Zealand; Kaiser Wilhelm Land, the Bismarck Archipelago, and the German possessions of the Solomon group from Australia. Both projects being "amphibious," Rear-Admiral Sir George Patey, with the battle-cruiser *Australia*, and the cruiser *Melbourne*, was to see them through.

The New Zealand Expedition left Wellington on August 15, 1914. Pending the arrival of the two Australian warships, the escort were the British light cruisers *Psyche*, *Pyramus* and *Philomel*. Though it was known that the German Pacific squadron had left Kiao-Chau, it was not known what course had been taken, and since the German squadron included the swift and powerful battle-cruisers *Gneisenau* and *Scharnhörst*, for precaution a course was shaped for New Caledonia. There the Australian ships were to pick the Expedition up. New Caledonia was reached on August 19.

---

1. *The Kaiser's Raider!* by Hellmuth von Mücke, *Two Accounts of the S. M. S. Emden During the First World War by One of its Officers: The "Emden" & The "Ayesha" Being the Adventures of the Landing Squad of the "Emden,"* also published by Leonaur.

On the station there was the French cruiser *Montcalm*, and she joined the convoy. In due course *Australia* and *Melbourne* appeared, and on August 23 the united force set out on the 1,000 miles voyage to Samoa. Though a brief call was made at Fiji, the trip was completed in six days. On August 30 they were off Apia, the port of Upolu. To the demand for surrender there was no resistance. After mine-sweeping operations the war-ships entered the harbour, landing parties of blue jackets took possession of the government buildings, the custom house, and the quays and bridges, the German flag was hauled down, the New Zealand ensign run up, the expeditionary force put ashore, and disposed in quarters, and all was over. Savaii was occupied in the same way.

Returning to Sydney, *Australia* and *Melbourne* convoyed the Commonwealth Expedition. This, of course, in view of the territory to be occupied, and the opposition looked for, was on larger lines, and comprised a total force of 4,000 men. The seat of the German administration was at Rabaul in New Pomerania, and near that place was one of the two powerful German wireless stations in the Pacific, the other being at Yap in the Carolines. For Simpsonshafen, the Expedition first made, and the port was occupied without resistance, and the other port of the island, Herbertshohe, captured also without a shot fired. All the same, the invasion was not a walk-over. One purpose of the attack was to take possession of the wireless station, and with as little delay as possible. This business was entrusted to Commander J. A. H. Beresford.

Immediately the flotilla had arrived off Simpsonshafen Beresford at daybreak was put ashore with a mobile column to push inland towards Rabaul, and seize the wireless installation before it could be wrecked. He found himself opposed by all the force the Germans had at their disposal. Part of the way it was a bush fight, but despite bush, snipers in the tree tops, land mines, and machine-guns, for every obstructive device had been resorted to, Beresford fought his way through. The fight lasted from daybreak until past midnight. It was the first flush of Australian fury, and bush-ranging resourcefulness. Both left the opposition staggered. Hot, tired, thirsty, but triumphant, Beresford and his men arrived at and in the early hours of November 12 mastered the wireless station, before the surprised and routed enemy could recover. And this was the only battle. All the Bismarck archipelago was occupied and the Germans on it rounded up. Even Kaiser Wilhelm Land was surrendered without a defence.

Coincidently, the Japanese Expedition had been going round the Pelew, Ladrone, Caroline and Marshall Islands collecting the Germans upon them. Commanding points were afterwards occupied by Australian posts.

We now pass to a different scene; from the gorgeous colouring and enchanted islands of the tropical ocean at the fairest season of the year, to the far north during the days of the Autumn rains. Not merely had the Government of Japan not forgiven the *démarche* of 1895, seeing that its inspiration from Berlin was well known, but to that insult, and the terms of the ultimatum to Japan had been studiously sarcastic and wounding to Japanese national self-respect, had been added the injury of the occupation of Kiao-Chau. This position, on the south-eastern coast of the Shantung peninsula, commanded the Yellow Sea, and such an occupation by Germany could only have one meaning—the exclusion of Japanese influence from the Asiatic mainland.

That it would have the effect of leading Japan to seek an alliance with Great Britain was not perhaps at Berlin foreseen, much less that the alliance *would* be concluded. But such an outcome, for Japan an obvious reply, had the effect of placing the Germans at Kiao-Chau in an awkward situation. They had stepped on to what had seemed a safe place and found that it had become a trap. Pride, however, forbade withdrawal, and at Kiao-Chau, pending development of their world-empire, the Germans meant to remain, trusting to the sequel proving fortunate. They had very largely rebuilt and transformed the town and port of Tsing-Tau to their own liking, for this in the Far East was to be the nucleus of great things, and the Eastern mind had to be impressed with the superiority and value of German *kultur*.

New docks were constructed; shipyards fitted up, and broad new streets driven across the town. Expensive and resplendent public buildings rose on these frontages. Gardens were laid out on the model of those in Berlin, and German officialdom took its leisure along an imitation *Unter den Linden*, or displayed itself in the novel tea-grounds. The natives, too, were given the benefit of schools, where the German language was taught. The possession was only a leasehold for a mere term of years, but the lessee evidently treated it as a perpetuity.

Comparatively, however, the civilian changes were a detail. Nor did they represent more than a fraction of Germany's outlay. Four-fifths of that outlay, and it ran into a good many millions sterling, was upon fortification. The bay of Kiao-Chau is a large, and almost land-locked inlet, one of the best natural harbours on the Chinese coast. On the east side of the bay there is a peninsula, the features of which lent themselves very peculiarly to military works. Across the peninsula extend two ranges of hills, an outer range and an inner, and between them lies a valley rather more than half-a- mile in breadth. Up the valley from the sea on one side and from the bay on the other run inlets, not easy to cross. The space between is narrow, a quarter of a mile wide at most. It was evident that the outer range of hills afforded a strong advanced position; that the valley, scientifically obstructed, could be made a very bad obstacle to negotiate, and that the inner range of hills could be turned into a powerful line of support. The town and port of Tsing-Tau lies behind the inner range of hills. To guard against attack from the sea the port was converted into a naval base and arsenal of the first class. To guard against attack from landward, not merely was the outer range of hills elaborately fortified, but on each of the three inner hills there were placed forts armed with long-range heavy pieces. The lighter armament was disposed in a line of redoubts laid out along the outer footing of the three hills, and designed to sweep with a cross-fire the gradual upward slope from the valley. This slope was left bare, denuded of every vestige of cover, and beyond it along and extending over the whole bottom of the valley, flat and swampy, were placed the entanglements, carried also up the opposite and farther slope. It may well have appeared that in the face of modern ordnance such a place was impregnable, and when for its defence there was maintained a garrison of more than 5,000 men, picked and specially trained, the Germans seemed not unjustified in believing they could defy every assault. What with their concentrated heavy, medium, and lighter guns, and machine-guns, the valley should be impassable. This was the other side of German *kultur*.

That Kiao-Chau had been selected because it could readily be converted into a first class fortress, as well as a naval base capable of almost unlimited extension— the bay of Kiao-Chau is large enough and deep enough to shelter and refit a great fleet—does not admit of doubt. Nor can it be doubted that the features of the place had beforehand been carefully studied. The quarrel picked with the Chinese while the German-Russian agreement yet held—that is to say, so long as the agreement suited the purposes of Germany—was deliberate, and had this acquisition in view. Japan, meanwhile, had no choice but to look on and see the Chinese bullied. But it is sometimes forgotten by Europeans that the Empires of the Far East are immensely old, and that there exists a sense of time and of its revenges little understood by those whose history and traditions date relatively from yesterday. At the beginning of the eighteenth century Prussia was a petty state. Hurry had always been the characteristic of its rulers, and a mark of the Prussian temperament. The temperament of the Far East, however, is before everything patience. The Entente concluded between Great Britain and France detached Russia from this co-operation with Germany against China and Japan. Having taken the profit of it, Germany viewed the defeat of Russia in the Manchurian War with complacency, if not with satisfaction. The British-Japanese alliance was the finishing touch. From that time Germany in the Far East played a lone hand.

Time certainly brought its revenges, and rarely more conspicuously than in 1914. The ultimatum which in the August of that year the government at Berlin received from Tokyo was word for word the mandate which in 1895 the German Government had presented to Japan. The only changes were the necessary alterations in names. The pompous and sarcastically polite phraseology in which Japan had been advised to evacuate Port Arthur now became the terms in which the German Government were advised to remove from Kiao-Chau. It was a touch of comedy rounded off by the solemn affability with which the Japanese Ambassador at Berlin carried the document over to the German Foreign Office, and there delivered it into the hands of von Bülow. Seven days were given for a reply. The answer of the German Government to this clean cut was that there was no reply. On August 23, the seven days' interval expired. On the same date, Japan declared war.

In the meantime, Admiral Meyer-Waldeck, the German Governor of Kiao-Chau, had received orders to hold out as long as possible. He had not only ample stocks of munitions and stores, but he had been liberally provided with land mines, and besides a tuning up of the forts, a stiffening of the redoubts, and a thickening of the entanglements, the valley beyond Tsing-Tau was sown with mines so contrived that they could in part be exploded by attempts to interfere with the obstacles, and in part by observation from the defence works. The equipment included also squadrons of aeroplanes, both bombers and scouts. Nothing apparently had been overlooked, and almost certainly there was at Berlin every confidence that the siege of Kiao-Chau, even should it succeed, would last during many months, and involve the Japanese in huge casualties. This was the contemplated revenge.

Nothing, apparently, had been overlooked, and yet sight had been lost of the one element in the business which mattered most—the skill, subtlety and resource of the attack. If German study of the defence had been thorough, Japanese study of the assault had been, if anything, more searching. There was not a detail of the defences that was not known; not a store of any kind that had not been sited; not a dump of munitions which was not marked down; not a trace along the works which had been left uncertain; not a line of barbed wire that had not been mapped; not a landmine unlocated.

For this very operation Japan had trained a special Expeditionary Corps of 23,000 men. From General Kamio in command down to the junior officers, every man knew his work. It was no intention of the Japanese to waste men in massed assaults on these fortifications. That was not science. The science lay in reducing the works to rubbish heaps, in firing the stores and oil tanks, in touching off the dumps, in causing the land-mines to explode themselves. The artillery for this purpose was part of the outfit, and it was not stinted. The pieces ranged up to naval guns of a calibre of 11 inches. For anything heavier reliance was placed on the warships, Japanese and British, which were to attack in enfilade from seaward. But more important even than the guns were the gunners. They knew what to hit. and they could be depended upon to hit it.

The remaining German ships being bottled up by the Allied fleet in the bay, the Expedition landed without opposition. The German land forces kept within their advanced lines. Activities began three days after the declaration of war.

The advanced forces of the expedition were landed at Lung-Kow on the north-western shore of the Shantung peninsula, and were to march across country south in order to reach Kiao-Chau from the inland, and seize the railway from that place. Formally this landing was a violation of Chinese neutrality, and formally the Chinese protested, but face having been saved there it ended. The main body of the expedition was put ashore at Laoshan bay, some thirty miles to the north-east of Tsing-Tau. This part of the force included a British contingent, the 2nd South Wales Borderers and the 36th Sikhs under the command of Brigadier-General N. W. Barnardiston. They had been embarked in three transports at Tientsin, and escorted by H.M.S. *Triumph* and destroyer *Usk*.

Over the preliminaries the Japanese displayed no haste. The laying out of a base, the making of roads, the movement and disposition of guns and supplies is work that usually receives but scant record. It is the tedium of war, not its glory; but it is the foundation of everything,

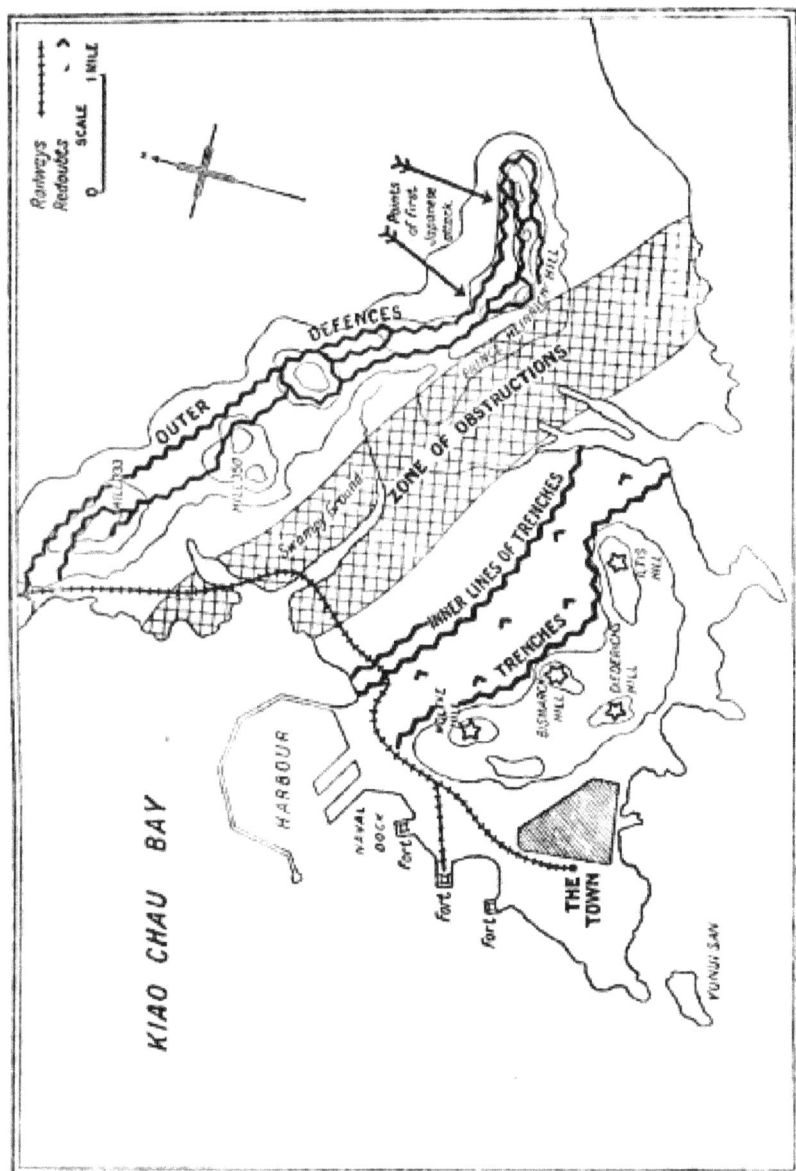

KIAO CHAU BAY

Railways
Redoubts

SCALE 1 MILE

0 1 MILE

OUTER DEFENCES

Points of first Japanese attack

PRINCE HEINRICH HILL

ZONE OF OBSTRUCTIONS

Swampy Ground

HILL 173

HILL 150

INNER LINES OF TRENCHES

TRENCHES

MOLTKE HILL

ILTIS HILL

BISMARCK HILL

DIEDERICHS HILL

HARBOUR

NAVAL DOCK

Fort B

Fort C

Fort D

Fort E

THE TOWN

FUNG SAN

and success or failure depends upon whether it be well or ill done. In this instance, it was well done. The conditions were adverse and might well have appeared disheartening. The autumn rains had set in, and day after day there was a torrential downpour, soaking everybody, and every object. Hereabouts the country is hilly, its surface a clay cut up by deep ravines.

Amid the rains there could hardly be worse ground, and the state of it churned by a multitude of men, guns, wagons, and thousands of horses and mules, can readily be imagined. But the Japanese took the conditions with philosophical stoicism. And the conditions, after all, had one advantage. At this stage the Germans had relied upon aeroplane attack, and bombing activity. The rains kept them off. Severed as their communications with the country outside now were—for the mobile force from Lung-Kow had seized the Kiao-Chau railway station, and Japanese posts had been drawn all round the beleaguered position to the north—the Germans must have wondered what was really going on behind the curtain of mist.

Three weeks thus went by. On the side of General Kamio, however, they had not been time lost, for when the weather began to clear towards the end of September he was ready for a move. He pushed inland and westward to Chimo, and disposed his forces for attack upon the German outer line. The enemy attempted to impede this move by bombarding the Japanese right from the remaining warships in Kiao-Chau bay, but the enterprise and daring of the Japanese airmen in bombing the squadron forced it to retire. Chimo was occupied on September 26. On September 29, the German advanced positions, extending across the Tsing-Tau tongue of land from Kiao-Chau bay to the sea were to have been assaulted.

After the Japanese artillery preparation they were found evacuated. The line of investment was now moved forward towards the main defences on Prince Heinrich Hill, and others of the outer elevations. A stiff resistance was looked for here. Prince Heinrich Hill, a crescent-shaped formation, is nearly 1,200 feet high, and the most elevated point of the region, and as an observation post it commanded not only the valley, but the inner hills and in part the town and bay. It hardly seemed probable that the enemy would let this work go without a severe struggle.

For three days the defences were hammered, and the shelling found the weak links. The works and obstructions were shot to rags, and it was more than the defence could stand. When on October 8 the

Japanese storming parties, fierce and agile, were thrown forward, they got home at the first try. The siege was proceeding with mathematical precision. In twelve days the besiegers had, move by move, pushed their lines forward four miles. Now having Prince Heinrich Hill in their possession they were in a situation to attack the inner defences with advantage.

This attack was to form the climax of the bombardment, and there was a pause in preparation for it. The necessary head of shell accumulated, the guns opened on the last day of October. Whether as an effect or as a spectacle it may be doubted if this sustained storm of fire has ever been surpassed. The three humps covering Tsing-Tau are: right Moltke Hill; centre Bismarck Hill; left Iltis Hill, and they range in height from approximately 270 to 500 feet. Each appeared a mass of powerful works. Under the cannonade, supported by the fire of the ships, the forts crumbled to ruins. The forts on Bismarck Hill were first silenced, and though the others yet held out, their reply was visibly enfeebled. At the same time, the bombardment, with a fatal accuracy, searched the port and storehouses, and the glare of fire rose over the town. Late in the day the oil-tanks caught, and enormous volumes of smoke floated skyward, like an eruption of a volcano.

When darkness fell a red glow shot through the base of the black fumes; the inner hills were outlined against the leaping flames beyond; the forts were burning. Now and then a dump went up. At rapid intervals the defences and the interlying valley were illuminated by nights of star shells. Amid this the roar of the bombardment went ceaselessly on, pounding the forts, crushing the redoubts, ploughing wide gaps in the entanglements. At the same time, the assaulting columns were moving forward to their allotted positions. They were in four sections, the British contingent the right centre. Under the cover of the guns three successive lines were to be taken up. The first was occupied on November 1; the second, a jumping off position for attack upon the redoubts, on November 3; the third, the line of the redoubts, on November 6. Five of these works were carried almost coincidently. The British troops assisted in the attack on the right.

The last stage, the assault on the hills, was reserved for the morrow. In the night Japanese skirmishers had gone forward and dealt with the obstacles and impediments. The main body of the troops were at dawn waiting in the ruins and trenches for the last rush, and with the first light the garrison began a cannonade with light guns, varied by an occasional shot from a heavy piece. The besieging batteries broke out in reply, a furious intense and destructive chorus. Then suddenly the white flag went up, and an enemy deputation came forward with a flag of truce.

Meyer-Waldeck had surrendered. A fortress which had been expected to withstand a siege of at least six months had fallen within six weeks. It had been, however, one of the most scientific sieges in history.

The Fall of Tsingtau

(extract)

GENERAL KAMIO
Commander-in-chief of the allied forces in the Kiaochow
campaign. The first representative of the yellow race to hold
command over a white force in battle

Contents

Preface   187

Japan's Dream of Domination   191

Preliminaries to the Declaration of War   196

The Violation of Neutrality   210

The Advance of the Japanese Army   215

Closing in the Offensive   219

The Germans Withdraw to Tsingtau   223

The Beginning of the Siege   227

The Fleet Bombards the City   233

The Surrender   239

After the City's Fall   243

Taking Possession   250

Sanitation and Discipline   254

To
My
Father

Preface

One of the most remarkable changes to be wrought in Christendom by the greatest of wars will be found, not in Europe or in Europe's dependencies, but in the Far East. The destiny of as many Chinese as there are white human beings in all Europe may be determined by the event of August, 1914.

In the following pages I have attempted to record, as a disinterested observer, just what happened in the Orient from the time Europe took up arms and Japan, as to the policy she was to play, was left alone in Asia. That Japan's part in the seizure of the German protectorate of Kiaochow was essentially a blind move in the making over of the Celestial Kingdom into a dependency of Japan, cannot be doubted by anyone who follows closely the moves of the Tokyo Government from the opening of the European war until China, after much harassing, acceded to the demands of Japan in May.

While China may nominally be in possession of many of its sovereign rights, the fact is, the power which controls Tokyo, for all intents and purposes, now controls the Government at Peking. Events yet to take place in the Far East may be depended on to prove this assertion.

Be that as it may, China, we believe, will yet be a nation—independent, possessing sovereign rights, and governed by its own people. For the Chinaman remains a Chinaman. Deprive him of his country, isolate him from his people, and whether you find him in Caracas, Cape Town, or Halifax, he, and his generations that follow, will cling to the customs of his former country. The Chinese have not learned what patriotism is. They will in time. Then let a leader arise to join in one cause the four hundred and fifty millions of people of China; let patriotism once be grasped by them after repeated humiliations, such as have already been their lot in the last thirty years, and then one will recall the words of Napoleon, who said of China, *"There lies a sleeping giant. Let him sleep; for when he moves he will move the world."*

Under the Tokyo domination, China is bound to learn by experience what it is to possess independent and sovereign rights; self-interest and the "squeeze" will become obsolescent words in the Chinese vocabulary, and gradually the nation that produced the philosopher Confucius will take on a national consciousness from which a truly awakened China will spring, and above all a China which will command from the world, not humiliating and jealous designs, but thorough-going respect.

From my experience as a resident in Tokyo, I feel there is much in the following pages that will strike the supersensitive hearts of the Japanese as an indication of my unfriendliness to the Nippon Kingdom. This is an impression which I do not wish for, as I think the Japanese a people of great ability and a nation the most patriotic and one of the most efficient in the world. My objection lies only against the diplomacy practiced by Japan during and since the siege of Tsing-tau, believing that it in no degree reflects credit on the glory of the Rising Sun. I base this statement upon the very words and actions of Japan herself; inconsistent words and actions which require no special emphasis from an observer in the Far East.

As I write this there has arisen opposition in the Diet of Japan, which, like all oppositions where bureaucracy controls, does not carry much weight. It has denounced the government's Chinese policy as one which has thrown a blight on the prestige of the nation. One of its radicals has publicly denounced Baron Kato, Foreign Minister, as a "traitor" to his government. Cabinet ministers have been called upon to explain certain actions of the Government in Japan, all of which has further brought out the inconsistency of Japan's diplomacy.

For example, in the opposition's denunciation of Japan's foreign policy, Mr. Motoda, ex-Minister of State, referred to the government's rushing troops and a battleship to China during the May breach in the negotiations on the twenty-one demands, as a forceful "threat" upon China. In reply to this. Baron Kato said that Japan was not increasing her troops in China as a threat, but the transaction was merely an exchange of guards. But as there was no exchange in troops,—that is, the troops in China did not return to Japan after the new troops arrived,—Mr. Tokohami, ex-president of the Imperial Railroad Board, became more inquisitive and called upon Lieutenant-General Oka, the Minister of War, to explain before the Diet just why the Government had sent fresh troops into China. To this the Japanese Minister of War replied that it was because of disturbances, an answer wholly aside from Baron Kato's statement.

But the opposition in the *diet* pressed for the answer and questioned Minister Oka as to what disturbances in China the troops had been rushed to put down. At length Oka replied there had been no disturbances in China warranting the dispatch of fresh troops, but there had been a likelihood of friction. To every foreigner in Japan who knows that the Japanese exchange of guards takes place annually in December, this measure taken by Tokyo during the days in May, when Japan had warned China that "harsh" steps would be taken unless the latter acceded to the demands then under negotiation in Peking, there is but one answer, one reason, as to the wherefore of the hasty dispatch of troops into Asia by Japan.

Since that date Premier Okuma's Cabinet has resigned and Japan is torn internally with political strife. The Britisher in Shanghai, Peking, Manchester, and the other industrial centres of Great Britain, is disturbed at the actions of her ally in the Far East, and presses his Government in London for an understanding. The utmost calmness over the recent turn of events in the Far East is the only answer that is allowed to escape the House of Parliament in London. Meanwhile those far-sighted rulers of Japan—the Elder Statesmen—seem to catch the future trend of events, for in July they were called together and considered the formation of an alliance with Russia, similar to the Anglo-Japanese alliance. In all probability definite action will be postponed until the treaty of peace in Europe or until the expiration of the British alliance.

With Russia, long a seeker for the partition of China, allied with Japan, events of international importance seem destined to follow. Will Russia's long-sought-after open-the-year-round Pacific port be a factor in the alliance? Will Taku, the port of Tientsin in northern China, come under Russian control with the consent of Tokyo, as rumour has it? In the mean time Japan's domination of China; the reconsideration of the demands at Peking which Japan explicitly labelled in May as only "postponed;" the "open door" in China and its latch; the treaty of peace in Europe, which will also terminate the Kiaochow affair, and the proposed Russian alliance—upon the outcome of these questions does the follower of events in the Far East look with eagerness.

As peace day by day nears its realisation in Europe, the clouds gather toward Asia, and with them a silence suggestive of the lull before the storm.

In closing, I wish to express my thanks and appreciation to General Kamio, commander of the Allied forces at Tsingtau, to Lieutenant Colonel Haraguchi, and to Mr. Zumota, civil *attaché* of the Japanese Army, for their many courtesies extended to me while within the lines of their army; also to Mr. Post Wheeler, Mr. B. W. Fleisher, and Mr. Carl Crow, my grateful acknowledgment for their assistance in getting me to the war front at Kiaochow.

J. J.

Minneapolis, August, 1916.

Chapter 1

Japan's Dream of Domination

The fall of Tsingtau and the wiping-out of the German colonies in Asia and in the Pacific, at any other time than as a side happening in the greatest of wars, would have attracted the attention of the whole world. With the rapid unfolding of events in Europe during early August, 1914, the nations focused attention on the continent, where the largeness of events had the effect of making minor the developments in the Far East. The passing of Germany from Asia, however, is of great international importance, for from it there may be traced the future remapping of Asia and even the dissolution of China as a nation.

Japan's participation in the European war and the events that followed may be divided into two parts; first, the "game" she played in going to war; second, the actions of her army in the overthrow of Germany in Asia.

In discussing the first of these divisions, it is necessary to note the "sayings" of the Japanese statesmen in conjunction with the actions that followed. In this way only will it be possible to reach an intelligent conclusion. It is not what we say we will do, but what we do, that really counts, and in no relation does this rule apply more positively than in diplomatic dealings. It will not be difficult to discover that Japan's part in the European war was not for the "peace of the Far East," as declared by her diplomats at the outset, but a move in her ambition to dominate China.

The opening of hostilities between Japan and Germany in August, 1914, gave to Japan another opportunity to express in words just what were her motives in going to war, and it afforded opportunity also for the distribution in publications in America and Great Britain of frequent references to Japan's "love" for China.

"We have always stood and will continue to stand for the territorial integrity" and "neutrality" of China, writes Count Okuma, Premier of Japan, at the opening of the war. By those unaquainted with Far Eastern politics, and especially those of Japan, this statement by a Japanese statesman may have been read with confidence. However, those familiar with Japanese affairs do not accept such statements as conclusive.

Many times before has Japan vouched for the territorial integrity and neutrality of China. We have followed her actions only to find that the declarations of her statesmen were mere diplomatic nothings, their actions the exact opposite of their printed resolutions. For these reasons the official utterances of the Tokyo Government, on the opening of hostilities against Kiaochow, came and went without leaving sincere impression.

"What is Japan's game?" was the question passed among foreigners in the Japanese capital late in August, 1914. A step in the acquisition of China, was of course the answer, but many accepted Japan's statements, this time with more faith. With Great Britain as her ally, they said Japan would play with her cards on the table. Later events proved that Japan was playing her usual concealed game.

In all diplomatic tangles in the Far East for the last twenty years, China has paid the bill, whether she has been involved in the transaction or not. All the Powers have gone on record as standing for the territorial integrity of China, and the preservation of China's neutrality, but there has been but one Power, in its dealings with China, that has always backed guaranties by actions, not words—the United States.

During the above period, while Japanese statesmen were addressing the world to the effect, as Baron Kato recently put it, that "Japan maintains to protect the peace of the Far East" and to "guard China from foreign encroachments," her government has taken from China, first, Formosa; then the Liaotung Peninsula; next, Korea; and now—shall we say Shantung?

While Japan's statesmen have been proclaiming that Japan is a friend to China, that she bears no ill-will against her, their hands have been slyly going into the pocket of China, and bit by bit has Celestial territory been taken. Is it to be wondered that during the recent war in the Far East the foreigner should look with distrust upon the actions of Japan?

Sunday, August 23, the day of Japan's declaration of war upon Germany, found the Japanese fleets in a semicircle in the Yellow Sea, making preparations for running the blockade to the Bay of Kiaochow.

Still farther north, off the Korean archipelago, Japanese transports had already sailed bearing three divisions of the Imperial regiments. The Japanese Minister at Peking at once started negotiations for fixing the war zone about Kiaochow, Germany's protectorate in Shantung, Tsingtau being the capital.

China proposed that the said zone should not extend farther westward than 20 *li* to the east of Wei-hsien, but Japan objected to this, and argued that such a boundary would be difficult to observe, as they might be considered "to have violated China's neutrality" if a few of the Japanese troops wandered beyond this boundary. China, however, declined to modify her proposal, and eventually Japan acceded to her wishes, adding that, while no troops would occupy the railroad beyond the war zone, it might be found necessary to send officers to Wei-hsien for the purchase of supplies. Upon this understanding did Japan send her troops into China to drive Germany from Shantung.

On September 2, news reached Peking that several Japanese transports had arrived at Lungkow, a port under Japanese influence in northern Shantung, and that troops were being disembarked. Just why Lungkow, a port situated one hundred and fifty miles from Tsingtau and in a mountainous district, practically devoid of roads suitable for military purposes, should have been the spot from which Japan first started war operations against Germany, remained a question that the Far East was unable to answer at the time, but events that followed after the disembarkation brought out the answer clearly.

With the German Kiaochow garrison miles away, Japan began the long, tedious journey across Shantung, where heavy rains and floods made difficult the advance of troops. Arriving at Tsimo the middle of September, the troops advanced westward, and about September 20, Peking was suddenly startled by the report that the Japanese troops had occupied Wei-hsien, and were advancing still farther westward along the Shantung railroad and beyond the defined war zone.

By this unnecessary action Japan had violated the neutrality of China. And, though England had joined in the European war because Germany had violated the neutrality of Belgium, the British Government, for some reason unknown, did not think it necessary, when all the eyes of the world were upon Europe, to protest loudly, to her ally in China, against the very thing that had seemingly so shocked her in Belgium.

Western Shantung was now in disorder and confusion. With the Japanese troops quartered over this district there were many clashes between the native soldiery and the Japanese troops, and it required a steady hand in Peking to check a revolution or a war.

And by this same action did Japan prove to the world that it was not "the maintenance of the peace of the Far East" that had brought her into the European struggle, but rather her political ambition.

So serious was the situation in Shantung, the Council of State at Peking was hurriedly called together to discuss Japan's breach of faith. A resolution was unanimously passed calling for interpretation of the Government's policy concerning China's neutrality. In moving the interpretation Liang Chi Chao, a member of the council, said:—

> Since the outbreak of the European war. President Yuan Shi Kai has represented the nature of China's diplomatic relations and we sympathize with the Government's difficult situation, but the events and the rapid movements of the last twenty days leads to the belief that his reports are incomplete. Since the people are most indignant, the duty has devolved upon us to ask the Government for an explanation. When Japan declared war upon Germany, we were forced to delineate a war zone. However, Japan has violated our neutrality by occupying Wei-hsien and preparing to seize the railroad beyond the limits set forth.
>
> I ask, are there any German soldiers west of Wei-hsien? The westward movement of the Japanese is nothing but a geographical movement? Judging from the actions of their army, Tsingtau is not their objective, but they are trying to occupy the whole of Shantung Province, which they will turn into another Manchuria. Britain cannot be excused for violating our neutrality, because its action is taken in concert with Japan. Britain has warred to uphold the neutrality of weak nations, thus gaining our respect, but in China it has followed a different policy, using the Allies' forces to violate the neutrality of Shantung. The Japanese outrages are facts and the Government should not look upon the people's sufferings with indifference.

Chen Kuo Hsiang, another member of the Council said:

> Japan, by attacking Tsingtau is following out a continental policy cherished for the last twenty years. Its purpose is to seize Tsinan-fu and the northern sections of the Tien-tsin-Pukow railways. The situation confronting us is most grave. I fear that Shantung will become a second Manchuria. If Japan takes

Shantung, what will become of the nation?

The Council of State even discussed war against Japan, when General Choa Wei Hsin jumped to his feet and shouted:—

> Should the people of China refuse to become slaves? There is hope that this country is becoming strong again. Should the people be abused? Then it is better for us to die than to live.

General Wang Yi Tang quickly responded:

> Yes, the people must unite to prevent their own destruction. Apparently Japan can seize anything it wants as a prize of war. This must be stopped. We are unprepared to face this emergency, but we must make immediate preparations to cope with the situation.

Looking with distrust upon Japan's actions, and regarding them as a serious breach of faith, China at once issued a protest to Japan. There followed the usual evasion by the Japanese diplomats. Japan intimated in her reply to the Foreign Office at Peking that she intended to go a step farther—to occupy the Shantung railroad from Kiaochow to Tsinan-fu. Again did China protest against the violation of her neutrality, adducing legal arguments this time to back up her claim. In reply to this a note was handed the Chinese Minister at Tokyo in which the Japanese Government:

> Announced its intentions of occupying the entire railroad from the coast to Tsinan-fu; that it had requested the withdrawal from the railroad area of all Chinese troops, and that it has declared that any opposition encountered from the Chinese authorities will be regarded as an act unfriendly to Japan and partial to Germany.

By this method Japan sought to drive the "mailed fist" policy of Germany from China in order that she could replace it with the "mailed fist" policy of Japan, which has been modelled after that of her former Teutonic tutor in arms.

In no position to resist the Japanese demands, and with everything to lose by defying her powerful neighbour, China was forced to be humiliated and accede to seeing her neutrality violated. It was but another example of how Japan tries to promote cordial relationship between China and herself. Japan was taking another step toward realizing her desire to dominate China.

CHAPTER 2

Preliminaries to the Declaration of War

In a war, such as Europe was thrown into, there is no neutral territory to feel so much the concussion as the Far East. With practically all the powers holding concessions in some part of the Orient, a diplomatic eruption in any other section of the world at once throws the foreign sections of the Far East into excitement.

The rising war clouds find Americans, Britishers, Germans, French, gathered together in the lobbies of hotels or at their respective clubs, all prophesying and discussing together the pros and cons of the question. By the time the actual declaration of war is served, the Far East is already at sword points, and the once cosmopolitan gatherings have become a clique affair with the Britishers at their club, the Germans at theirs, the French at their quarters, and the Americans free to go to whichever their membership entitles them to, And then the war starts—in the actual field of battle by the deep undertoned voices of siegers and the *phut-phut* of rifles; in diplomatic centres by column after column of communications for publication to the editors of the various foreign newspapers.

The British Resident in Shanghai writes a communication denouncing the German and his methods, to which the Germans promptly reply. Other foreigners take sides and join in the "communication" battle, and gradually the fight broadens. Before the battle is half over the editor finds himself swamped with mail and a truce is therefore declared. But by this time the political, the commercial, the religious, and in fact every side of life of the "warring nations" has absorbed the discussion and there is little left for the fighters to do but to hold their chagrin for distribution among their fellow nationals, and to watch and await developments from the actual field of war.

In such a condition was the Far East during the first week of August, 1914. With the European Powers at war with each other, there was a hasty call for reservists throughout the Orient. Immediately there was a rush, business was dropped, and everybody journeyed to the railway stations or to the piers to see the farewell of departing troops. In Yokohama and Kobe were great crowds of Japanese at the stations shouting "*banzai*" and waving a "*sayonnara*" to their departing French, British, Austrian, and German friends, who were all going over to Europe on the same boat to fight each other. And Shanghai and Hongkong witnessed like scenes with the enmity showing a little more bitter by the gathering in cliques: Germans on one side of the pier or on one side of the deck—the British on the other.

It was the publication in the foreign press of Japan, on August 4, of the reported seizure of the Russian volunteer fleet steamer *Riazan*, by the German cruiser *Emden*,[1] from Tsingtau, which first bristled the back of the Far East with talk of actual war within its boundaries. The capture, so the report stated, took place near the Korean archipelago, while the steamer was on its way to Vladivostok, and as such was considered a heavy blow to Japanese sovereign rights and neutrality.

Whatever may be the truth of this reported German interference with trade in the Orient, the fact is that the Foreign Office at Tokyo had already seen in Germany's war against Europe a most opportune time to pay back that "grudge" against Germany for the part Berlin had played at the close of the Chino-Japanese War, in forcing Japan later to renounce the definite possession of the Liao-tung Peninsula, her fruit of the war. Then, too, the European war gave Japan an exceptionally favourable opportunity to realize her ambitions for the last ten years—the domination and control of China, and with England, Germany, Russia, and France all busy at home, there would be no Power left to check Japan but the United States.

It was not, therefore, a surprise to those foreigners who resided in Tokyo to learn on August 2 that the Foreign Office at Tokyo had sent a formal note to the Foreign Office in London in regard to the Mikado's willingness at once to put in force the Anglo-Japanese Alliance, which was negotiated in July, 1911. The note from Japan specifically referred to Article II of the Alliance, which stated:

---

1. *The Kaiser's Raider!* by Hellmuth von Mücke, *Two Accounts of the S. M. S. Emden During the First World War by One of its Officers: The "Emden" & The "Ayesha" Being the Adventures of the Landing Squad of the "Emden,"* also published by Leonaur.

If by reason of an unprovoked attack or aggressive action, wherever arising, on the part of any other Power; (or, if) either of the High Contracting Parties should be involved in war in defence of its territorial rights or special interests, the other High Contracting Party will at once come to the assistance of its ally and will conduct the war in common and make peace in mutual agreement with it.

Japan's offer to London to join in the European war by banishing the German menace from the Far East, signalized the approach of exciting and busy days in diplomatic circles of the Nippon Empire.

Scarcely had the note been handed to Sir Conyngham Greene, the British ambassador to Tokyo, than the French ambassador, Eugene L. G. Regnault, and the Russian ambassador, Nicolas Malewsky-Malewitch, drove up to the compound of the English Embassy in Tokyo where an exciting discussion was held with the British Ambassador as to the practicability of allowing Japan to enter the war.

The conferences of the three ambassadors was continued for three or four days, but just what stand was taken by the representatives was never known, except that harmony must have been reached, for on August 7 the British ambassador handed to the Foreign Office at Tokyo a request that Japan join in the European war.

The exact contents of the note were never made public, but the rumour in diplomatic circles in Tokyo the following day had it that England had asked that Japan, in case she joined in the war, should confine her war operations to the actions of the German and Austrian warships, and to the protection of British merchantmen in Far Eastern waters, or to the negative help to British warships in Oriental waters.

Japan, it appears, was not content with restricted action, since she was to participate in the war under the terms of the Anglo-Japanese Alliance, but desired rather to play a more important part in the war operations than were proposed for the Far East.

On the same evening that the British ambassador handed the Foreign Office in Tokyo the request from Sir Edward Grey, Count Okuma, Premier of Japan, called a meeting of the Cabinet which did not break up its session to well beyond 2 a.m. the following morning. At that meeting it was decided to go further into action in the Far East than to control the Pacific waters and aid British merchantmen and British warships; instead, to drive Germany from Kiaochow and Asia.

With this in mind. Baron Kato, Foreign Minister, proceeded the same morning to Nikko to advise the Emperor of Japan of the situation. At the same time an important conference was held at the Navy Office in Tokyo, at which Vice-Admiral Yashiro, Minister of Marine, Fleet Admiral Togo, and other prominent officials of the Navy Department conferred upon the possible part the Japanese fleet was to play in Oriental waters.

Germany at this time began to scent danger in the Anglo-Japanese Alliance and its possible effect upon Kiaochow and her other colonial possessions in the Pacific, and so on August 8 the German Embassy issued the following *communiqué* stating the relative position of the German Far Eastern fleet with Japanese commerce:—

> It will be of interest to learn that the German authorities have taken proper measures to avoid all unnecessary interference with neutral shipping, especially Japanese. Thus it is known that the German cruiser *Emden*, when meeting the Japanese steamship, *Sakaki Maru*, in hazy weather, requested her to show her flag in order to ascertain her nationality, and, when this request was complied with, immediately allowed her to proceed, observing all the usual courtesies.

Great Britain, now being advised of Japan's desires of pushing Germany out of Asia, began to hesitate in approving the start of Japan's war operations, and this led naturally to a delay in Japan's declaration to the world of her actions. The question that seemed to interest the Foreign Office in London was whether or not, if Japan drove Germany from Asia, Kiaochow should be placed under the control of Great Britain or of Japan.

Japanese diplomatists evidently decided that they should be supreme, for already their Government had mobilised an army of 25,000 men, transports had been hired, and the vessels of the Japanese Navy, which were later to blockade the Bay of Kiaochow, were already at their yards at Sasebo, Kure, and Yokosuka, coaling, loading with ammunition and supplies, and preparing for the first move—in case war should be declared against Germany.

Meanwhile notes were being exchanged between London and Tokyo upon the issue at stake—whether Kiaochow at the conclusion of the European war was to be given to Great Britain to do with as she pleased, or should pass into the hands of the Japanese Empire. With Germany busy warring in Europe and unable, therefore, to offer her colonies in Asia and the Pacific any assistance, there was no thought in the minds of London officials that the little German garrison at Kiaochow could show any substantial resistance against the overwhelming odds that Japan would put against it—if allowed to carry out her desires.

The Foreign Offices at London and Tokyo, evidently being deadlocked upon the question, matters took a more favourable turn when Sir Edward Grey addressed a note to Japan in which he stated that Great Britain would grant Japan's wish—to drive Germany from Kiaochow—provided she "would confine her war operation to the China Sea" and "eventually turn over Kiaochow to China."

In this move of depriving Germany of her Far Eastern naval base, Great Britain saw an opportunity of furthering her immense trade in China at the expense of Germany, at the same time depriving German commerce of a great asset in Asia. It sounded the death-knell of the "mailed fist" in Asia and, as Great Britain thought, would eventually see the restoration of Kiaochow to China, its rightful owner.

The British note, under the new terms, being delivered to Japan, the Nippon capital at once took on busy conferences. First, the Elder Statesmen and the Cabinet conferred, then the War Office was consulted, and at length, on August 9, Sir Conyngham Greene, the British ambassador, was notified that Japan was ready to carry on the war against Germany according to the last note.

In the evening of the same day Count von Rex, the German ambassador in Tokyo, was notified informally that a breach between the two governments was pending. In fact, with the happenings that had occurred in Tokyo for the past several days, the German Ambassador had not been long in scenting danger, and days before had notified Berlin, as well as the Kiaochow Government, of the fast approaching war clouds in the Orient. His government had therefore acted accordingly.

On August 1, the day that Germany declared war upon England, the Norddeutscher Lloyd liner, *Prinz Eitel Friedrich*, which had called at Shanghai, on its voyage to Bremen, was notified by the Berlin Government to disembark all passengers and to proceed at once to Tsingtau. The following day it arrived at the Shantung port, and on August 3, Tsingtau was declared under martial law.

The British steamer, *Kanchow*, which was in port, was notified late that evening that she would have but two hours to leave the port or she would be seized. She moved out at once. Early the following morning Britishers, Russians, and Americans summering at Tsingtau awoke to find the city posted with proclamations. Every train running into the city brought handfuls of German reservists from Tientsin and other cities in the hinterland, and all business in the city seemed to have ceased; instead there were preparations for war. Vice-Admiral Meyer Waldeck, Governor of Kiaochow, issued shortly afterward a note informing all non-combatants that they would be given a twenty-four-hour notice to leave. That evening, however, found the train running from Tsingtau to Tsinan-fu packed with foreigners as well as Chinese, all greatly excited and hoping to get out of Kiaochow before the war broke.

During this time quite another scene was being enacted in the harbour of Tsingtau. On August 3, the *Prinz Eitel Friedrich*, which had rushed from Shanghai two days before with her full speed of eighteen knots, was in Tsingtau being converted into a battle cruiser. Searchlights were placed on the vessel and the gunboats *Iltis* and *Tiger*, which stood alongside, were quickly stripped of their guns to be mounted on the faster boat. In the greater harbour lay the gunboats *Jaguar* and *Lucks*, with sailors busy about their decks dismantling the vessels of guns and war equipment.

With the exception of these ships the only other war-vessel in port was the Austrian cruiser, *Kaiserin Elisabeth*. All Tsingtau now seemed to be preparing for war and the busy and mysterious way the German residents went about the city quickly threw into panic the Chinese *coolies* of Tapautau, the Chinese section of the city, and many began to leave the district. Prompt action was taken by the German authorities however, who brought back two hundred *coolies* under guard and set them to work helping to dismantle the gunboats and equipping the *Prinz Eitel Friedrich*.

Likewise were other war operations carried on about Tsingtau. Along the fortifications that skirted the woods on Iltis, Bismarck, and Moltke hills in the rear of the city, members of the German *Landsturm* stationed in Tsingtau were busy mounting machine guns and artillery. The German freighters *Longmoon*, *Gouverneur Jaeschke*, and *Stattssekretaer Kraetke* had been requisitioned as colliers by the Government, and after entering port and coaling had gone out upon the Yellow Sea twenty miles to where the *Emden*, *Scharnhost*, and *Gneisenau* were standing ready to fight or retire into the harbour, according to the strength of the enemy. At the same time Chinese *junks* heavily loaded with crates and boxes made their way down the Yang-tse River from Haicheng and interned at Tsingtau. Then started the long file of coolies from the piers to the military warehouses and fortifications with the crates on their backs.

Tsingtau was preparing for war—the war clouds had gathered so quickly that she found herself unprepared, with the result that powder, shells, and ammunition were being brought into the port from somewhere in the hinterland of northern China. British residents in Tsingtau, seeing these war preparations under way, became uneasy, and on August 7 more than sixty left the city for Peking. On the same day the governor-general had the following notice posted throughout the city:—

> All British nationals are allowed to continue to reside at the port and engage in their business as hitherto if they will give their word of honour through the British Consul not to engage in any acts which may be regarded as inimical to the German Empire.

At Hongkong quite the same warlike scene was being enacted as at Tsingtau. August 1 found the city seething with excitement over the secret preparations that were being made to guard the city against attack. Throughout the previous night British-owned launches in the harbour had been steaming to and from the naval jetty, with all lights out, and heavily loaded with ammunition, stores, and guns. In the harbour was H.M.S. *Triumph* and the Canadian Pacific liner, the *Empress of Asia*, which had been requisitioned by the government and was mounting guns over her sides. All the British river gunboats on the Yang-tse had been recalled and the crews paid off and commissioned to the *Triumph*. Large red handbills placarded the naval yards announcing to service men that divulgence of what was progressing meant seven years' penal servitude.

The British bluejackets were confined to the dockyard, the troops to their barracks, and none were allowed to leave the place. Sentries were placed at every outpost boundary to guard the four hundred square miles of the colony, while the Royal Garrison Artillery and the Hongkong and Singapore battalions were stationed at the posts on the Peak. Within the city the Governor of Hongkong journeyed throughout the centres of employment, addressing the workers at noon-day meetings and urging all able-bodied men to join the volunteers or reserves.

In this way, with sentries at attention armed with rifles and fixed bayonets, did the war clouds from Europe arise from the Pacific to greet the British settlement of Hongkong.

On August 10 war rumours which had been circulating throughout the Orient for the past two weeks, took decided form when Count Okuma called all journalists in Tokyo together for a conference at his home. At the appointed hour more than one hundred newspapermen were in attendance to listen to the remarks of Japan's veteran statesman. It was the writer's fortune to be one of the listeners at the conference, and to hear Count Okuma go over the war situation then existing in Europe. He broached the situation as it related to the United States and denounced as "false" the report, printed throughout the vernacular papers a few days before, in which it was stated that the United States had dispatched a note to the Japanese Government in regard to its proposition to join in the European war. The report further stated that the Atlantic fleet was being rushed through the Panama Canal to Japan to back up the note.

The Premier said:

> How can the United States make such an interference, when Japan has practically done nothing in reference to the present war? Besides, judging from the holiday[2] of the United States, and the traits of her people, no one will believe in such an allegation of the American intervention with Japan's attitude.

Count Okuma then laughed at the fear of the alleged approach of the American navy and advised the Japanese journalists to read Congressman Hobson's book on the United States before being disturbed by any thoughts of America.

Lieutenant-General Oshima, Vice-Minister of War, Rear-Admiral Suzuki, Vice-Minister of Marine, and Mr. Matsui, Vice-Minister of Foreign Affairs, in turn addressed the gathering and each hinted at the approaching war with Germany. The pressmen were notified that in the future no news about the movement of the Japanese fleet or its army could be printed without fear of the suppression of their papers by the government. That evening the torpedo boats *Kiji* and *Kamome* were guarding the harbour at Yokohama, while a Japanese fleet under the command of Admiral Kato had put to sea and was sailing in the direction of Formosa.

For the next five days about Tokyo the Elder Statesmen, the Cabinet, the War and Navy Offices and the Foreign Office were busy in

---

2. Meaning in Japanese interpretation that the United States is at peace with the world.

JAPANESE INFANTRYMEN
Showing the equipment that makes up the
fifty-pound pack-sack

GENERAL YAMASHITA
Chief of the Japanese Staff. He planned the
strategy of the allied troops in Kiaochow

completing the final negotiations for the entry of Japan into the war. The Admiralty, to safeguard the actions of its fleet and army from the outsider, had issued drastic censorship regulations for newspapers. On the first days of its issuance several newspapers were suspended for publishing the whereabouts of the fleet or troops. On August 15 the Emperor of Japan with the empress repaired from his summer residence at Nikko to the Imperial Palace at Tokyo, where late that afternoon the Elder Statesmen, as well as the chiefs of the General Staff and Naval Board, assembled before the throne to confer with His Majesty upon the Far Eastern situation and to arrange for the official rescript announcing the declaration of war upon Germany. The session before the Imperial Throne lasted until 7 in the evening, and but a few minutes later, Count von Rex, the German Ambassador, was presented with the following note:—

The Imperial Government, in view of the present situation, deems it important for the permanent peace of the Orient to see that causes of disturbance of peace in the Far East are removed and to take steps to protect the general interests of the Anglo-Japanese alliance. So, herewith the Imperial Government makes the following demands on the German Government:—

1. The German war-vessels shall at once withdraw from the waters of Japan and the China Sea. Those vessels which cannot withdraw shall be disarmed.

2. The German Government, with the object of its return to China, shall hand over the leased territory in Kiaochow to the Japanese Government on or after September 15 without condition and without compensation.

If a reply, agreeing unconditionally to those demands, is not received by noon on August 23, 1914, the Japanese Government shall take whatever steps it deems necessary."

A few days after the deliverance of the ultimatum. Count Okuma called a conference at his residence of the business and commercial heads of Japan. The writer attended the conference with a Japanese interpreter and the following is part of Count Okuma's declaration made that day. The reader will note that the Japanese Premier states that the Japanese participation in the war is for no "territorial aggrandizement," nor for any other "selfish end," and also that the Government will take no action to give other Powers "any cause of anxiety

205

or uneasiness regarding the safety of their territories and possessions." The Premier spoke as follows:—

Japan's object is to eliminate from the continent of China the root of the German influence which forms a constant menace to the peace of the Far East, and thus to secure the aim of the alliance with Great Britain. She harbours no design for territorial aggrandizement nor entertains any desire to promote any other selfish end. Japan's warlike operations will not, therefore, extend beyond the limits necessary for the attainment of that object and for the defence for her own legitimate interests. Accordingly the Imperial Government have no hesitation in announcing to the world that the Imperial Government will take no such action as to give third Powers any cause of anxiety or uneasiness regarding the safety of their territories and possessions.

On the same day the Japanese Government sent the following *communiqué* to the Foreign Office of Peking:—

Owing to the aggressive actions of Germany, unfortunately a war has been started between England and Germany and the peace in the Far East is about to be disturbed. The Japanese Government, after consultation with England and considering the present circumstances and the future of the Far East, has been obliged to take this last course for the assurance of peace of the Far East and the preservation of China's territorial integrity and the maintenance of peace and order in the same country.

Just what the *Kaiser* thought of the Japanese ultimatum can be gathered from the fact that two days after its deliverance Count von Rex, the German Ambassador in Tokyo, with his legation staffs, started to pack their belongings initial to final leave-taking. War between the two countries, he knew, was inevitable. Only the German ambassador at Peking held out hopes that the German ruler would not be humiliated by its tone, and he started a vain negotiation with the Berlin Government for the transfer of Kiaochow to China.

Mr. Buttmann, of the German Embassy, when I called upon him a few days later said:

But this action of Japan's I cannot understand. Who is it that is hostile to the power of Japan in the Far East? It certainly is not

Germany. It is none other than Russia who is still looking for a harbour that is not ice-bound, and where she can carry on her commerce.

Of course the whole war is nothing but political nonsense, and the jealousy of Great Britain over the fast-growing German Navy is what has led to this conflict in which practically all Europe is involved. It had been the hope of German government officials to form some sort of alliance with Great Britain, in which one Power supreme on sea, and the other Power supreme on land, could thus combine to maintain peace throughout Europe. But the English politicians in their narrowness would have none of it and they were bound to keep the English navy supreme on sea. The German navy has seen a wonderful growth in the past few years, but for every ship they built England built two.

Then, too. Great Britain has shown her narrowness again by combining with the Slav to fight her own race, the Teuton. But Russia drew them on, for Russia saw in supporting Servia her chance to extend her power into the Balkan States and possibly Austria-Hungary. And that is why Germany sent a note to Russia at the beginning of the conflict asking her to stop mobilization, for if Russia extended her sway into Austria-Hungary it would be but a step into Germany, and that would be her aim. But Russia refused to end her mobilization, and so with the mobilization of the German troops France was brought in. With revenge for Alsace-Lorraine still in her mind, France realized that with her rise or fall the question of who should dictate upon the Continent rested.

As to Germany and Kiaochow, that is not the big fundamental question that Germany has to contend with today. It is a mere nothing to them and does not loom up as anything vital at all. Kiaochow can really only be called a sentimental question as far as Germany is concerned at the present.

On August 19, Count von Rex received word from Governor-General Meyer Waldeck of Kiaochow that the Berlin Government had instructed him to defend Kiaochow to the last man. At the same time Berlin cabled the following message to America:—

Should Japan intend to take possession of Kiaochow it would frighten us as little as did England's attack on Africa. This is only a new manoeuvre on the part of England, and though painful it will have little influence on the campaign. Germany will be obliged to refuse Japan's claim. If Germany thereby suffers any loss, she will take her satisfaction in other ways.

All that Count von Rex had expected from Berlin in reply to the Japanese ultimatum was vouched for four days later—Sunday, August 23—when that memorable hour of 12 o'clock noon was reached and not a word from his Government. A few hours later he was handed his passports as well as the following Imperial decree announcing the declaration of war:—

We, by the Grace of Heaven, Emperor of Japan, seated on the throne occupied by the same dynasty from time immemorial, do hereby make the following proclamation to all our loyal and brave subjects:—

We hereby declare war against Germany and we command our army and navy to carry on hostilities against that empire with all their strength, and we also command all our competent authorities to make every effort, in pursuance of their respective duties, to attain the national aim, by all the means within the limits of the law of nations.

Since the outbreak of the present war in Europe, the calamitous effects of which we view with grave concern. We, on our part, have entertained hopes of preserving the peace of the Far East by the maintenance of strict neutrality. But the action of Germany has at length compelled Great Britain, our ally, to open hostilities against that country, and Germany is, at Kiaochow, its leased territory in China, busy with warlike preparations, while its armed vessels cruising the seas of Eastern Asia are threatening our commerce and that of our Ally. The peace of the Far East is thus in jeopardy. Accordingly, our government and that of His Britannic Majesty, after a full and frank communication with each other, agreed to take such measures as may be necessary for the protection of the general interests contemplated in the Agreement of Alliance, and we, on our part, being desirous to attain that object by peaceful means, commanded our government to offer, with sincerity, an advice to the Imperial German Government. By the last day appointed for the purpose, however. Our government failed to receive an answer accepting their advice.

It is with profound regret that we, in spite of our ardent devotion to the cause of peace, are thus compelled to declare war, especially at this early period of our reign and while we are still in mourning for our lamented mother.

It is our earnest wish that, by the loyalty and valour of our faithful subjects, peace may soon be restored and the glory of the empire be enhanced."

CHAPTER 3

The Violation of Neutrality

It was to be expected that while the German offensive movement in Belgium was developing, during the first month of the war in Europe, observers would centre attention upon the countries in Europe, to the exclusion of all war events elsewhere. This accounts probably for the somewhat indifferent attitude that was taken toward the war that Japan was waging against the German protectorate at Kiaochow. However, the events in the Far East had primarily a more important meaning to America than events in Europe, for they brought to the fore Japan's seizure of the German islands in Pacific waters. In case Japan should ever war against the United States, these islands might play a very important part; for the once German possessions in the Pacific can be utilized as a block in the communication between the colonial possessions of the United States, namely, Hawaii, Guam, and the Philippine Islands.

While Japan had actually started her war operations against Kiaochow days before her declaration of war against Germany, the first event in the war was the blockading of the Bay of Kiaochow. On August 26, three days after the declaration of war, Vice-Admiral S. Kato, in command of the second Japanese squadron, consisting of the Suwo, Iwami, and Tango, which had been the Pobjeda, Orel, and Poltawa of the Russian fleet before their capture by the Japanese in 1905, steamed from their base on the island of Formosa and drew up in a semi-circle ten miles out from Tsingtau. Admiral Kato sent a wireless message to Governor Meyer Waldeck of Kiaochow asking that he receive a *parlementaire* from the Japanese Government to consider the surrender of the protectorate. The Governor of Kiaochow refused the request unless the desires of the Japanese Government were specifically expressed, whereupon the Bay of Kiaochow was immediately declared by the Japanese to be blockaded.

Days before the German garrison at Tsingtau had expected this development, and so after calling in her Far Eastern fleet consisting of the flagship *Scharnhorst*, under command of Admiral von Spee, the *Emden* and the *Gneisenau*, the war-vessels were reprovisioned and dispatched from the Bay of Kiaochow on a raiding cruise which proved one of the most melodramatic of the war. Germany had learned her lesson from the Russians and she decided that she was not going to do what the *Czar's* commanders had done at Port Arthur during her war with Japan—allow the bottling-up of her fleet.

With the departure of Admiral von Spee's fleet from Tsingtau, the entrance to the Bay of Kiaochow was sown with more than five thousand mines behind which barrier steamed the disarmed Austrian cruiser *Kaiserin Elisabeth*, as well as the German destroyer, *S-90*.

For the next several days the war operations of both Japan and Germany were seemingly veiled. The first fleet of the Japanese Navy, under command of Admiral K. Kato, was still steaming about Formosa and the China coast, evidently searching for German prey, while the British cruiser *Triumph* and the British gun boat *Kennet*, which were scheduled to join in the Kiaochow action, were cruising off Hongkong and Shanghai guarding the China coast from the approach of the German Far Eastern fleet. The latter, however, was cruising about the South Pacific islands, searching for British merchantmen and otherwise guarding the German possessions.

To the extreme north of the Yellow Sea were the Japanese transports steaming toward northern Shantung and bearing twenty thousand fighting men, all eager to put into effect "the game" of the *mikado's* protectorate in China and the driving of Germany from Asia.

Within Kiaochow and Tsingtau final preparations were being made for the Japanese attack. With a permanent garrison of only sixteen hundred men, Berlin had issued a call for the reservists in the Far East to report at Tsingtau, and into the German protectorate they poured—from Singapore, Hongkong, Shanghai, Kobe, and Tokyo; every train from Tsinan-fu into Tsingtau brought its quota of Germany's finest men. The majority of the reservists were traders, men who had spent years in the Far East in learning native languages and fostering German trade. By the first week in September there were about forty-five hundred fighting men gathered about the fortifications of Tsingtau.

All were busy along the fortification walls that skirt the rear of the city. Trenches were being dug, the ground in front mined, redoubts with bomb-proof shelters constructed, barbed-wire entanglements set up, and guns mounted. The garrison was expecting the landing of the Japanese land forces at any minute and the Tsingtau fortifications were alive with moving men both day and night.

But the German garrison of Kiaochow had seemingly forgotten, during their exciting preparations for war, that the Japanese diplomats are shrewd, and that even an army bent on war sometimes halts to gather fruit by the wayside. And so the German garrison worked hard and laboured in preparation for news of the landing in Kiaochow of the Japanese expeditionary force and their advance upon Tsingtau, but the Japanese did not come.

Expectancy always kindles excitement. And so it did in Tsingtau during the last week in August. At night the bright flares and flashes from the searchlights on the blockading squadron could be seen reflected like signals on the clouds that hung over the Yellow Sea, suggesting "tomorrow the attack" in the minds of the Tsingtau garrison. But the days came and went without much change in manoeuvres.

One day, however, the blockading squadron approached within the nine-mile zone to the entrance to Kiaochow Bay, and then it was that the residents in Tsingtau heard the deep undertone reports of their twenty-four-centimetre guns on Iltis Fort and knew that the war in the Far East had actually started.

And the "tomorrow,"—well, it came and with no signs of the approaching expeditionary forces, until, on September 3, the German garrison at Tsingtau received a report that the Japanese troops had landed at Lungkow, one hundred and fifty miles to the north.

The news was received with surprise and was instantly followed by the ordering of three detachments of the German troops into the hinterland of Kiaochow. One detachment, called the eastern detachment, proceeded in the direction of Chinchiakow to guard the road to Chefoo; another proceeded to Kaomi to check the advance of the Japanese on the road from Lungkow; and the third, or western, detachment stationed themselves at Chucheng to guard the southern seacoast.

Beyond Lungkow, the Japanese army began to violate China's neutrality, which, at the opening of hostilities, they had guaranteed to uphold. With the troops already landed upon Chinese soil, and with the Peking Government too weak to carry on any aggressive action against Japan, no matter how much her citizens desired it, there was but one thing China could do—place a limitation upon the actions of the Japanese troops in northern Shantung. In this connection the Chinese Government on September 4 sent the following note to the foreign legations in Peking:—

> The Government of China declared its neutrality toward the present European war and is faithfully maintaining it. According to reports from the Chinese local authorities in the province of Shantung, the Germans have commenced war operations at Kiaochow Bay and their sphere of influence there, and the allied forces of Japan and Britain have also started war operations at Lungkow, Kiaochow, Laichow, and in their neighbouring districts. Germany, Japan, and England are all in friendly relations with China, and it is to be regretted that unfortunately these powers have taken such unexpected courses in China's territory, therefore the Chinese Government has decided to propose special limitations as regards the extent of the present war operations as China limited the scope of war operations at Liao-tung Peninsula at the time of the Russo-Japanese War in 1904. The Chinese Government will not accept responsibility for the passing of troops or any war operations at Lungkow, Laichow, Kiaochow, and their adjacent districts, but in the other districts in China the government will strictly enforce neutrality as declared. The territory and diplomatic negotiations of China are recognized by the Powers and they will likewise protect the property of the inhabitants in the region to be affected by the war operations."

Though Peking and all China looked with distrust upon Japan's actions, the government issued a proclamation stating that "as Japan and England are cooperating in the attack upon Tsingtau at this time, in order to return Kiaochow to China, our people should show their goodwill toward them. If any Chinese officials should meet Japanese or British soldiers they should show their goodwill toward them, should act peacefully and avoid all conflicts. Should the Japanese or British soldiers come outside of the war zone, our soldiers and citizens should not act independently, but should await instructions from Peking."

On September 11, Japanese forces entered Tsimo, ninety miles from Lungkow, after battling nine days with heavy rains which flooded rivers and made the advancement of military operations practically impossible. The roads were mere quagmires in which the heavy military carts sank to their hubs.

From Tsimo the troops pushed on to Wei-hsien, again going out of the defined war zone and violating the neutrality of China.

This last action seems to have been the straw that broke the camel's back, for all of northern China rose in revolt against the Japanese action. The Japanese troops took command of the Shantung railroad, shooting down native employees who seemingly rebelled at the invasion. The troops pushed on to Tsinan-fu, leaving small garrisons in every Chinese town to keep "Japan's peace," and in a few days western Shantung was practically in the control of Japan.

CHAPTER 4

The Advance of the Japanese Army

On September 11, while officials in Peking were still discussing Japan's violation of China's neutrality, the Imperial Japanese army with its cavalry arrived at Pingtau, about forty miles from Tsingtau. There had been no sight of the enemy, but reports were current that a detachment of Germans were garrisoned in the little city of Tsimo, about twenty miles distant. The same night the troops advanced toward Tsingtau, and on the following morning the first encounter of the war with Germany took place at Tsimo.

The little German garrison, consisting of but ten men, was driven off easily after an exchange of a few shots, in which two of the Germans fell wounded and Tsimo, a Chinese city of thirty thousand population, passed into the hands of Japan. The Japanese army officers, to soften the hostile feeling of the Chinese residents against them, at once journeyed to the shrines of Confucius, devout Shintoists and Buddhists as they were, and knelt in prayer before the great philosopher of the Celestial Kingdom. In this way did the Japanese army officers gain the respect of the Chinese natives in Tsimo.

While these warlike events were taking place about Tsimo, Tsingtau was suddenly thrown into great confusion by the flight of a Japanese aeroplane over the city dropping bombs. The aeroplane, which was attached to the blockading squadron, had previously made one or two reconnoitring flights over the Tsingtau fortifications, but had confined its actions simply to observation. The gaping holes in the roofs of the Moltke Barracks and Governor Waldeck's residence, which marked the damage done by Japan's first use of the aeroplane in modern warfare, put the residents of Tsingtau in great excitement. From then until the first week of November and the siege of Tsingtau, the little city lived in an atmosphere of trembling expectancy.

JAPANESE AEROPLANE
Preparing for a flight over the city of Tsingtau from its base
along the Tschangtsun River. The long tubular bomb-carrier
can be seen on each side of the aviator's wind-shield

THE MOLTKE BARRACKS AT TSINGTAU
The roof shows the work of bombs from the Japanese
aeroplanes. The concussion from the guns in the nearby
forts had shattered every window

With the "game" in the landing of troops at Lungkow now fulfilled,—the occupation of western Shantung,—Japan now set about to bring her war operations to a close in the brushing of Germany from Asia. The first step taken toward this end was in the transferring of her base of supplies from Lungkow, one hundred and fifty miles from Tsingtau, to Lauschan, but fifteen miles from the German city. The district lies just without the limits of Kiaochow and, having a large bay, well sheltered by the Lauschan Mountains, which rise up in the Yellow Sea at its southern end, it furnished an ideal location for a base of supplies.

On September 14, Commander Aoki, in command of the destroyer flotilla before Tsingtau, forced a reconnoissance into Lauschan Bay and drove back the handful of German sentinels that were posted about the district. The following day other units of the blockading squadron were brought into effect at Lauschan and within a few days Japanese transports appeared in the bay bearing fifteen thousand additional troops.

Siege guns were unloaded, ammunition and supplies of all kinds, as well as several aeroplanes and portable wireless outfits, and soon Lauschan was a bustling little war-city. Chinese *coolies* of the district were forced into service and work was started on the construction of a narrow-gauged railroad into the hinterland to carry supplies to the attacking army.

Tsingtau by now was practically cut off from all communication with the world. The Shantung railroad had been cut by the Japanese Army and troops had already entered the Chinese city of Kiaochow, outside the protectorate. The Tsingtau cable line had been cut, and only the wireless in the rear of Governor Waldeck's residence remained as a source for news of anything happening outside the little protectorate. Through messages transmitted by wireless from German vessels anchored at Woosung, near Shanghai, Tsingtau was able to get a few scattered messages of events in the European situation, but these were meagre and only served as an appetiser for more. Japanese aviators had on one or two occasions tried to destroy the Tsingtau wireless station by bombs, but only once did the effort prove effective, and then the damage done was repaired in a few days by the Germans and communication was again opened.

On September 18, the Japanese troops which had landed at Lauschan advanced into the hinterland eight miles, where they suddenly met with resistance from a detachment of about one hundred

Germans who had strongly fortified themselves in one of the mountainous passes, behind machine guns. No casualties were suffered in the fighting, but the Germans were forced to retreat toward Tsingtau.

On the same day Captain Zenji Sakuma, of the Japanese cavalry corps, was killed in a skirmish of his force with an advanced guard of Germans near Liuting on the River Paisha, the western boundary of Kiaochow. It was the first Japanese casualty of the war. In the same engagement Baron Leadsell, second secretary of the German Legation at Peking, was also killed.

For the next two weeks there were many clashes and skirmishes between small detachments of the two opposing forces, and all tended to the gradual retreat of the Germans toward their fortifications at Tsingtau.

During the next week the Japanese Army centred its fighting in the mountainous districts south of Lauschan and gradually the small German detachments were driven back toward Tsingtau. With the occupation of Sanpiaoshan Peak, nine hundred feet high, on September 22, the Japanese were able to secure a first-class observatory position, from which to view the movements of the German front line, four miles distant at Litsun and Shatsekau.

Two days later the attacking force was further strengthened by the landing of the British expeditionary force at Lauschan, under the command of Major-General Barnardiston. The British force consisted of the Tientsin garrison of South Wales Borderers, comprising nine hundred and twenty-five men with three hundred additional Sikhs.

CHAPTER 5

Closing in the Offensive

The war operations of the combined Anglo-Japanese force in Ki-aochow, from the last week in September until the siege of Tsingtau late in October, offered little of interest to the outside reader, such as was furnished by the war raging in Europe. With a battle front of scarcely five miles, and with the German garrison at Tsingtau able to put only two thousand trained soldiers in the field, the fighting in Kiaochow during the above-stated period took the form more or less of mere skirmishes.

Governor-General Meyer-Waldeck at Tsingtau had scattered his trained force in small detachments about the hinterland, there to guard the roads and, if possible, hinder the advance of the Japanese troops, but so overwhelmingly were the odds against him that the resistance was very little.

From a military standpoint, however, the manoeuvring of the troops during these four weeks had proved beneficial to the Japanese Army, in that it gave the aviation corps a chance to show the value of the aeroplane in modern fighting. It was the first time the Japanese army had ever utilized the air machine in their war operations. Five or six machines were in flight throughout the day marking movements of the Tsingtau garrison. Through this form of communication the Japanese staff officers were constantly in touch with the movement of the German field force, and gradually they were able to cut through the German front defence and force the latter to withdraw toward the Tsingtau fortifications.

Bringing the gunboat *Jaguar* and the Austrian cruiser *Kaiserin Elis-abeth* up the Bay of Kiaochow, the Germans opened fire upon the advancing force, both from sea and land, in an effort to check the advance, but the Japanese retaliated by sending a bomb attack from their aeroplanes against the ships and gradually they were forced out of range of the land operations.

At the same time the fourth detachment of the Japanese blockading fleet before Tsingtau in the Yellow Sea advanced into the bay at the foot of the Lauschan range, and, after landing marines, forced back the left wing of the German defence line to within three miles of Tsingtau. Four old field guns, German trophies of the Franco-Prussian War, were all the spoils that the Japanese gained in the attack. The German outposts in the mountains, however, before withdrawing, applied the torch to Mecklenberg Inn, a mountain summer resort for the Tsingtau residents, and destroyed all the bridges in the mountain gorges that the German Government had built in constructing the macadamized automobile road from the capital of the protectorate into the mountains.

In the same way did the German outposts along the Bay of Kiaochow hinder the advance of the Japanese Army by dynamiting all railroad bridges and the like along the route of the Shantung railroad.

During this time Japanese trawlers were busy at work in the Yellow Sea sweeping the entrance to the bay of mines that the Germans had placed in the waters. The Tsingtau promontory forts all attempted to harass the work by firing upon the trawlers, but the guns were not equal to the range and no damage was reported. A German aeroplane also made continuous flights over the vessels at sea, dropping bombs, and the Japanese retaliated by dispatching two hydroplanes in pursuit of the German air machine. In each such case the German machine easily outdistanced the Japanese flying corps and flew back in range of the Tsingtau fortifications before the Japanese aviators could head it off.

By October 12, the Japanese investing army, with the British expeditionary force making up the right wing, had advanced to Litsun, about eight miles from Tsingtau. Here the German front line seemed to take a stubborn stand and backed by the Kiaochow cavalry and artillery the fighting took on more desperate form. During the week the Germans were firing more than fifteen hundred shells daily from their field pieces and the Japanese casualties for the total operations had passed the two hundred mark.

So hot did the operations before Litsun eventually become that the Governor-General of Kiaochow forwarded a dispatch to General Kamio, commander of the investing force, asking for a suspension of hostilities in order that time could be taken to bury the dead. Just

On the march through a chinese village in
Kiaochow

Trophy relics from the Franco-Prussian War
Used by the Germans in the defence of Tsingtau. Rather than
leave them as useful prizes of war to the enemy, they blew the
breech-block off each gun

what were the German losses in the engagement is not known, but a few hours later, when the bombardment was resumed, the Japanese force in advancing came upon a trench with twenty-eight dead Germans, evidently overlooked by the Tsingtau garrison during the truce, and it is thought the German casualties for the day amounted to more than two hundred.

In preparation for the final investment of Tsingtau, however, the Japanese staff officers decided to notify all non-combatants in the city of the situation and, if possible, give them an opportunity to leave the war zone before the operations became more serious. In this connection the following communication was sent by wireless to Governor-General Waldeck at Tsingtau on October 10:—

> The undersigned have the honour to convey to Your Excellency the most gracious wishes of the Emperor of Japan, who desires to save non-combatants of the belligerent country as well as the subjects of neutral countries at Tsingtau who desire to escape from the loss that may arise from the attack on the fortified port. If Your Excellency desires to accept the proposal of the Emperor of Japan, you are requested to furnish us with a detailed *communiqué* about it.
>
> [Signed]   Lieutenant-Geneeal Kamio.
>   Vice-Admiral Kato.

A few days later the Kiaochow Governor notified his approval of the Japanese note and Captain Yamada, with ten Japanese soldiers, was sent to the gates of Tsingtau to escort the non-combatants who desired to leave the ill-fated city and the war zone. Only about a dozen persons desired to take advantage of the Japanese humanitarian note, one being Mr. Peck, the American Consul at Tsingtau, who had remained in the city to protect American interests, until notified from Washington to proceed to Peking.

CHAPTER 6

The Germans Withdraw to Tsingtau

With the field guns of the attacking force now thundering at the very door of Tsingtau, and with the final leave-taking of non-combatants, the little German city commenced to stir with excitement. Up to this time the city had not been cheered by any optimistic reports from the field of battle, but events shortly took on a different aspect when on the midnight of October 17 a report went circulating through the city that a Japanese warship had been sunk outside the Bay of Kiaochow by the German destroyer *S-90*.

The report was true, but not until days later did the little German city learn the extent of the damage. It seems that the German destroyer, which was supposedly interned in the harbour of Tsingtau, had made its way out through the mined entrance to the harbour under cover of darkness and had attacked the *Takachiho*, a second-class defence boat of the Japanese blockading fleet, which was doing outpost duty near Lauschan Bay. Suddenly the other units of the Japanese fleet, which were standing out at sea about nine miles, saw a flash, and a few minutes later the report of an explosion was heard. Putting on full speed, the vessels rushed to the aid of the *Takachiho*, but when they arrived in the waters they found the vessel already sunk and a few of its crew scattered about in the sea. As the relief ships approached they caught the sound of the Japanese national anthem, "*Kimigayo*," which the survivors were singing. Only one officer and twelve of the crew were picked up as survivors of the incident. Twenty-eight officers and two hundred and forty-four of the. crew had gone down with the vessel.

It was a sorry day for the Japanese Navy, not only from the standpoint of the loss of its many officers, but because of the sinking of the vessel around which was wrapped so much historical sentiment.

The *Takachiho* had been the flagship of the Japanese navy during the Chinese-Japanese War, and as such had played a prominent part in the naval battles of that war which had left Japan supreme among Asiatic nations. It had also seen service at Port Arthur in the Russian war, and had come to be looked upon by the Japanese as the foundation of their present first-class navy, much as the American people regard the *Constitution*.

Following its successful attack upon the *Takachiho*, the German destroyer broke through the Japanese blockading squadron and, its movements unnoticed, cruised along the China coast to Shihsuehso, a Chinese port sixty miles south of the Bay of Kiaochow where the vessel was beached and disarmed by its crew. The crew was then placed under guard by Chinese soldiers, by orders from Peking, and was held at Nanking.

With the report of the escape of the *S-90* in Japanese hands, the blockading fleet at once closed up on Tsingtau and started a bombardment upon the forts, from a point nine miles at sea. The British cruiser *Triumph* also joined in the action, but upon approaching within gun range of the Tsingtau promontory forts she received damage on her port side. One sailor was killed and several wounded in the attack.

In co-operation with the sea attack upon Tsingtau the investing land forces started their operations for the final investment of the city from land. One regiment started an assault upon Prince Heinrich Berg, a mountain rising one thousand feet, and but three miles from Tsingtau, on which a detachment of thirty Germans had been stationed. Barbed-wire entanglements had been placed on the mountain-side, already strongly fortified behind the rocky crags that characterized the cliff. The little German detachment was able successfully to hold its own for more than four hours. One Japanese major and more than fifty men were killed in the storming of Prince Heinrich, but by a *coup* a few of the regiment were able to gain the summit of the mountain from the rear, without their approach being noticed by the Germans, who, surrounded on all sides, laid down their arms and surrendered.

Following this incident the Japanese and British forces were suddenly thrown into bewilderment by the disappearance across the Yellow Sea of one of the German observatory balloons from Tsingtau. The balloon, which corresponded to the type being used by the Japanese army from their rear line, was seen to contain the figure of a man using field-glasses, and during the middle of October it was every morning above the Tsingtau fortifications. The attacking army had tried to reach the balloon with shrapnel, but the attempt had proved unsuccessful. Suddenly one day in a heavy wind the balloon, with its observer,—afterwards learned to be a stuffed dummy,—took to the air and went whirling across the sea. Japanese and British officers followed it with their glasses, wondering what the movement could mean, and it was several days before it was known to have been a hoax.

With the disappearance of their war balloon from Tsingtau, the German garrison was forced to rely upon its one Taube for information of the Japanese Army movements. In all the heroic work of the German defenders in Kiaochow, probably no incident stands out more than the work of Lieutenant Pluschow, who, days before the Japanese Army had approached to gunshot distance of the Tsingtau forts, was flying about the hinterland of Kiaochow spotting the movements of the opposing force. With only three months' training, he had taken charge of the German aircraft, and high in the air above the entrenched British and Japanese forces, he had braved shrapnel fire and shells from field guns in order to keep the German staff at Tsingtau acquainted with any changes on the battle line.

Back in Tschang-tsun, where was stationed, two weeks before the siege of Tsingtau, the headquarters of the Japanese staff officers, no alarm clock was needed to tell when daylight was rising from the Yellow Sea. Simultaneously with the first streaks of dawn in the east could be heard the whirr and hum of Lieutenant Pluschow's Taube as he set out from Tsingtau, and over the hills in the hinterland, to see what was stirring in the enemy's camp. Swooping low over the village of the Japanese staff officers, he dropped many a bomb upon the Chinese thatched roofs. The hum of the German aeroplane was the signal that a new day had arrived, and promptly the little village was astir, each of its residents hurriedly dressing and scanning the sky for the fast-disappearing Taube. Each day he visited the Japanese headquarters, and though, on occasions, a Japanese field piece, hidden behind some embankment, would try to cut short these flying expeditions, Lieutenant Pluschow was undaunted, and a few hours later would be back again flying over the village.

But the investing forces slowly pushed on their operations. There was not much hurry, not much excitement in their movements, for the Japanese staff officers, as well as the Tsingtau garrison, knew that it was only a question of time before Kiaochow would have to bow to the inevitable and be handed over to Japan. General Kamio, commander

1. *The Only One Who Got Away* by Gunther Plüschow also published by Leonaur.

of the Japanese forces, knew that he was master of the situation, that Tsingtau was practically isolated from the world, and especially Germany, and that no aid could possibly reach the little protectorate.

And so the Japanese staff officers allowed events to progress slowly, not especially because it would lessen loss of life, but because the political situation, then developing in Japan, was very critical for the Tokyo Government. The Cabinet, which in conjunction with the Elder Statesmen had shaped the policy that the nation was following in the war, stood in danger of falling, and with the *diet* meeting in December to shape the government's budget and to decide on other bills and measures, it was deemed necessary that the war operations should progress slowly until the right moment should present itself for bringing the Kiaochow issue to a close.

Under such a scheme the government thought the successful culmination of its war operations would sweep the island nation with patriotism and the opposition to the government at home would at once have to accede to public demand. In this way the Okuma Cabinet would remain in power after the *diet* session, and would be able to further the policy that it had under construction when it first suggested to England that it be allowed to wipe out the German naval base at Kiaochow under the terms of the Anglo-Japanese Alliance.

CHAPTER 7

The Beginning of the Siege

War from a grandstand seat! I had never before heard of the possibility of witnessing modern warfare—the attack of warships, the fire
of infantry and battery, the reconnoitring of airships over the enemy's
lines, the rolling up from the rear of reinforcements and supplies—all
at one sweep of the eye, yet after watching for three days the siege of
Tsingtau, from a position on Prince Heinrich Berg, one thousand feet
above sea level and but three miles from the besieged city, I am sure
there is actually such a thing as a theatre of war.

On October 31, the anniversary of Mutsuhito's accession to the
throne of Japan, the actual bombardment of Tsingtau began. All the
residents in the little Chinese village of Tschang-tsun had been awakened early in the morning by the whirr of the German Taube as it
made its usual inspection of the headquarters of the Japanese staff officers. Everyone quickly dressed and after a hasty breakfast was out at
the southern edge of the village gazing toward Tsingtau.

A great black column of smoke was arising from the city and hung
like a pall over the besieged. At first glance it seemed that one of the
neighbouring hills had turned into an active volcano and was emit-
ting this column of smoke, but officers who stood about enlightened
onlookers by explaining that the oil tanks in Tsingtau were on fire.

As the bombardment of Tsingtau was scheduled to start early in
the morning, we were invited to accompany members of the staffs
of the Japanese and British expeditionary forces on a trip to Prince
Heinrich Berg, there to watch the investment of the city.

When we arrived at the summit there was the theatre of war laid
out before us like a map. To the left were the Japanese and British
cruisers in the Yellow Sea, preparing for the bombardment of Tsingtau. Below was a Japanese battery, stationed near the Mecker house,

227

HEADQUARTERS OF THE GENERAL STAFF OF THE JAPANESE
FORCES AT TSCHANG-TSUN

TSINGTAU ON THE MORNING OF OCTOBER 31

As it appeared from the Japanese Staff Office at Tschang-
tsun, when the bombardment began. Japanese shells had fired
the oil-tanks, and the smoke hung like a pall over the city
throughout the day

which the Germans had burned in their retreat from the mountains. Directly ahead was the city of Tsingtau with the Austrian cruiser *Kaiserin Elisabeth* steaming about in the harbour, while to the right one could see the German coast and central forts and redoubts and the entrenched Japanese and British camps.

We had just couched ourselves comfortably between some large jagged rocks, where we felt sure we were not on a direct line with the enemy's guns, when suddenly there was a flash as if some one had turned a large golden mirror in the field down beyond to the right. A little column of black smoke drifted away from one of the Japanese "saps," or trenches, and in a minute later those of us on the peak of Prince Heinrich heard the sharp report of a field gun.

"Gentlemen, the show has started," said the British captain, as he removed his cap and started adjusting his "opera" glasses. No sooner had he said this than the report of guns came from all directions, with a continuous rumble, as if a giant bowling-alley were in use.

Everywhere the valley at the rear of Tsingtau was alive with golden flashes or the flashing from discharging guns, and at the same time great clouds of bluish-white smoke would suddenly spring up around the German batteries, where some Japanese shell had burst.

Over near the greater harbour of Tsingtau could be seen flames licking up the Standard Oil and Asiatic Petroleum Companies' large tanks. We afterwards learned that they had been ignited from the huge shells that had been turned upon the tanks from the Japanese guns, and the bursting tanks had thrown burning oil on to the naval buildings and wharves adjoining.

The warships in the Yellow Sea opened fire on Iltis Fort, and for three hours we continually played our glasses on the field, on Tsingtau, and on the warships. With glasses on the central redoubt of the Germans, we watched the effects of the Japanese fire until the boom of guns from the German fort A, on a little peninsula jutting out from Kiaochow Bay, toward the east, attracted our attention there. We could see the big siege gun on this fort rise up over the bunker, aim at a warship in the sea, fire, and then quickly go down again. And then we would turn our eyes toward the warships in time to see a fountain of water, two hundred yards from the vessel, where the shell had struck. We scanned the city of Tsingtau.

The one hundred and fifty-ton crane on the greater harbour, which we had seen earlier in the day, and which was said to be the largest crane in the world, had disappeared and only its base remained standing. A Japanese shell had carried away the crane.

As the sun started to drop behind the Pearl Mountains in the west, our eyes were suddenly attracted by wavering flashes from fire close to Moltke Fort. Turning our glasses on the spot, we saw an armoured car pushed by a locomotive suddenly dart out from the shadows of the fortress, run a short distance along the tracks of the Shantung railroad that skirt the Bay of Kiaochow, come to a stop, and then open fire upon the entrenched British force on its right. There were quick flashes of flames from its side as its guns poured round after round into the trenches, and then the engine would quickly pull the armoured battery back behind the hill and from view.

But this first day's firing of the Japanese investing troops was mainly to test the range of the different batteries. The attempt also was made to silence the line of forts extending in the east from Iltis Hill, near the wireless and signal stations at the rear of Tsingtau, to the coast fort near the burning oil tank on the west. In this they were partly successful, two guns at Iltis Fort being silenced by the guns at sea.

On November 1, the second day of the bombardment, we again stationed ourselves on the peak of Prince Heinrich Berg. From the earliest hours of morning the Japanese and British forces had kept up a continuous fire on the German redoubts, in front of the Iltis, Moltke, and Bismarck forts, and when we arrived at our seat for the theatre of war, it seemed as though the shells were dropping around the German trenches every minute. Particularly on the redoubt of Tai-tung-chen was the Japanese fire heavy, and by early afternoon, viewed through field-glasses, this German redoubt appeared to have an attack of small-pox, so pitted was it from the holes made by bursting Japanese shells. By nightfall many parts of the German redoubts had been destroyed, together with some machine guns. The result was the advancement of the Japanese front line several hundred yards forward from the bottom of hills where they had rested earlier in the day.

It was not until the third day of the bombardment that those of us stationed on *Prince Heinrich* observed that our theatre of war had a curtain, a real asbestos one that screened the fire in the drops directly ahead of us from our eyes. We had learned that the theatre was equipped with pits, drops, a gallery for onlookers, exits, and an orchestra of booming cannon and rippling, roaring pom-poms, but that nature had provided it with a curtain—that was something new to us.

We had reached the summit of the mountain about 11 a. m., just as some heavy clouds, evidently disturbed by the heavy bombardment

JAPANESE SUPPLY COLUMN ON THE WAY TO THE REAR LINE
On the day of the opening of the siege, October 31. Two
smoke-columns from the burning oil-tanks in Tsingtau can
be seen in the distance

JAPANESE STAFF OFFICERS VIEWING THE OPERATIONS
OF THE SIEGE
On the top of Prince Heinrich Berg, a mountain
1000 feet high

during the previous night, were dropping down into Litsun valley and in front of Tsingtau. For three hours we sat on the peak shivering in a blast from the sea and all the while wondering just what was being enacted beyond the curtain. The firing had suddenly ceased, and with the filmy haze before our eyes we conjectured pictures of the Japanese troops making the general attack upon Iltis Fort, evidently the key to Tsingtau, while the curtain of the theatre of war was down.

By early afternoon the clouds lifted, however, and with glasses we were able to distinguish fresh sappings of the Japanese infantry nearer to the German redoubts. The Japanese battery, which the day before was stationed below us to the left, near the Meeker house, had advanced half a mile and was quartered just outside the village of Ta-Pau. Turning our glasses on Kiaochow Bay we discovered the Austrian cruiser *Kaiserin Elisabeth* missing, nor could a search of the shore line reveal it. We afterwards learned that the Germans had sunk the vessel in the Bay of Kiaochow early in the morning, after stripping it of all its useful war equipment.

CHAPTER 8

The Fleet Bombards the City

The fourth day of fighting at Tsingtau was undoubtedly the most severe of the siege. With two guns on Iltis Fort already silenced, and with the Japanese force pressing the Germans hard in front of their redoubt walls, the Tsingtau garrison practically gave up the defence of their seacoast forts, and, with the exception of an occasional shot from Iltis, the battleships in the Yellow Sea were free to bombard Tsingtau at will.

Then it was that the Japanese, already famous for their military science, put into use, probably for the first time since naval warfare began, the wireless, as a means of marking the shots from the guns at sea. At the rear of the Japanese lines, a naval lookout had been erected, and there behind a bomb-proof shelter were entrenched several marines with horned telescopes focused on the Tsingtau forts. As soon as a shell landed, one of the marines would telephone the exact location of the bursting shell to the wireless station near Lauschan and immediately the message would be relayed to the warships standing out at sea. In this way gunners on the Japanese and British warships knew, a moment after each shot, whether the great shells were finding their marks in the German forts. As a result few shells were wasted.

Well provided with maps, the gunners' officers could locate the spot where the shell dropped. If it was not a "hit," the big gun's aim would be changed, guided always by the wireless.

On land, the Japanese were regulating their gun-fire in somewhat the same way. An observation balloon was anchored each morning on the rear line, and with telephone connection running to every part of the field, the observers were able to make the gun-fire much more efficient. Slowly the German redoubts and casement walls commenced to crumple under the severe pounding they were receiving, and at the same time the zigzag lines of the Japanese saps were noticed to be continually nearing the German front defence line.

Over on the extreme right, near the Bay of Kiaochow, the gunfire was extremely heavy. General Johoji, with General Barnardiston on his left, was pressing hard the entrenched Germans, in front of Moltke Fort. Early in the morning General Johoji had sent a detachment against the triangular pumping station fort, as it was deemed wise not to turn the siege guns on the place, because the fort might be destroyed and the supply of water be cut off in the city when the troops entered. The detachment approached the fort without any resistance from the Germans and surrounding it, discovered that there was a small garrison which had barred itself inside. The Japanese commanded the men to surrender, threatening to dynamite the place. The steel door was opened and twenty-three Germans walked out.

The capture of this fort was the key for the final attack of the Japanese, as it left the central fort and redoubts exposed to fire.

We had left Commanding-General Kamio early in the morning, after taking tea with him in his little dugout close to the base of Prince Heinrich Berg, and had started for the rear line, there to watch the fire of the new twenty-eight centimetre siege guns that were just being put in position near the Litsun River. As we approached the line Japanese batteries in our rear would open up and we could hear a shell go tearing through the air with a noise like a giant skyrocket.

Through zigzag saps, ten feet deep, we crept along, now hugging the bank of the trench, with occasional stops, to make way for stretchers bearing the wounded from the front line. The wounded and the dead appeared the same, just a stretcher with its bearers, a large, heavy, blood-stained canvas, with, perhaps, an arm dangling or a heavy boot protruding.

We spent the whole day on the rear line, until a snowstorm, not unlike those of western Canada, drove us to the charcoal fire of the naval lookout, near by.

Here, with telescope, were entrenched several marines, all seeking to mark the fire of the vessels in the Yellow Sea.

Late in the afternoon the fire became extremely heavy. The Germans seemed to be making sharp resistance to the Japanese, lest they advance within the quarter-mile zone of the redoubt walls. The Japanese infantry, however, were sapping away, and as dusk settled over the field we saw the bright flash of bursting shrapnel from the German forts. It was the first shrapnel sent out by the Germans during the siege.

Ten, twelve, fifteen, and sometimes even twenty shrapnel shells could be counted bursting at one time, all in a straight line, over the Japanese front line, and then the big German searchlights would flash about the field. They would fall on fifteen or twenty Japanese sappers on the top of their trenches placing sandbags, and then the flash would disappear. A lull for a minute and then *pom-pom-pom-pom-pom!* the machine guns along the redoubt walls would open up and for fifteen minutes would pour shot into the fresh trenches. It was woe to a man in such a fire who was wounded away from his trench. Exposed to all guns. Red Cross workers would be unable to get to him and he would be left to die the death of a soldier.

All night long the firing kept up, and for miles into the hinterland the ground trembled and echoed from the discharging guns. Tsingtau was now in darkness, Japanese shells having disabled the electric power plant and the flash of the German searchlights from the forts was missing. Instead star-shells took their place, and bursting high in the heavens above the entrenched British and Japanese forces they flooded the country with daylight and gave a spectacular touch to the fighting.

Thursday, November 5, seemed only a repetition of what had been witnessed the day before. The Tsingtau forts were a cloud of smoke and dust from the hundreds of shells that were falling upon their slopes.

I took tea with General Kamio in the morning, and he told me he would notify me ahead of time when he would order the final attack on the forts, so I could witness it. Night, of course, was to be used to screen the attack, and from what I gathered from the staff officers' remarks, it was to be a stubborn affair, with, perhaps, the loss of more than an entire regiment—eight hundred men.

Captain Shaw, back in the British Red Cross camp, a few hours later said:

Oh, the Japanese are getting too impatient. It will be a shame if they make that attack, for I am going to lose all my men if they do. And that's what hurts. I know all these men, I've worked with the most of them for years, and they are all good chaps. I hate to give them up.

In fact all the British officers at Tsingtau, when they heard that the Japanese staff officers were planning on an assault of the Tsingtau fortifications, were down in heart. The British preference was for slower

QUARTERS OF THE JAPANESE STAFF OFFICERS DURING
THE CLOSING DAYS OF THE SIEGE

Within a hundred yards of the rear line of the attacking force
and the big 24-centimeter siege guns. The large lean-to in
the foreground was the home of General Kamio

GERMAN MACHINE-GUNS ON THE REDOUBT WALLS OF
THE TSINGTAU FORTS

The pom-pom-pom of these guns and the shriek and whistle
of shrapnel made a nightmare of the starlight hours during
the closing days of the siege

236

and less costly methods than those insisted upon by the Japanese commander. The viewpoints of the two armies seemed to hinge on the judgment of the professional soldier, such as Great Britain's, and the soldier of conscription, as Japan's. But of the professional soldiers there were not and could not be enough. And being so few, General Barnardiston, as well as the other officers, were reluctant to sacrifice them. But the British general, being under the orders of General Kamio, the commander-in-chief of the investing forces, had to abide by the plans of the latter. Due to the lack of ammunition in Tsingtau, the assault, when it did take place two days later, did not prove so costly of life as was first expected.

Late in the afternoon the Japanese blockading fleet closed in on the southern end of the entrance to the Bay of Kiaochow and started a bombardment of the city of Tsingtau. At first the Tsingtau residents were unable to locate the source of the gun-fire as the ships were shielded in the sea by Cape Jaeschke. However, to the city itself it was the one exciting moment of the whole war.

With shells coming right into the city front and around the Prince Heinrich Hotel, which was being utilized as a hospital, there was a hasty retreat for cover farther into the city. Every one took to the basements and there spent the night, in deadly fear of the large shells which were crashing into building fronts every few minutes.

That night the Japanese forces advanced two hundred yards under a heavy shrapnel fire from the Germans. A snowstorm, followed by rain, had filled the trenches with water a foot deep, and it was in these that the Japanese and British forces found themselves during the closing day of the siege. Friday, November 6, was a bitter morning. A forty-mile gale was blowing off the Yellow Sea, and with the thermometer at two below zero it was not any too comfortable even for those of us who were fortunate enough to get near a charcoal burner.

Out in the trenches stood the troops, in water over their shoe-tops, no overcoats, many without mittens, their hands on cold steel, without the warmth of a fire for the last three days, and only an extra ration of hot tea to keep them up.

All day the shrieks from the shells continued, but when I returned to General Kamio's quarters, everyone was of the opinion there would be only one more day of this and then the night attack of the infantry.

BRITISH TROOPS ARRIVE IN TSINGTAU

CHAPTER 9

The Surrender

The fighting during the closing hours of November 6 found the little German garrison at Tsingtau pressed to their utmost resistance against the inevitable. For more than two months they had been at war with the small khaki-clad soldiers of the Nippon Empire, not with any hope of finally coming out victorious in the struggle, but simply to stave off the hour when they must lay down their guns and be humiliated by seeing the Rising Sun flag replace the banner of the Fatherland above the fortresses of the German protectorate. That hour had come.

But twenty-five yards from the front wall that skirted the Tsingtau fortresses for three miles from the Bay of Kiaochow on the right, to the Yellow Sea on the left, was entrenched the front line of the Japanese and British expeditionary forces. Behind this line of underground fighters was another line, a third, and then the large, massive twenty-eight-centimetre siege guns of the Japanese, which at various intervals of the day had been hurling projectiles with a deafening roar, scattering death within the walls of the fortress as a reminder to its garrison members that Germany must leave Asia.

As I stood on the rear Japanese line that night, close to General Kamio's dugout, and gazed toward the German fortresses at Tsingtau, the scene before me appeared much like a spectacular pyrotechnic exhibition. Star-shells continually fired from the German walls would burst in the heavens above and for several minutes would continually keep lit the field below. Japanese infantrymen could be seen outside fresh trenches placing sandbags and the like, and with darkness covering the field again there would be a few seconds of deathly stillness and then the machine guns along the redoubt walls of the Tsingtau forts would open up. From all about the field in front there appeared the bright red flash of flames as field and siege guns went into action, and the echo of their deep roaring undertones would at length subside into the ripping *pom-pom-pom* of the German machine guns as they attempted to check the advance of the Japanese sappers.

Toward midnight, the fire from the Tsingtau forts had slackened somewhat,—due, as afterwards learned, to the giving-out of ammunition supplies,—and noting this condition of affairs, General Yamada, whose men were entrenched in front of Forts 2 and 3, sent out a detachment to learn the condition of the garrison opposing him.

The men approached the redoubt walls of the forts, climbed down ten feet to the bottom, and found themselves facing wire entanglements, ten yards wide and running the length of the wall. No Germans were seen. Reinforcements were called for while the advance guard was cutting the entanglements, and by 1 a.m. on the morning of November 7, General Yamada with more than three hundred men was behind the central redoubt walls of the German forts.

In the meantime, heavily protected on all sides by planks and sandbags, a detachment of two hundred Germans, with machine guns, was watching the approach of General Barnardiston's men, who had been stationed to the right of General Yamada. The Germans were unaware that the Japanese had gained the wall when suddenly a sentry heard Japanese voices in the inky blackness before him and the signal was given.

Rushing from their little sandbag fortress, the German detachment hurried in the shadow of the redoubt wall toward the casemate approaches, hoping, in so doing, to reach their comrades stationed five hundred yards back along the casemate walls. Some undoubtedly reached their destination, but the majority of the men were shot down by the Japanese as they ran toward the approaches unconscious that Japanese guards were there.

The capture of Forts 2 and 3 by General Yamada was quickly reported to General Horiuchi, and within an hour his men had captured Forts 4 and 5 with little resistance. General Johoji, on the extreme right, with the British expeditionary force to his left, under General Barnardiston, also advanced with the news of the capture of the positions, but the Tsingtau garrison seemed to have concentrated its attack at this position and General Johoji's advance was met with stubborn resistance.

Utilizing the high-banked macadam roadway that runs from Litsun into Tsingtau as a cover, the British force was able to advance to

GERMAN BARBED-WIRE ENTANGLEMENTS
Along the redoubt walls of the Tsingtau forts

GENERAL HORIUCHI ON THE CREST OF MOLTKE FORT
He stands smiling, with a chrysanthemum, the Japanese national emblem, in front of him. He and his men had captured this fort

the Tsingtau redoubt walls without suffering much damage, and, after tearing a hole through the stone guard, was able to capture the fort. The capture of Fort No. 1 by the British was closely followed by General Johoji's capture of the coast fort at 6.30 a.m.

The German front and second line of defence was now in full retreat toward the three mountain forts, Iltis, Bismarck, and Moltke, about a quarter of a mile in the rear of the captured redoubt and casemate fortifications. General Yamashita, chief of the Japanese staff, realizing now the weakened condition of the Germans, ordered General Yamada and General Horiuchi to advance with detachments of engineers and infantrymen and to begin the general attack.

After weeks in rain-filled trenches, the attacking force was only too eager to begin the hand-to-hand encounter that would eventually mean the surrender of Tsingtau, and so with orders given, they rushed from their trenches over the redoubt walls and behind the advance Japanese guard started their charge up the steep slopes of the Tsingtau mountainous fortresses that rose one thousand feet high.

With bayonets in front of them gleaming in the glow of the morning sun, just rising as a ball of fire from above the horizon of the Yellow Sea, the attacking force charged up the slopes. Two guns on Iltis Fort had been silenced; the four big twenty-eight-centimetre mortars on the same fort were useless for work at the base of Iltis, while the other guns, making up the German equipment, had been so placed and sandbagged at the rear of the forts that they could not be quickly brought forward and utilized for work along the steep slopes leading to their summit. Rifles and machine guns were resorted to.

The Japanese, as they charged up the slopes, were mowed down by the machine guns, but on they came from all sides—17,000 men against 3800. The German garrison could not hold out and the white flag was seen suddenly to be hoisted from near the Governor-General Meyer-Waldeck's residence. The surrender came at 7.05 a.m.

As the white flag struck the top of its mast the air about the forts was suddenly rent by the "*banzaiing*" of the victorious troops. For twenty minutes the cheering kept up, until at length it was replaced by the appearance of the Rising Sun flag floating from the peak of every fort and hill in the neighbourhood. Thus had Germany's dream of domain in the East come suddenly to an end.

CHAPTER 10

After the City's Fall

Scenes of havoc met the eyes of the Japanese staff officers when they entered the fallen forts of Tsingtau. With dynamite and nitro-glycerine the German defenders had destroyed the guns and demolished all that might be taken by the captors as trophies of war. Along the casemate walls of the forts still lay the German and Japanese soldiers who had been killed in the final assault, while the concrete forts themselves were just a mass of shale and twisted steel rods where dynamite or falling shells had done their work.

Into the forts the Japanese filed and, collecting all the German soldiers together in lots, marched them to the barbed-wire entanglements in the rear of the city and after a short rest took them to the foot of Prince Heinrich Berg, where a prison camp had been improvised. The German officers, however, through the courtesy of the Japanese commander, were allowed to remain in Tsingtau.

The courtesy of the Japanese, for which the Orient is already famous, received an excellent demonstration in the surrender of Tsingtau. General Kamio, commander-in-chief, realizing that to march his victorious troops through the city of Tsingtau would throw the residents into much confusion and disorder, made the direct surrender appear like a capitulation on terms. All German officers, including Governor-General Meyer-Waldeck, were allowed to go about Tsingtau at their freedom after the surrender, and General Kamio at once posted orders that only the Japanese staff officers would be allowed to enter the city for several days. Japanese pickets were placed along the roads outside of the city to see that this regulation was enforced.

For several days, then, while the Japanese troops were quartered in Moltke and Bismarck Barracks in the rear of Tsingtau, and the British force was also in German barracks, the residents of Tsingtau were

243

given free opportunity to recover from their besieged life without being ruffled by the sight of marching and quartered troops.

During that period between the surrender of the Tsingtau forts and November 16, when the British and Japanese expeditionary forces made their triumphal entry into the city, the Japanese officers busied themselves in the final preparations for the transfer of the German possessions into the hands of Dai Nippon. The rest of the troops spent the days in examining the Tsingtau forts and gradually the "why-fore" of their surrender was answered.

On Iltis Fort were mounted six twelve-centimetre guns, two of which had been captured from the French in the siege of Paris in 1871. On the left of this battery and toward the rear of the fort had been placed four twenty-eight-centimetre mortars, while two 10.5-centimetre guns cast in 1889, which had seen service in the siege of Taku in 1900, made up the remainder of the fort's equipment.

Bismarck Fort, to the left of Iltis, seemed to be the most strongly fortified of any of the Tsingtau defences. Besides four twenty-eight-centimetre howitzers and two twenty-one-centimetre guns, it contained the Tsingtau battery of four fifteen-centimetre guns.

At Moltke Fort, on the bay side of the city, the German garrison had mounted two fifteen-centimetre guns stripped from the Austrian cruiser *Kaiserin Elisabeth*, a field battery of ten pieces, three field howitzers, and several small guns taken from the second-class German gunboats and cruisers that had been allowed to be bottled up in the Bay of Kiaochow.

The two German forts which commanded the sea approaches were Huit-chien-huk and Tscha-nui-va. The first was equipped with two twenty-four-centimetre guns and three fifteen-centimetre guns, while the latter's equipment consisted of two twenty-one-centimetre guns which had been taken from the Chinese Taku forts in 1900.

The German garrison at Tsingtau at the opening of the war, knowing that their surrender was inevitable, had made all plans to keep as far as possible all trophies of war from falling into the enemy's hands after surrender. The result was that early on the morning of the 7th, after the Japanese infantry had gained the redoubt walls, all preparations were made by the garrison for destroying the guns.

The breech-block of each was wound with nitro-glycerine and dynamite was placed in the cannons up to the muzzle edge. The white flag was the signal. A few minutes later, when the Japanese forces swarmed the forts, they found the place a mass of wreckage. Big twenty-four-centimetre guns were split in two as evenly and neatly as if they had been cut by a jack-knife, while one hundred or more yards distant could be found all that remained of the breechblock. The four twenty-eight-centimetre mortars on Iltis had been dynamited and just a mass of twisted steel and splintered plates remained.

On Bismarck and Moltke Forts, many of the guns had been backed in against the sandbag walls and dynamited on their carriages. The discharge had left the place scattered with the broken pieces of the carriages and split sandbags. The guns in the majority of cases had fallen down to the foot of the casemate walls. The explosions of the dynamite also appeared to have wrecked adjacent walls, for the concrete work about the gun-stands seemed to be so much shale. Exposed to sight were the steel pipes and wire used in the construction of the forts, all twisted and broken.

This desire to keep trophies of war from the hands of the enemy was not confined alone to guns. From the various post-offices German officials gathered the colony's issue of postage stamps and all were burned. Men had evidently been detailed to handle the storehouses, for all about them I found large cans of corned beef, sausages, milk, *sauerkraut* and German delicacies opened and lying in heaps, their contents untouched.

All valuable papers in the vaults of government buildings that contained military secrets or maps of fortifications throughout the Far East, were also made way with; in fact the German garrison left little that the Japanese could boast about, except the city of Tsingtau itself.

As officially given out by the War Office, the Japanese forces had a total of 142 guns on the firing line. They consisted of 6 28-centimetre howitzers, 72 other siege guns of 15- and 24-centimetres, 18 mountain guns, 36 field pieces, and 8 4.7 and 6-inch guns of the marine detachment.

According to figures given me by General Kamio, the total active fighting force of the Japanese during the siege was 20,000 men, while the British expedition force consisted of 925 regulars, with a regiment of 300 Sikhs.

Opposing them was the German force of 4500 men, more than 700 of whom were sick or wounded or captured before the actual siege started.

Among the criticisms directed against the defenders of Tsingtau, which I heard after the surrender, especially in the British camp, was that the Germans fired away great quantities of ammunition at the

THE FOOT OF THE CASEMATE WALLS THIRTY MINUTES
AFTER THE SURRENDER

Fatigued by their past thirty-six hours of work in storming
the German forts, the attacking force dropped wherever the
white flag found them, and there they slumbered while the
soldiers of the German garrison (in the background) smiled
upon their conquerors

THE MOLTKE BARRACKS AFTER THE SURRENDER

Showing the effects of Japanese shrapnel. Sandbags were
placed about buildings in the city to keep shells from un-
dermining them

beginning of the bombardment of the fortifications so that, with their supply exhausted, an excuse for the surrender could be made. In proof of this they referred to the large number of shells which fell daily about the Japanese forces while they were getting the big siege guns into position. The estimate of "more than two thousand German shells in twelve hours' firing with no casualties to the Japanese or British forces," was further evidence given.

On my first trip into Tsingtau I met a German officer in the Prince Heinrich Hotel, who had taken part in the siege, and questioned him as to the truth of the statement.

Maybe that is what they say, but the facts are the garrison had expected Tsingtau to fall sooner than it did. Our heavy artillery fire was not kept up for the purpose of throwing away our shells,—it would have been less dangerous to have dropped them in the bay,—but solely to do as much damage to the Japanese as possible before the assault on the fortifications could be made. We regulated our fire with the one purpose of covering the country with shells before they had a chance to get under cover. When they attempted to mount their siege guns at the start of the bombardment their forces were exposed to us. We could see their ammunition columns and supply wagons rolling up on open roads and, by spreading our fire about the valley, we were attempting solely to postpone the fall of Tsingtau as much as possible by hindering the allied forces in their work.

The officer then went on to tell me of the ruse Lieutenant Trendel, manager of the Wagonlits Hotel at Peking, who took part in the siege, played on the Japanese. Trendel was in command of a battery of six old nine-centimetre ships' guns which were in an exposed position on a ridge near Iltis Fort. This battery received a fire from both the ship and land guns, and the men could be seen on the first day of the bombardment building bomb-proofs in the dust and smoke from exploding shells.

In the night Lieutenant Trendel put up wooden guns, roughly shaped from beams, at a distance of two hundred yards from his own guns. In the morning, he exploded powder near them to give an appearance of firing from them. By his ruse he diverted the Japanese fire and saved all his men, dynamiting his guns before the surrender.

Governor-General Waldeck, after the surrender, made the following statement as to the bombardment:—

The combatant force at Tsingtau did not amount to more than forty-five hundred. The permanent garrison consisted of eighteen hundred men nominally, but was, in reality, about two hundred short. Some of those under arms were mere boys. Each fort was defended by about two hundred men.

The Tsingtau guns were mostly weapons captured from the Boxers during their rebellion, or trophies of the Franco-German War, and were no match for modern arms. The Huichuan and Bismarck Forts, however, had some modern pieces. Altogether there were, for the defence, about sixty guns and a hundred machine guns.

The Iltis fort was guarded by sixty men. The Japanese in their assault charged up under a hot fire as if unconscious of their danger, and gained the position before the defenders could call reinforcements.

The Bismarck and Moltke Forts were also taken by a charge, but for the most part the Japanese conducted their attack under cover of their trenches, and concealed themselves so well that the most searching German fire could not stop their advance. At length the supply of ammunition ran out, and further defence was futile. I thought the Japanese casualties would be very heavy, as they fought bravely and charged desperately, and I estimated their loss at five to six thousand. I have been astonished to learn that the loss in killed and wounded amounts to only seventeen hundred. They certainly showed remarkable skill in taking cover.

Tsingtau was not an ideal fortification, such as Antwerp. Strictly speaking, it was merely a defended position. As possible enemies in the Far East, Germany had calculated only on England, France, and Russia. It was quite unexpected that the blow would come from so good a friend as Japan.

The fire from the Japanese squadron was not so furious as to cause any great inconvenience, except once when a shell landed in the Huichan Point Fort, killed thirteen and severely wounded three. In respect of accuracy of range the fire of the British cruiser *Triumph* was inferior to that of Japanese ships. The land fire, however, was terrible. A perfect rain of shells fell on the Bismarck, Iltis, and Hsiaochau Forts, and the central batteries suffered severely. One of them received as many as a hundred shells, and it was death to leave the trenches for an instant.

Two days after the surrender I was able to get through the picket line thrown about the rear of the city of Tsingtau, and could observe better just what damage had been done to the city during the seven days of bombardment.

The city appeared as if a typhoon had passed through it. Its wide asphalt and macadamized streets, fronted by beautiful four and five story buildings of German architecture, were vacant. Giant shells, some three feet long and a foot in diameter, were lying about on sidewalk and street still unexploded. Trees, splintered at their bases, lay toppled over in the avenues. Windows in the houses were shattered, while gaunt holes in the sides of buildings, where shells had torn their way, made the residence blocks appear to be gasping for air.

Out in the harbour could be seen the spars of the Rickmers and two or three other German freighters, which had been sunk at the opening of hostilities about the city, while farther out in the channel was the grave of the Austrian cruiser, *Kaiserin Elisabeth*, which had been sunk by the Germans.

The whole scene seemed one of devastation. Streets deserted of people, show-fronts of stores completely gone, as was also the merchandise, harbours deserted of ships, and not even a sign of a *rickshaw* to remind you of the Orient.

Such was Tsingtau as I first saw it two days after its surrender. But for the continual sight of the Rising Sun flag flapping from every peak in the rear of the city, as well as from every Government building, and its message of "occupied," one would have thought Tsingtau a city deserted.

CHAPTER 11

Taking Possession

The transfer of Tsingtau to the allied forces was commenced on November 11, and, two days later, the majority of the German officers who were not needed by the Japanese in spotting the land mines were marched off to Sesheco to be transported to Japan. During the final transfer I lingered about the field below Moltke Barracks, on which had gathered about one thousand German prisoners of war, with their officers. As Governor-General Waldeck and his officers were going through roll-call, the *scuff-scuff-scuff* sound of marching troops was heard along the roadway near by leading over a small slope. The sound of the heavy boots hitting the ground was shortly followed by the whistling of many men, and all the heads in the field below quickly turned toward the crest of the hill, where the road disappeared.

In a few minutes they appeared in sight—first four bayonets, four khaki-coloured helmets, then four men, another four men—nine hundred strong, the British expeditionary force, marching to the German barracks, whistling "*Everybody's Doing It.*"

At the sight the heads in the field below immediately turned toward Governor-General Waldeck, while the faces of neutrals on the side lines turned into smiles. That tune whistled by the Britishers evidently grated on the field below, and a few minutes later, when an officer shouted in German for the men to form on the roadway, one thousand voices burst into a German war song.

I stood by the roadway as they formed; some with heavy packs strapped to their backs, others carrying accordions, mandolins, and guitars in their hands. As they marched by me, all stared.

"English or American?" some would ask.

With the nod of my head to the latter they seemed to rest content and would pass the remark on to the other, "newspaperman."

Five days later, the formal entry of the allied forces took place at Tsingtau. Following the review of the forces by General Kamio and his staff, the troops marched to the Strand on the Yellow Sea, where a wooden monument, much like Cleopatra's Needle, stood banked in the centre of the sands. Large straw-wrapped casks of sake, or Japanese wine, stood on each side of the monument, a gift to the departed souls of the Japanese dead, from their emperor and empress. Heaped on top of the casks were thousands of cigarettes, bowls of rice, chrysanthemums, the national flower of the Empire, and many eatables much prized by the Japanese.

After all the troops had assembled facing the monument. General Kamio approached it with a large scroll in his hand. All helmets and caps of the troops in front of him went off. He stepped on to the path leading directly to the monument, took off his cap, bowed, and then approached. Stopping within a foot of the monument. General Kamio bowed again, and then slowly opened the scroll. Not a sound could be heard in that gathering of thousands in front of the monument, except an occasional neigh of a cavalry horse.

The scroll opened, he read from it in Japanese the following message to the dead:——

I, the humble General Kamio, commander-in-chief of the Japanese forces, express my hearty condolences to the souls of the dead who have been killed in battle or who have passed away from illness contracted during our days of war.

My Imperial Majesty's reason for declaring war against Germany was because Germany had expanded her war politics to the Far East. They occupied Tsingtau, and forced our neighbouring Government, China, to give it up, thus destroying the peace of the Far East. Our Imperial Majesty was therefore called upon to drive the disturbing element from our hitherto peaceful shores.

I, the humble General Kamio, was appointed to be commander-in-chief of the allied army in its operation against Tsingtau. I and my staff, from early morning until late at night, have laboured hard to achieve the desire of our Imperial Majesty and now Tsingtau is occupied by the allied army.

Its surrender is the result of the grace of heaven, the virtues of our Emperor and Empress, and the bravery of those passed souls which we honour today. We are assembled here to com-

TRIUMPHAL ENTRY OF THE JAPANESE TROOPS INTO
TSINGTAU
The military attaches of the United States, Greece, Spain, and
France on the left, in front of the Asiatic-Deutsch bank

PAYING RESPECT TO THE SOULS OF THE JAPANESE DEAD
Before the monument erected on the shores of the Yellow Sea
at Tsingtau

fort you, O souls, and I ask that you receive the condolences which I, representing the surviving army, give to you today.

The rites were those of Shintoism and, as believed, the souls of the men killed and buried during the war, all gathered at this monument. As General Kamio finished reading from the scroll, an aide stepped up and handed him a pine branch—the Japanese symbol for long life— and the commander-in-chief placed it upon the monument, bowed, and stepped down along the path that faced the troops. The impressive ceremony was over.

The troops then returned to their quarters, while the officers of the Japanese and British forces were entertained at a banquet in Bismarck Barracks.

Tsingtau had now formally passed into the hands of Japan, and but two weeks later the British expeditionary force returned to Hongkong on the *Triumph*, and later embarked again for the war in Europe. The *Triumph* proceeded to the Suez Canal, afterwards distinguishing herself in the siege of the Dardanelles, but was sunk later by the enemy's torpedo.

CHAPTER 12

Sanitation and Discipline

As to the military organization of the Japanese, I think the operations of their troops in Shantung will add little to their reputation for scientific work. Surely on one point—that of sanitation—the military *attachés* of Holland, Spain, France, Greece, and the United States, who were present with the Japanese army during their war operations, if they can speak, will bear me out on the point that sanitation was something wholly lacking in the Japanese war-camps.

Military experts will tell you that in a campaign when the troops move camp, ditches should be dug almost before tents are pitched. The Japanese war-camps I found the exception; to this rule. Even in the question of "mess refuse," I found upon inspection that the Japanese provided no ditches. Rivers and creeks, already typhoidal, were principally used as the dumping-grounds of camp refuse, and days after the camps had passed, the bivouacking spot would stand out as a stain upon nature: tin cans and rubbish all about, with old meat, and rice, paper, and other refuse cluttering.

Even during my days with the Japanese Army in the model German barracks of Moltke Fort, I found this same Japanese lack of sanitation. Unprintable, is the way to describe the conditions resulting from the complaisance of the Japanese officers in permitting the soldier inmates to litter doorsteps and hallways with refuse.

But this disorder of Japanese camps, not only applied to sanitation, but as well to the handling of their troops after the surrender.

With the recent history of Japan showing that the little island nation goes to war at intervals of every ten years, and with its large army of conscription not knowing what defeat is, they are continuously kept under the intoxication of victory, with the result that carelessness is bred among them.

With the surrender of Tsingtau the Japanese generals appeared to have lost control over their men. "There was quite a little looting going on by the Japanese yesterday," said a British captain to me the day after the surrender; but for the next several days when I visited the city I found that the statement applied to more than "yesterday." Wherever I went I was met by faces of Japanese soldiers peering from deserted German residences. Upon a further inspection I found them searching through bureau drawers and going out of back doors with articles of various sorts.

Not for an instant do I think the officers of the Japanese army allow their troops to loot, for I think the Japanese Empire passed that stage of affairs after the relief of Peking, during the Boxer Rebellion. But what I saw taking place in Tsingtau after the surrender only bears out the statement that the Japanese Army is becoming careless.

I do not think the Tokyo Government can dispute the point, when it accounts for the many deaths that occurred to its soldiers during the week after the surrender, from exploding land mines and the like. With practically every one in the war zone after the surrender knowing the vicinities of the dangerous mined ground, and with German officers right on the spot with maps showing the exact location of each mine, there seems very little excuse for such accidents, except as control of the army is lax and men are allowed to roam around at will.

On November 8, I heard a rumour in Tsingtau that forty Japanese soldiers and one officer had been killed in an explosion of a land mine near Moltke Fort. When I questioned Japanese officers regarding the matter, none denied that my version of the accident was correct. When I returned to Tokyo after the war I looked up the newspaper accounts to see if the War Office had given out anything on the matter, and in the *Japan Advertiser* I found the following:—

The following report was officially given out by the War Office: Ten men and an officer were killed in an accident at Tsingtau today.

To be sure, it was an accident that killed the men, whether eleven or forty-one, but will the War Office deny that the men met their death through carelessness? There were several other such accidents at Tsingtau to the Japanese Army, but there were no casualties reported in the British camp after the surrender, and no one could find a British soldier away from his barracks unless on picket duty along the nearby roads. Days afterwards there was that same discipline about the British barracks.

255

Editor's Note

The remainder of this book-published it should be noted-1916-goes on to speculate on Japan's aspirations for the region and upon what this fortune might bring it. As can be gathered from these pages, the author proved to be chillingly accurate.

LEONAUR

ALSO FROM LEONAUR

AVAILABLE IN SOFTCOVER OR HARDCOVER WITH DUST JACKET

THE RELUCTANT REBEL *by William G. Stevenson*—A young Kentuckian's experiences in the Confederate Infantry & Cavalry during the American Civil War..

BOOTS AND SADDLES *by Elizabeth B. Custer*—The experiences of General Custer's Wife on the Western Plains.

FANNIE BEERS' CIVIL WAR *by Fannie A. Beers*—A Confederate Lady's Experiences of Nursing During the Campaigns & Battles of the American Civil War.

LADY SALE'S AFGHANISTAN *by Florentia Sale*—An Indomitable Victorian Lady's Account of the Retreat from Kabul During the First Afghan War.

THE TWO WARS OF MRS DUBERLY *by Frances Isabella Duberly*—An Intrepid Victorian Lady's Experience of the Crimea and Indian Mutiny.

THE REBELLIOUS DUCHESS *by Paul F. S. Dermoncourt*—The Adventures of the Duchess of Berri and Her Attempt to Overthrow French Monarchy.

LADIES OF WATERLOO *by Charlotte A. Eaton, Magdalene de Lancey & Juana Smith*—The Experiences of Three Women During the Campaign of 1815: Waterloo Days by Charlotte A. Eaton, A Week at Waterloo by Magdalene de Lancey & Juana's Story by Juana Smith.

TWO YEARS BEFORE THE MAST *by Richard Henry Dana. Jr.*—The account of one young man's experiences serving on board a sailing brig—the Penelope—bound for California, between the years 1834-36.

A SAILOR OF KING GEORGE *by Frederick Hoffman*—From Midshipman to Captain—Recollections of War at Sea in the Napoleonic Age 1793-1815.

LORDS OF THE SEA *by A. T. Mahan*—Great Captains of the Royal Navy During the Age of Sail.

COGGESHALL'S VOYAGES: VOLUME 1 *by George Coggeshall*—The Recollections of an American Schooner Captain.

COGGESHALL'S VOYAGES: VOLUME 2 *by George Coggeshall*—The Recollections of an American Schooner Captain.

TWILIGHT OF EMPIRE *by Sir Thomas Ussher & Sir George Cockburn*—Two accounts of Napoleon's Journeys in Exile to Elba and St. Helena: Narrative of Events by Sir Thomas Ussher & Napoleon's Last Voyage: Extract of a diary by Sir George Cockburn.